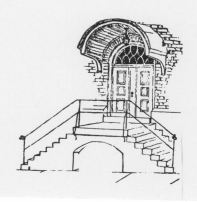

Reading Tudor-Stuart Texts
Through Cultural Historicism

"Frontispiece" of Sir Walter Raleigh's *History of the World*, 1614,
C 38110. By permission of The British Library.

Reading Tudor-Stuart Texts Through Cultural Historicism

Albert H. Tricomi

University Press of Florida
Gainesville/Tallahassee/Tampa/Boca Raton
Pensacola/Orlando/Miami/Jacksonville

01 00 99 98 97 96 6 5 4 3 2 1

Library of Congress Cataloging-in-Publication Data
Tricomi, Albert H., 1942–
Reading Tudor-Stuart texts through cultural historicism / Albert
H. Tricomi.
  p. cm.
Includes bibliographical references and index.
ISBN 0-8130-1435-2 (alk. paper)
1. English literature—Early modern, 1500-1700—History and
criticism—Theory, etc. 2. Literature and history—Great Britain—
History—16th century. 3. Literature and history—Great Britain—
History—17th century. 4. Great Britain—History—Tudors, 1485–1603—
Historiography. 5. Great Britain—History-Stuarts,
1603–1714—Historiography. 6. Historicism. I. Title.
PR421.T75   1996   95-45465
820.9′003—dc20

The University Press of Florida is the scholarly publishing agency for the State
University System of Florida, comprised of Florida A & M University, Florida Atlantic
University, Florida International University, Florida State University, University of
Central Florida, University of Florida, University of North Florida, University of South
Florida, and University of West Florida.

University Press of Florida
15 Northwest 15th Street
Gainesville, Florida 32611

To my father
and
the memory of my mother

Contents

Illustrations

Preface

This book is the product of my engagement with new historicism and my concern to reform several of its methods and to see it develop into what I have called "cultural historicism." In writing it, two purposes have guided me. The first, which came more and more clearly into focus as I concluded my earlier monograph *Anticourt Drama in England, 1603–42* (1989), is methodological and theoretical: to explore the problem of historical knowledge in relation to the production of literary history and culture. The second is historical and literary: to produce a self-conscious form of cultural historicism by perusing the representations of surveillance and the sexual body in the popular literature, particularly the drama, of early modern England. The relationship between representation and culture is a new-historicist thematic that presents unplumbed opportunities and problems. In attempting to explore both, I have chosen as my subjects of inquiry two related activities that appear prominently in Tudor-Stuart drama and literature—governmental surveillance and the social oversight of the sexual body.

The study is intended for those readers concerned with the relationships between history, anthropology, and literature as well as between new historicism, history, and literature. The subject of the book, Elizabethan-Jacobean literature and drama, will be of interest to students seeking new readings in these areas. Students interested in theory and its applications will find Michel Foucault to be an informing presence throughout this study, even when my thinking goes in a different direction. My concerns with representation, particularly in respect to symbolic forms of cultural signification, have led me to use a range of visual sources beyond the theatrical. This kind of contextualization has been of great interest to art historians for some time now. The chapters treating "problem-play" drama in terms of the oversight of female sexuality and the final chapter on affectivity in criticism and the ideological representations of the mothering body in Jacobean theater should be of particular interest to students of women's history. Throughout the book, I have tried to make my criticism accessible to graduate students and advanced undergraduates, as well as professional academicians.

In writing the book, I have been grateful for the assistance of colleagues with expertise in many areas of Renaissance studies, and some beyond. Brook Thomas, Walter Cohen, and Arthur Kinney offered valuable criticism and needed support when the manuscript was in its formative and middle stages. Louis Montrose's admonitions about treating Foucault in respect to modern "utopian" thought helped me theorize an important chapter. Ira Clark provided an astute reading of the entire manuscript and the exhortation to have reproduced engravings and photographs important to the argument. Stephen Collins also read the entire manuscript, some sections more than once. I am especially grateful to him for his perspicuity, detailed commentary, and encouragement on matters epistemological and historical. I am fortunate that the press secured such good readers, and I appreciate very much the contributions made by the staff of the University Press of Florida, especially Walda Metcalf, associate director and editor in chief, Alex Leader, and production editor Judy Goffman, and of copyeditor Trudie Calvert and indexer Roberta Engleman .

To my colleagues at Binghamton, I recognize a genuine community of scholars across the disciplines among whom I am proud to be a part. Ellen Brand's editorial expertise helped me to bring the manuscript to near-final form. In the final stages before submission, Joseph Church provided extremely valuable advice on developing various features of the manuscript to attract a wider audience. For their intellectual and editorial contributions along the way, I thank David Bartine, Norman Burns, Albert Higgins, Phillip Kraft, Bernard Rosenthal, Melvin Seiden, Biswarup Sen, Patricia Speyser, and Kenneth Straus and take special notice of my close colleague in Renaissance studies, Alvin Vos. For their assistance in helping to provide photographs for the book, I am grateful to Lucie Nelson, Robin Oggins, Dagmar Gabard, and my secretary, Diane Kalmen, who prepared the paperwork. I also wish to thank our provost, Mary Ann Swain, who in celebrating the completion of the project helped free me for the work ahead in the provost's office.

In concert with our children, Eebie, Will, and Al, this homespun book was happily made. Bet provided, as she always has, the steady encouragement and care that sustain me in my work and life. For all she is to our family and to me, I thank her with love.

1

The Problem and the Project

"Being Historical"

The most useful beginning, I think, is to explain the perspective from which I write, which is to foster the development of the new-historicist initiative while challenging—with the idea of reforming—some of its current practices. This book is, then, both an assessment of the movement and of the most notable practices that emerge from it. As an assessment, it addresses a number of issues to which I will turn in due course, but the central one, the one that underlies everything else, is the relationship of the new literary historicism to historiography. From my perspective, the central task facing the profession is how a genuine "new *historicism*" is to be developed. To inflect the issue somewhat differently, the broader project is how a viable *cultural historicism* can issue from new-historicist practices.

In pursuing this enterprise, I have taken as my subject two mutually informing topics that devolve from modern critiques of the disciplinary society. These are presented in the two parts of this study. Part One treats Tudor-Stuart representations of surveillance, Part Two the discourse in Elizabethan-Jacobean drama pertaining to the production and control of the sexual body. In both parts I intend to show how literary and theatrical representations contribute to the reproduction of the disciplines of power while also participating in the continual process of remaking English society. My purpose is to revise the dominant new-historicist proposition that texts reproduce culture and to demonstrate the more complex proposition that they simultaneously make and reproduce culture. In the Elizabethan-Jacobean theater especially, we see that plays participate ceaselessly in the masking as well as the unmasking and readjustment of cultural power.

My second agenda is to situate this study within the new-historicist project and then to move beyond it to press the claims of a new cultural historicism. To do this, I will present in this first chapter an epistemological assessment of new-historicist practices along with a critique in this and subsequent chapters of their methodological strengths and weaknesses. It is to separate myself from several of the dominant practices of new historicism, but not its charter, that I apply the term *cultural historicism* to my own work. In employing this term I do not mean a return to a traditional historiography with an anthropological subject matter (rituals, rites of passage, marital and child-rearing practices) tacked on; rather I mean a criticism committed to an understanding of history as an ongoing cultural, not merely event-based, process.

At the same time, by showing how notions of time are implied even in synchronic readings of texts, I mean to break down the dichotomous practice new historicists observe of excluding diachronic readings of culture while embracing synchronic ones. In this manner, I intend to exhibit a more robust kind of historicism, one in which functional analyses can be joined with a conception of history that can recognize both events and processes as taking place over time. Throughout these chapters, I urge a cultural historicism committed to examining the relationship between social structure and social practices and textual articulations (which can themselves be practices). Invariably, the historicism presented is informed by the new-historicist goal of deciphering the symbolic codes that underlie semiotic processes.

In attempting to achieve these ends, I recognize that some readers may expect me to stipulate from the beginning my principles or theoretical premises and throughout this study to be perhaps less conversational. I have determined to do otherwise. I believe in conversations as a way of expressing perspectives and showing the contexts out of which operating principles emerge. I do not particularly endorse the formal statement of principles on terms divorced from or privileged above the conversations out of which they appear. My own voice is important to me and to the relationship I wish to establish with my readers. Whatever the perspectives these chapters endorse, they are inseparable from the way of thinking that emerges out of the contexts I establish along the way.

Both as a practice and an epistemology the new historicism is still discovering itself. Everyone knows by now that there is no settled praxis offering itself as *the* new historicism. Rather, the term is an abstraction used to describe what Louis Montrose characterizes as a mere "historical *orientation*" ("New Historicisms" 406). At the theoretical level, new historicism's hostility to traditional historiography, frequently represented in a caricaturist's way, points to a problem whose center is elsewhere—for the new-historicist attack against older forms of criticism has been more effective than new historicism's articulation of its own relationship to historiography. In part this reserve can be attributed to new historicism's own suspicion that theory will lead to a prescriptive, totalizing strategy. Theory itself has been seen as a repression or else as promoting a procrustean authoritarianism.[1] To settle, therefore, on a term that captures the movement's vigor without misleadingly suggesting a settled set of procedures, I think it is better to speak of the new-historicist initiative rather than the new-historicist practice because there is no one practice. So various, in fact, is the conception, assessment, and practice of new historicism that H. Aram Veeser, editor of *The New Historicism*, has opined that the conflicting readings in his edition prove that "'the New Historicism' remains a phrase without an adequate referent" (Veeser x).

But there are numerous referents that make the term meaningful if not precise. Jean Howard identifies the "crux" of new historicism as the conviction that history, like the concept of "man," is a "*construct* made up of textualized traces" and that it is, as Hayden White has theorized, "produced" rather than discovered.[2] Montrose's chiastic characterization of new historicism as a practice that concerns itself with "*the historicity of texts*" and "*the textuality of history*" ("Professing" 20) emphasizes the social embeddedness of all writing. Stephen Greenblatt's pronouncement that new historicism probes "both the social presence to the world of the literary text and the social presence of the world in the literary text" (*Self-Fashioning* 5) reiterates this emphasis while laying greater stress on the text's role in producing and reproducing the dominant ideologies and practices within culture. The implicit rejection in all these formulations of interpretive strategies attempting to recover authorial intention or the "themes" of (literary) texts proceeds from the view that texts perform cultural functions and contain a plenitude of covert meanings that traditional methods of interpretation cannot treat.

The interesting thing about these well-known statements characterizing new historicism is that although they function as descriptions, they are abstract. None of them, for example, specifies *how* new historicism is to be practiced, in part at least because there is no defined practice. What they do emphasize is the mutually constituting character of texts as socially productive discourse, and this fundamental belief is rooted in the understanding that meaning itself is always immanent, always contingent. From this limited but widely circulated sampling we see that although the epistemology guiding new-historicist practice appears to be widely shared, it is not rigorously theorized. We also see that its procedures, as they might be prescribed theoretically, are quite underdetermined.

Among the tangled questions confronting new historicism the most crucial, to my mind, is whether the theoretical assumptions underlying it actually foreclose the notion of a retrievable past. Typically, the explicators of new historicism have been quick to contrast its theoretical orientation with empirical and even positivist notions of history in which evidence is taken to present itself "self-evidently" and factually.[3] When it comes to defining new historicism's own understanding of history, what we get are descriptions of other people's descriptions, usually reported from a distance. Montrose, in a careful formulation that appeared in "Renaissance Literary Studies" (5) and was reiterated in "New Historicisms" (412), observes that current invocations of "History" seem to be a reaction against "various structuralist and poststructuralist formalisms that have seemed, to some, to put into question the very possibility of historical understanding and historical experience." In this way he distances himself from the distressing possibility of new historicism's being a nonhistorical formalism. The reason he does so is clearly that such a development threatens the entire historicist part of the project.

Jean Howard, who echoes these concerns, faces up to the somber prospect. Seizing on the notion that poststructural linguistics and epistemology have put under the gravest doubt the referentiality of language, she poses two questions: "If literature refers to no ground extrinsic to itself, what can be the nature of its relationship to an historical context or to material reality? In fact, if one accepts certain tendencies in poststructuralist thought, is the possibility of an historical criticism even conceivable?" ("New Historicism" 8–9). Indeed, if new historicism is examined from this perspective, its very existence can be viewed (Howard's caveat notwithstanding) as an attempt to forestall or postpone radical indeterminacy by performing tropological analyses on a select number of parallel texts. Consequently, dazzling discoveries of the discontinuities of cultural moments substitute for knowledge of a continuous past that cannot be had. Bringing the issue to an excruciatingly fine point, Joseph Litvak says the question is "how can we make *historical* sense out of an essentially *linguistic* unreliability?" (123; cf. Thomas, *New Historicism* 79–81). This is the crucial problem.

Heavily indebted to deconstructionism as it is, new historicism exhibits a troubled relationship to things "historical." The irony that a movement calling itself "new historicism" may possibly not admit of historical knowledge underlines a continuing epistemological crisis from which, as Brook Thomas frankly puts it, "the Western world has not yet recovered" (*New Historicism* 78). Merely to state the problem helps to explain why the term *cultural poetics* has fitfully been offered in substitution for "new historicism." Obviously, the two terms are not equivalent. A cultural poetics makes no historical claims; it only promises to lead literary criticism by investigating "the collective making of distinct cultural practices."[4] But the label *new-historicism* raises the ante. It signifies that the cultural analysis of texts gives us access to a historical past and can enhance our understanding of that past.

Nevertheless, new historicism has hardly addressed the epistemological tension implicit in its historicist label and its characteristically synchronic analyses. One explanation for this neglect is simply that new historicism emerged as a practice, not a theory, in a poststructuralist environment. Another is that present social concerns have impressed themselves upon new historicism. Even as the pressures exerted by deconstructionism in its doctrine of radical indeterminacy have tended to foster an ahistorical and apolitical quietism (as the revelations in the late 1980s about Paul De Man's involvement with Nazi anti-Semitism have shown in a new demonstration of "blindness" and "forgetting"), the urgency of present social and political needs—to which England's cultural materialists and a few notable new historicists have given repeated voice—has propelled new historicism toward history and politics. For this reason, present-minded practitioners, Montrose chief among them, have held fast to the notion that study of the past can be managed to improve present conditions. Despite new historicism's deconstructionist legacy, then, its social conscience, its need to be a force for cultural understanding and change, moves it away from the epistemological impasse that defines our cultural horizon (De Man's cultural aporia). It is this social need to be in some fashion "present"—to use the past with conscious political purpose as England's cultural materialists have done to engage present social needs—that has impelled a diffident literary movement to accept the term *historicism* as part of its charter. These circumstances do not solve the theoretical problem; they do help us to understand it: the conflicting methodological and social pressures that have made new historicism the exciting thing it is help to explain why the movement's epistemology is uncertain and its practice fluid.

If new historicism is to articulate an adequate epistemology, it must distinguish conflated presuppositions. The pressure exerted by Saussurian linguistics in its discovery of the constitutive character of language might, but does not necessarily, raise the bald question of whether there is an object-world out there to know. The deconstructionist proposition that language is a self-constituting (hence indeterminate) signifying system does, however, release a closely related metaphysical anxiety: if all we have is "language" and language does not "refer," perhaps we cannot "know" anything about the world. Devastating as this eventuality would be to any new-historicist project, it does not leave us without recourse, for the issue turns on what the verb *to know* is taken to mean.

In the very limited sense that the world, perceived through the mediation of language, cannot be apprehended or communicated to others as "the thing in itself," the statement that "we cannot know" may be accepted. From this poststructuralist perspective, which derives from Ferdinand de Saussure's *General Course in Linguistics,* the past as a thing in itself is, indeed, *not* recoverable, perhaps not even knowable (hence the term *traces*). But the crucial point is that this condition need not preclude the making of histories or the meaningful use of the term *knowledge*. It is precisely because our encounter with the past is made possible by present ways of seeing and constructing that the practice of history must be defined as an ongoing dialogic activity. This manner of conceiving the project of historiography allows us to account for a signal feature of historical writing—that its practice always eludes the historian's ability to present the case definitively, not because the full facts are elusive or even because of disagreements about interpretation but because the very concept of evidence is subtly, sometimes dramatically, reconstituted over time. The past we recover may not be and never was *the* past, but it can be for all that a historicized past.

This means that histories can still be written and called by that name. The impossibility of composing grand histories in the manner of Spengler, Toynbee, or Gardiner—as if definitive histories can be achieved if they are comprehensive and detailed enough—should not make us so timid that our narratives attempt no more than to record a succession of "local undecidabilities" (Litvak 126). This assessment of the historical enterprise argues for a cultural historicism that constrains the play of the deconstructionist and purely structuralist impulses within it. If histories are written with an awareness that their founding categories are metahistorical constructions and that these co-determine outcomes,[5] it will be possible to engage the reasons why one such set of assumptions is more appropriate to the evidence and the goal sought than another set. It is from such premises that a new cultural historicism can be attempted.

But even the poststructuralism that derives from Saussurian linguistics leaves us with an epistemology that concedes too much. The weakness of Saussure's argument—that because the sign is "arbitrary" or "unmotivated" there can be no intrinsic resemblance between language and phenomena or events—has been exposed by Emile Benveniste. In the interplay between signifier and signified, the third term, "the thing itself, the reality" is missing, but it creeps back as it must, Benveniste notices, when Saussure, speaking of the arbitrariness of the words "*b-ö-f*" and "*o-k-s*," shows "he was referring in spite of himself to the fact that these two terms applied to the same *reality*" (44). This means that the object-world is not unmediated by experience, either for us or our ancestors, but it is at once both present and under interpretation. For these reasons we have a mediated access to the world of the past, even though the manner of its constitution is different (though never entirely) from our own. Sign, signifier, and object-world together constitute a mutually interdependent reality.

These terms are consistent with Charles S. Peirce's triadic semiology, especially in the redactions of his contemporary explicators. Peirce's description of the signifying process contains three distinct but interrelated elements—sign, object, and interpretant. This semiotic escapes the dichotomous epistemology of poststructuralist thought in which there is only the sign (or signified) and signifier. As interpreted by James Hoopes, for example, the consequence of Peirce's triadic is that "objective knowledge is relative because objective reality comes into being in its fullest in relation to thought. The idea that knowledge is relative does not mean that it is subjective" (1551). Moreover, thinking cannot be an arbitrary or unfettered activity in Peirce's philosophy because it is constituted by our relationship with the world and with the signs that give objects meaning. As Hoopes puts it, "thought is in signs" (1553). Richard Rorty's oppositionalist reading correctly places Peirce among the "correspondence" theorists,[6] but this identification simplifies Peirce's distinctive contribution to epistemology. Peirce's triadic does set forth a semiotic of reference; the world is there in its objectness, but it is always constituted by both sign and interpretant and therefore, in the interpretation of its redactors, always under interpretation.[7]

In one form or another new historicism must acknowledge this pastness of the past if its historicism is to be practicable. However silent its practitioners may be on the subject, they are constrained to assume such pastness despite their synchronic analysis of systems of power. For processes, practices, and even systems make the fullest sense when conceived over time. A process is meaningless without a temporal aspect. The absence of such a recognition is a concealed contradiction in new-historicist analyses, and it is associated with another. In new-historicist practice synchronous accounts of sixteenth-century culture implicitly assume diachronicity (present critic engages things past, situating the reading by reference to a date, period, or event) even though the practice does not actively engage that diachronicity as method. There is no place for recursivity, for self-conscious contemplation of system, for agency. Under this purely structural epistemology, "history here is still understood as a succession of synchronic systems" (Giddens, *Central Problems* 28). But diachrony and synchrony must be reconciled inasmuch as diachrony is a constitutive part of new-historicist procedure (and epistemology), even though new historicism does not account for diachrony at the level of theory and method. Clearly, our attention to method behooves us to do so.

Because the past was once, in some sense, *us,* we feel it should be possible to make it speak to us once again in the present. And yet if our historicist goals are to be at all achievable, we must contend with its strange familiarity by consciously reconstructing it. For this reason we must respond to the past in its dialogic relation to us, and to do this effectively necessitates attending to its sometimes disorienting affective power. This means remaining alert to the ways that texts situated in the past make claims on us by engaging our feelings, thereby subtly informing our present values. The past, however we come to engage it, is a present experience, not just a form of intellectual knowledge. By our dialogic recognition (i.e., our affective, historiographical re-cognition) the strange familiarity of the past is summoned to consciousness so that its unrecognized hold over us is broken, thereby opening the way to a future that does not blindly replicate the past.[8]

As we have seen, new historicism's relationship to history is problematic because the concepts of knowledge and the historical are themselves in question. Having just argued that an effective cultural historicism ought to construe knowledge in relational (rather than objective) terms and that it encompasses affectivity as well as cognition, I would like to take up the most fundamental question of all: what is meant when we say we are or are not "being historical." The idea underlying this concept is obviously crucial to any articulation of what history or historicism is.

One of the ironies about the new-historicist project is that its indebtedness at the theoretical level to poststructuralist indeterminacy, an indebtedness that if carried far enough could preclude new historicism's viability as a historical method, has been swept away in practice by a proclivity toward its opposite, totalizing interpretations. Partially explainable by new historicism's attempt to establish its presentist credentials by reading the past in explicitly political ways, this proclivity, which we see in essays throughout the 1980s—there is some hope of a change in orientation (see below)—has sparked a modest body of essays on the nature of new historicism.

Among the most important of these is Carolyn Porter's essay "Are We Being Historical Yet?"[9] Treating Greenblatt's "Invisible Bullets" as a characteristic expression of new-historicist methodology, Porter identifies the method as ahistorical. The governing procedure in Greenblatt's argument, Porter observes, is the development of an analogical relationship between the subversive playfulness of Falstaff in *Henry IV, Part One* and an equally absolutist theatricality that appears in Thomas Harriot's *Brief and True Report of the New Found Land of Virginia* (758–63). In Greenblatt's reading, Harriot capitalizes on the potentially subversive Machiavellian doctrine that religion can be imposed on a more ignorant people by attributing one's own superior power and technology to God's own favor. But as in the treatment of Falstaff, Harriot's narrative then contains this subversive "Machiavellian anthropology" by using it to reinscribe the Christian religion among the Algonkian people ("Invisible Bullets" 27–30).

Reviewing the structure of this argument, Porter points out that the analogy between these two texts holds firm so long as we are speaking about discrete sites. However, Greenblatt's strategy moves from analyzing these particular textual tensions, which belong to a "cultural poetics," to a larger, let us say "new-historicist," claim that this analogical relationship reproduces the structure of the entire culture. The problem with Greenblatt's method, in Porter's felicitous terminology, is that it makes "functional resemblance" into "structural equivalence" (762). A description that begins richly clothed in local specificity ("thickly described," as it were, with the stuff anthropologists recognize as evidence) yields to a totalizing claim based on an essentialized conception of power. The latter is itself hypostatized as a numbing kind of universal ether infusing all human activity. The governing logic of the essay, as Graham Bradshaw shows, ends up assuming the very thing for which it argues (86), namely the repetitive monotony of a process that produces subversion and then systematically subverts that subversion by containing it. Simply put, the larger conclusion, the one that moves from a localized cultural poetics to a historical account of the nature of Elizabethan power, rests on an unsubstantiated generalization. And although no one practice can stand for the movement as a whole, that of drawing cultural generalizations from the analysis of parallel texts *is* widespread.[10]

Several associated epistemologies fortify this new-historicist predilection for making generalizations based on extremely limited samples. Porter, among many others, attributes new historicism's totalizing penchant to the importation of a Foucaultian model (in one reading of his work) of transhistorical "power" (764–65). Further underwriting this conception is the structuralist linguistics of Claude Lévi-Straus (Giddens, *Central Problems* 22–28) and Clifford Geertz's functionalist anthropology, in which distinctive practices in one part of the culture are seen as symbolic revelations of the operation of the culture as a whole.[11] To these may be added Lee Patterson's contribution: "the skeptical self-cancellations of contemporary [including new-historicist] textuality" are brought on by deconstructionism, whose qualities of irresolution and undecidability foster a dazzling world of self-contradiction in which, ironically, nothing finally happens because "the continually renegotiated antagonisms of Renaissance culture are always already inscribed within a space of stasis," disclosing "a world strangely drained of dynamism" (63). Without trying to piece out the degree of influence of each school of thought, we clearly see that new historicism's identity as a practice offering a self-contained, and in that sense totalizing, interpretation of culture has not been accidental.

The practical criticism of Leonard Tennenhouse, Jonathan Goldberg, and Stephen Orgel has gone a long way toward defining what new historicism is. With their virtually exclusive focus on the power of the court and the monarch, their work has provided a concrete illustration of the practice, from which I believe new-historicist criticism must break. In this prominent brand of new historicism, the king's power to represent the monarchy and its authority is seen to suffuse everything and to be virtually synonymous with the reality of seventeenth-century life. The gaze that is directed in the first instance to king and court is found to be maintained in all the other representations, literal and symbolic, that radiate from that central power—in portraits, poems, plays, miniatures, coins, and so on—to the culture at large.

Often, the accusation that new historicism "totalizes" actually refers to something else—its "imperialistic" emphasis on texts alone as the only operative reality. In this critique, the claim is that new historicism not only establishes an analogic relation between text and culture; it ends up as a new formalism that denies a difference between textual representation and any material power external to it. James Holstun's "Ranting at the New Historicism" uses the example of a Jacobean masque to explain that in a new-historicist purview the masque "contains within itself not just a partial model of monarchical power, but all of that power and all conceivable kinds of resistance to it" (202). The result is that each artifact examined is treated as a representative "cultural synecdoche" (203). The system of interpretation is thus a closed one; it needs or searches for no reference to something outside itself. Pursuing a similar line of reasoning, Lee Patterson concludes that "New Historicism sets itself against the monologic idealism of traditional *Geistesgeschichte*, with its insistence upon cultural homogeneity, and yet . . . ends up presenting a Renaissance as synchronically isolated and politically uniform as anything we find in Tillyard's *Elizabethan World Picture*" (63). Implicit in this criticism is that the new-historicist method has no way of testing itself, no means of introducing contradictory external evidence; it functions like a closed system (Bradshaw 86). Such critiques may even urge that new-historicist readings lack an internal mechanism to assess whether the paradigmatic canonical artifact functions, as the critic claims it does, to challenge, repress, or reinscribe (as the case may be) the dominant culture. The "poetics" can call itself "cultural" but it is in fact "formal."

The charge that new historicism is a totalizing project is thus closely tied up with the question of whether it is a historical method. Feminist historian Martha Howell confronts this complex issue and flatly states her negative evaluation. "Essentially, my problem is that the new historicism is not historical, that is, it does not focus on the questions which motivate my research or adopt methods that I can use" (142). In particular, she charges that new historicism reifies power as a totalizing abstraction (as used, for example, in *patriarchy* as an all-embracing term) and that it is unable "to show texts doing social work, even to illustrate how they shore up the hierarchy; instead they tend to imply, and occasionally assert, that texts do this work" (142).[12] A version of this view appears in Stephen Collins's essay "Where's the History in the New Historicism?" There Collins defines what he calls the "new literary historicism" as an enterprise that "trivializes human agency and ignores the social production of the history of order" because it "privileges preconceived cultural contexts such as 'state power,' 'the court,' and 'patriarchal norms'" (232). After stating that "they"—the new historicists—"refuse to appreciate that order and stability are as much social products as is change," Collins goes on to call for a more "historical" method—one that attends to "historical particulars and process" so that agency and the social production of both change and order can be accounted for (232–34).[13]

Are these criticisms just? Are they even answerable? In substantial measure, the issue depends on how closely new-historicist practices are to be identified with new historicism itself. At what point, in other words, do a myriad number of practices become new historicism itself? I, for one, am loath to treat its methodology as being as fixed as these critiques suggest.

So too, if we return to Carolyn Porter's critique of new-historicist practice, we find that her powerful argument is not without its underlying difficulties. The critical issue is what Porter means by "being historical." If being historical means adducing causal evidence of the sort that *a* causes *b*, then Porter is right that Greenblatt's analogical argument fails because causation is not demonstrated. But does all historical evidence need be of this causal sort? Stephen Collins's argument raises similar problems. When he exhorts new historicists to attend to "historical particulars" and to social order as a productive and not merely a restraining process, his admonition is fair and constructive. But when, after characterizing new historicism as a "literary imperialism" (234)—a phrase borrowed from Murray Krieger— he goes on to call for a more "historical" method, demanding that structural/functional analyses be "abandoned," it becomes clear that the only method he recognizes as being "historical" is one that makes "human agency" central to understanding (234). But if analyzing human agency be judged as the only acceptable way of carrying out a historical project, then Porter's argument and Collins's too are based on a reductive view of what constitutes being historical.

Why should not the description of an economic system or a semiotic system (in which individual agency may be viewed as negligible)—also count as being historical? History is concerned not only with what happened but with how systems work, in short with ongoing processes between and within groups and institutions. In any of these circumstances, the agency of individuals may be present, but their presence may not be very useful in accounting for the orderly and dynamic features of the system under study. Indeed, it is perfectly obvious that apparent event-based "causes"—Shakespeare's writing *The Tempest* after reading the Bermuda pamphlets; James I's and Charles I's repeated prohibitions against monopolies; and Thomas Middleton's arrest after a performance of his anti-Spanish, papist-baiting play *A Game at Chesse*—may be mere effects disguising deeper cultural transactions.

Those who claim categorically that event-based arguments of the sequential sort are *the* way to write history, often citing precedent and authority, tend to be impatient with evidence that does not present itself empirically, in its "thingness," or at the level of intentions with the palpability of identifiable motive. In other words, positivist proponents of event-based analyses may too easily rest satisfied with a causal criterion for truth while failing to concern themselves with the cultural processes, including linguistic ones, that underlie or predetermine what presents itself as a determining cause. For this reason, some of the ablest materialist critics such as Fredric Jameson, Raymond Williams, and Frank Lentriccia have found subtle ways of treating the principle of causality. Deterministic as a fundamentalist Marxism is, its adherents approach the question of causation as revisionists, cagily, gingerly, admitting of analyses that are not necessarily structural (institutional), and from this vantage offer qualified statements to the effect that questions of agency and causation cannot be brushed aside. In this spirit, a cautious Lentriccia speaks of the necessity of modern historicism's showing "a complicated commitment to the principle of causality, for without causal explanation there is," in this view, "no historicism, old or new" (231).

Against even this revisionist position, I would contest the necessity of causal explanations. First, new-historicist interpretations of how the parts of any social system worked together in a given era *is* historical study of a valuable kind. For example, Marxist interpretations that read major changes in economy—from feudal, to capitalist, to socialist—in terms of an inherent telos are not causal in the usual sense that *a* causes *b* sequentially; they are descriptions (often including supporting, causative arguments) of a stipulated, internal economic logic or process. But for all that, Marxist criticism *is* a method of historical analysis and contributes to our historical understanding. Significantly, this strength is also a weakness inasmuch as the functional methods of Marxist criticism operate within a paradigm that makes no provision for the creation of alternative hypotheses. This is why strong versions of ideological criticism can be procrustean and are accused of being ahistorical. Nonetheless, I would insist that such criticism is historical (all criticism is based on foundational assumptions), while conceding that the inability of any school to revise or modify its categories of historical analysis reduces its effectiveness over time.

Second, the concept of change must be distinguished from cause. Change simply means the substitution of one state of affairs for another, in short, alteration or variation. Cause, normatively understood, entails the identification of one or more agents, let us say *a*, that bring about a result—*b*.

Causal arguments are exacting. They demand that b could not occur without a and, further, that the presence of a will necessarily beget b. These are conditions that may be met in the physical sciences but hardly in (the making of) cultural or literary histories, or histories of any sort. In these latter endeavors, causal arguments are usually explanatory rather than strictly causal. Louis Mink, writing well before the appearance of new historicism, contended that the "causal language" we employ in describing human affairs is not really helpful because a multitude of prior intentions and circumstances extending far into the past continuously engender the world, and to illustrate the case he presented examples of how such causal language can be "translated into non-causal language without significant loss of meaning" (23).

Third, long before Mink, Friedrich Nietzsche, to whom Foucault owed so much, lodged several trenchant critiques of cause-and-effect reasoning, asserting that the latter is a dangerous concept "so long as people believe in something that *causes*, and a something that is *caused*" (*Will to Power* 15:58–59). He called the search for causes no more than an urge "to trace something unfamiliar back to something familiar" and "already *known*" (*Twilight of the Idols* 39; *Will to Power* 58). The truth is not simply something out there; "it is something *which has to be created* and which *gives* its name *to a process*" (*Will to Power* 60). Although I don't believe causal arguments are useless, I would certainly maintain that the attribution of causes is a construction, one manner of being historical, and it ought not to be privileged over functional historical narratives.

This leads to a fourth consideration. In a system of cultural analysis a is often inseparable from b and may neither precede nor cause b because the features of sequentiality and separability may not apply. But even when a specific cause cannot be attributed (and may not be pertinent), change within a system (as against an inert structure of power) may still be discerned. The main point, therefore, is not that synchronic analyses must at some point become diachronic, though that is true as well, but that all human reality is simultaneously synchronic and diachronic. An effective cultural historicism must treat both. Although Anthony Giddens prefers to avoid these terms, this simultaneity is exactly what emerges from his argument that "the structural properties of social systems are both the medium and the outcome of the practices that constitute those systems" (*Central Problems* 69).

If traditional historians often commit themselves to an overly restrictive conception of being historical, new-historicist practice too frequently ignores the entire process whereby change occurs within cultural systems. This is the problem seen from the other direction. When Collins argues that new historicism errs in disregarding Giddens's insight about the structural properties of social systems being both the medium and the outcome, he makes the excellent point that "structures are not barriers to action or to change," or at least not necessarily (233). Order and stability must be seen as processual, not merely as something imposed from without tyrannically.

This, of course, does not mean that the task confronting new historicism is that it must meet a traditional standard of historical proof, whose champions appropriate the category of the historical as if their practice alone were the thing itself. Functionalist reading of texts in the new-historicist mode is a legitimate historical method, especially when we recognize that the category of the "historical" is itself a historical term subject to revision.[14] But having acknowledged as much, we should also recognize that it is possible to treat "the textuality of history" and "the history of textuality" without yielding to a dualistic, either-or epistemology. The synchronic and diachronic can and should be seen as mutually constitutive, nonexclusive categories, an insight to which chiastically inclined new historicists should warm.

Still, the nagging problem remains as to whether this is a possible direction for new historicism. Collins, for example, characterizes new historicism's avoidance of the categories of change, agency, and diachrony as "theoretical" (232–33). Perhaps he is right. Nonetheless, the evidence he offers with reference to essays by Montrose, Goldberg, Greenblatt, Jonathan Dollimore, Terry Eagleton, and Franco Moretti shows that it is the practice he is talking about. This distinction is crucial. A theoretical assumption is foundational, altered only by resituating the enterprise; an orientation can be realigned and a particular practice reformed. To come to a fine point, the question shakes down to this: Does new historicism have an essential character or nature, or is it more aptly characterized as an association of practices, whose nature is fluid and changing or changeable?

Fortified though new historicism's critics are with multiple illustrations of essays exhibiting such a closed, formal, ahistorical system of inquiry, the accusation rests on an overgeneralization. The reason is that counterillustrations—theoretical ones—can be adduced to illustrate what new historicism is. I will select three prominent new-historicist critics to make this point.

In her widely cited account of new historicism, Jean Howard explains that a central feature of new historicism is its displacement of an older, "unproblematic binarism" between literature and history, one that sometimes removed literature from the realm of the "real," or, alternatively, under the sway of an older mimetic literary theory, one that treated literature as a mere backdrop to "the historical" ("New Historicism" 16). In opposition to this older historiography, Howard endorses new historicism by pointing to Foucault in support of her view that the discursive practices of any age never exactly coincide. Recognizing the essentially Bakhtinian point that "there is always some gap between what discourse authorizes and what people do," she argues that literature, one of the primary means by which a culture represents reality to itself, helps "to form its discourse on the family, the state, the individual" and "to make the world intelligible, though not necessarily . . . to represent it 'accurately'" (16–17). Here Howard's understanding of new historicism discerns a dialogic relationship between literature and history. This relationship differs from traditional historiography by focusing on the ways that texts (legal, literary, medical, theological) function in the discursive construction of such categories as "women," "wife," "family," and "state." Clearly, in Howard's conception, new historicism's formalism, its intimate embrace of textuality, does not exclude a relationship to the object-world, nor does it demand a totalizing interpretation of culture.

So too, Montrose's account in "New Historicisms" is notable for its denunciation of the way in which Renaissance new historicists have come to pose a "simplistic, reductive, and hypostatized opposition between 'containment' and 'subversion'" (402). The determinism implicit in this form of criticism can be identified with the "now-notorious argument" of "Invisible Bullets" (402). Observing the hopelessness implied in a practice that would leave no room for "a direct intervention in the process of ideological reproduction" and that would employ Foucault to support a monolithic conception of power that emphasizes "the inescapable subjection of subjects" (403), Montrose brackets the approach. Characterizing it as an "extreme" of new historicism, he points out that the "containment of subversion" hypothesis does not characterize the full body of the work of either Greenblatt or Foucault and so shields both authors from the generalization that theirs is a totalizing criticism (403).

In his more recent writings, Greenblatt himself has been at pains to dispel the generalizations that have arisen around his work. Notably, in *Learning to Curse* (1990), Greenblatt complains bitterly that he never proposed that "all manifestation of resistance in all literature . . . were coopted";

yet characterizations of "Invisible Bullets" and of new historicism in general "repeatedly refer to a supposed argument that any resistance is impossible" (165–66).

Attempting to describe a more positive direction for new historicism, Montrose recommends that critics adopt a "heterogeneous" and "processual" model and urges that texts be approached as "open, changing, and contradictory *discourse[s]*" that are "cumulatively produced and appropriated *within history*" ("New Historicisms" 404, 406; second emphasis mine). Unwilling to accept certain current practices or disparaging methodological generalizations about them as being *the* project, Montrose is clearly fighting for a far more fluid identity for the new-historicist project.[15] The stakes are high. Time has brought new historicism to a crossroads. Despite its varied theoretical commitments, new historicism's heralded lack of theoretical definition has now become a signal weakness. Such weakness must be redressed, for generalizations based on the practices themselves threaten to identify the project itself.

Whether the kind of reconceived historicist project I have described above ought to be called a species of new historicism or redesignated by the new term I have introduced, *cultural historicism,* is hard to say. New historicism is a widely recognized, developing interdisciplinary critical method. It would be salutary if that project could shed its associations with the "containment" hypothesis and with totalizing readings of culture. It ought also to accommodate itself to synchronic/diachronic readings of history without becoming the "establishment" history it opposed in the first place. But whether it can or cannot do these things, the cultural-historicist readings of this present study are dedicated to these goals.

To spell these out, the project of generating a new cultural historicism begins from within the new-historicist paradigm: it distinguishes itself from documentary historicism by its concern to treat the cultural power encoded in and transmitted through textual representations. The project also seeks to move beyond current new-historicist practices by challenging the predilection for treating any one textual feature of culture as indicative of the entirety (sometimes called the anecdotal method). Following this same logic, it challenges the new-historicist habit of offering synchronic readings of culture while ignoring diachronic ones. Synchronicity and diachronicity ought to be seen as mutually constitutive aspects of an inseparable process of cultural reproduction and change.

To come to the subjects of this book, the chapters following explore the manifest and covert expressions of an extensive Tudor-Stuart practice—surveillance. I treat surveillance both in the restrictive sense of the observation of or spying upon suspected persons and, more broadly, as the social oversight of individual behavior, especially sexual behavior. My purpose is to contribute to an understanding of the pervasive phenomenon of surveillance in early modern English culture through distinctive but convergent perspectives. That is, each chapter exhibits its own method, eschewing any notion about the necessity for a definitive or single method in every chapter. In this respect the book displays a strong exploratory rather than a programmatic impulse. Especially in Part One (chapters 2–4), the discussion begins from a new-historicist perspective and moves outward. The idea is to present effective methods of producing a historicized, decentered, cultural criticism.

The following chapter brings Foucault to the center, not because he is a new historicist—he is not—but because his antihumanistic critique of Western culture as a totalizing disciplinary project is a dominant theme in the new-historicist enterprise.[16] Sir Thomas More's *Utopia* is taken as my subject to show, in the first instance, the radical perspective that a Foucaultian/new-historicist analysis of surveillance casts on More's canonical, "humanistic" work of social engineering. In the second instance, the chapter seeks to respond to a troubling question in new-historicist criticism: what politics ought to mark new historicism as a movement? The prospect of fashioning a utopian society provides the occasion for turning the method back upon itself to reflect on the limitations of a presentist politics implicit in a Foucaultian assessment of Western disciplinary society.

Chapter 3 makes G. R. Elton's study *Policy and Police* in Thomas Cromwell's England the point of departure for examining the limitations of a documentary-based historicism. In opposition to Elton's traditional conception of what counts as evidence, this chapter presents a psychosocial account of the effects of surveillance as registered metaphorically in imaginative texts. A form of *mentalité* criticism—that is, a criticism associated with recovering attitudes and beliefs held (especially) by nonelite groups—this approach uses the tropes of surveillance in the poetry of Shakespeare and Jonson to provide insight in a way that documentary historicism cannot into the self-conscious representation of conscience and the divided construction of the self in Tudor-Stuart England.

Chapter 4 pursues the implications of the third from explicitly social perspectives. After considering surveillance as an officially sanctioned mechanism of social control, it proceeds to stress the social process of representation that both reproduces and recreates the informer's identity in culture. The initial focal point is the Rainbow Portrait displaying Queen Elizabeth's gown embroidered with little eyes and ears, symbolically indicating that the queen sees and hears all. Proleptic as it may be of Jeremy Bentham's device of the prison panopticon (Foucault, *Discipline* 195–228), Elizabeth's gown is different from a technology of power. Yet the display of royal omniscience offers the opportunity to test the prevalent new-historicist premise that any one element may be taken to reveal the whole. The question is, How closely did the Tudor-Stuart regime of surveillance, with its tribe of informers, actually fulfill the imperial vaunt emblazoned on Elizabeth's gown? An extensive popular literature wholly at odds with the official valorization of informers indicates the need to employ a processual model of society that can show culture divided among itself and being constituted by and through those divisions. It also suggests the necessity of distinguishing between the display or masquerade of power and its effective practice.

If Part One treats the institutional and psychosocial effects of the regime of early modern surveillance, Part Two (chapters 5–7) turns to surveillance as cultural oversight and takes for its subject the gendered sexual body. The reason for this emphasis is, first, that no other form of behavior is so carefully monitored, so fully subject to oversight, and yet so intractable. Second, recent studies in women's history have alerted us to the differential application of control mechanisms for women as contrasted with men. The dramatic representation of the oversight of sexual behavior thus offers an important subject for examining the operation of power within power.

I treat only in passing lesbian and male homosexual desire, not because it is unimportant—to the contrary, a significant literary criticism on these subjects continues to burgeon—but because homosexuality, as Alan Bray has shown, was not constituted as a sexual identity before the late seventeenth century. Rather, male homosexuality was immersed in a larger discourse of "debauchery," which bespoke the dissolution of order and included lechery, incest, adultery, and drunkenness (16, 30–31). Moreover, homosexual acts were condemned not because they marked a specific, abhorrent, idiosyncratic identity but because they bespoke one of the many depravities "to which *all* mankind is subject" (B. Smith 11). The identification of homosexual activity per se was thus secondary to the regulation of disorderly conduct in general. Because homosexual acts were not very visible, the activities of the "sodomite" or "catamite" could be condemned as they often were, sometimes vitriolicly in high cultural texts, without much being invested in their regulation.[17] Moreover, because such acts did not result in illegitimate children and had little relationship to the transmission of property, they were far less the object of regulation and surveillance than heterosexual desire. For these reasons my treatment of surveillance in respect to the sexual body treats the subject in its heterosexual relations.

My approach to this extensive subject is also limited by its focus on the cultural functions of Elizabethan-Jacobean theater. Theater was a public place where images of the sexual body were reproduced within a received order of virtue. Like television today, Elizabethan-Jacobean theater was a crucial site where the problematic relationship between high-cultural "literary" texts and cultural reproduction itself may still be investigated in dramatic texts from the period. The claim I wish to press in this respect is that Elizabethan-Jacobean stages did not merely reproduce the disciplines of cultural surveillance; they simultaneously reproduced *and* contested the disciplines of oversight and control.[18]

To establish the distinctive possibilities this method offers, Chapter 5 takes for its subject the Shakespearean problem play, a subgenre hitherto treated in terms of aesthetic form, and locates its cultural functions in the social/sexual issues of late Victorian England. The chapter provides a cultural analysis of the problem play as a genre whose special province is the representation and critique of sexual oversight. Chapter 6 carries the argument further. Challenging the very notion of the problem play as an exclusive phenomenon of Shakespeare's drama, it contends that this manner of cultural understanding must be extended to Shakespeare's Jacobean contemporaries. It subsequently identifies a select number of what are designated *Jacobean* problem plays. From this new category it examines three exemplary plays—*The Widow's Tears, The Dutch Courtesan,* and *The Tragedy of Bussy D'Ambois*—finding in them the relentless surveillance of sexual desire and yet an insistence on surveilling the surveillers.

The final chapter attempts to show how the representations of the sexual mothering body are deployed ideologically. Attempting to recuperate the social power of John Webster's *Duchess of Malfi,* Thomas Drue's *Duchess of Suffolk,* and Lope de Vega's *El mayordomo de la duquesa de Amalfi,* this chapter shows that these plays were among the first to represent the affective nuclear family as "natural." Accordingly, each represents the Duchess figure as sexual, fertile, and nurturing. The depiction establishes a counterpoint to the operations of early modern governments, which are reconstituted as invasive, "unnatural," and repressive. Read as a form of cultural history, these plays accord the family a discrete space separate from and opposed to the spreading incursions of princes of state.

The affective power of these plays, which centers on the corporeality of the Duchess figure, poses a challenge to literary/historicist criticism. The emotional distance many British materialists, Marxists, and new historicists adopt when approaching texts usually takes the forms of "scientific" detachment or outright hostility (Cohen 21; Belsey, *Critical Practice* 128). Frank Lentriccia, for example, recommends approaching the text with "suspicion" and then "interrogating" it "so as to reproduce it as a social text in the teeth of the usual critical lyricism that would deny the social text power and social specificity in the name of 'literature.' The activist intellectual needs a theory of reading that will instigate a culturally suspicious, trouble-making readership."[19] Edward Pechter summed up this attitude of antagonism in the phrase that holds that we had better "master the text before it masters [us]" (302).

But the question is whether this tonality of suspicion, authorized in the name of an ideological self-awareness, is necessary to new-historicist criticism or to poststructuralist practice in general. I don't believe it is. And the costs are high. In literary criticism especially what is needed is an affective, not merely a cerebral, critical practice. When professional readers study "poetic" texts, among others, critics need in some way to give voice to the affective messages they are interpreting. An unalterable strategy of opposition in effect demands the suppression of emotional responsiveness and impoverishes the cultural inheritance that must be engaged.[20]

There is a further consideration. When critics encourage an antagonistic relation between reader and text, they presume that texts are all the product of repressive culture. But such a perspective is itself totalizing and leaves no room for progressive impulses. Not all texts, and certainly not all parts of all texts, ought to be treated with contumely. If power is everywhere, and if it always implies a jostling within itself, not all of its textual manifestations ought to be viewed as negative. Indeed, if various texts take up distinctive sites in an ongoing discourse of power, a uniform response to the abstraction "power" is impossible. Were this not the case, political criticism would make no sense. Far, then, from ignoring or resisting affectivity, cultural historicists must find ways of engaging the affectivity of texts because that is how they exerted—and may perhaps continue to exert—their cultural effects. Simply put, criticism ought not to relinquish the task of recovering the diverse ways in which texts do their cultural work.

Although this study eschews any singular scheme for reforming new-historicist practices, it presents throughout interventions that seek to evaluate and enhance the potential for developing a fuller *historical* practice. As a concrete means toward this goal, I have taken as my subjects Tudor-Stuart surveillance practices and the cultural oversight of the sexual body, especially as these themes recursively appear in the poetry and drama of the period. The result, as readers will see, is a generally converging but not uniform view of Tudor-Stuart culture.

My hope is that out of such interventions as these there will emerge a more sustained—and sustainable—new cultural historicism.

Part One

Surveillance

2

Foucault and *Utopia*

Politics and New Historicism

My purpose in this chapter is a double one—first, to illustrate several ways in which new-historicist methods reconstitute our understanding of the past and, second, to make visible the politics that informs method, and so to assess both. Establishing the methodology that both creates and critiques the past is one important new-historicist activity; so too interrogating the politics of method even as method works to constitute the past must be another.[1]

Since the disinterested pursuit of knowledge has been shown to be saturated with concealed ideology, the impetus to announce the politics that informs one's method (in hopes of avoiding complicity in a covert ideological practice) has become almost mandatory. So has the pressure to write with explicit political commitment, not just awareness. But in marked contrast to various feminisms and versions of Marxism, including England's highly polemical movement in cultural materialism, the new historicism has exhibited unimpressive credentials. It lacks a discernible political identity. Because it emerged as a series of alternative practices without any founding ideology or announced presentist concern it has also been insufficiently theorized. Its uncertain political allegiances continue to concern numerous theorists of new historicism, including Montrose and Peter Erickson, who have been frank to acknowledge the ways in which a merely academic practice of new historicism—that is, one that closes off its study of the past from present concerns—may enthrone new historicism as the new (comfortable) academic orthodoxy ("New Historicisms" 406; "Rewriting" 336).

My own response to this set of concerns is to attempt a critique of the implicit politics that informs many new-historicist readings. To do this, I propose to use Michel Foucault, the figure whose methods inform new-historicist practices, and to show how a Foucaultian analysis functions to subvert Western culture and ideology. Clearly, a Foucaultian critique, unlike certain apolitical Derridean deconstructionisms, particularly as exhibited in Paul De Man's work, does not merely "reconstruct" the historical past (Simpson 727); it exposes Western culture as disciplinary and repressive. But far from being content to demonstrate that Foucaultian-inspired, new-historicist approaches work to subvert dominant "truths," I want to use utopian texts to show that power/knowledge is an inherent condition of social organization itself. And if this is the case, practitioners of the new historicism ought to respond to that recognition by setting aside the fantasy of a world outside power. Once that happens, it will be possible to face the political issue still being avoided, namely, the kinds of power/knowledge that ought to be endorsed in moving toward a better society, a "eutopia."

To come to cases, Foucault's analysis of the disciplinary powers in the West, especially the devolution of surveillance in modern "carceral" institutions,[2] allows us to examine a canonical master text, More's *Utopia,* from an alienating distance. From our post-1984 vantage, Utopia is best interpreted neither as a redaction of monastic Christian communalism nor as a prophetic text heralding capitalism's end and the advent of a propertyless, socialistic state.[3] It is no longer even best understood from a liberal-democratic perspective (exemplified by Lewis Mumford's essay) as a society in which the controls are external, the tyranny imposed on resistant, autonomous persons. Rather, *Utopia* is best viewed today as a canonical text best expressing the Western urge to fashion a practicable, systematically controlled society in the name of equity, justice, and the social good.

My perspective, however, is not as alienated as Foucault's. The latter's critique of the disciplinary society of the eighteenth century permits us to see that the strategies of surveillance are built into the very concept of rational organization. By rational I refer to that self-reflecting activity traceable at least to the Greeks, by which the concept of the "good society" is imagined and planned according to a logic of organization that reduces the whole to a system of practices. Once the rule-laden, perforce coercive strategies undergirding every serious utopian narrative are recognized, it becomes important—to me—to interrogate Foucault's own master critique of Western culture in respect to his general silence in identifying the kinds of power that ought to be legitimated. For us as political creatures it is important to know what utopian society, in the original, weaker sense of "improved" or perhaps "optimal" social organization, might plausibly be established, or seriously imagined, as an alternative to a disciplinary culture. On the answer to this question the viability and character of a presentist, new-historicist political criticism depends.

In Foucault's analysis, the episteme of horrific, exemplary punishment as employed from the Inquisition through the sixteenth century was replaced in the eighteenth by the rupturing episteme of disciplinary surveillance. In contrast to horrific punishment which operated on the "body," disciplinary surveillance emerged as the systematic form of social control because it effectively made—makes—subjects willing agents in the social construction of their own subjectivity (identity); it operates on the "soul," the better to discipline the body for its own good (16–19).[4] This assessment, that Enlightenment reformers branded exemplary punishment as "barbaric" and replaced it with an ideology of crime prevention and criminal rehabilitation via surveillance, is important to our analysis because it makes Foucault's philosophy of punishment empirical: Foucault's history of the disciplines purports to corroborate his epistemic method.

But does it? If the history of disciplinary regulation were to prove to be more processual, how would that affect the construction of a presentist politics? To come to a central point, if Foucault, writing in the 1970s and 1980s, erringly identified the Enlightenment as the source of comprehensive, disciplinary organization, then the object of attack would have to be, not Enlightenment practices, but possibly systematic social thinking itself. At that point it would be important to ask whether we believe such thinking to be inimical to the development of Western civilization. In short, what ought we to ask of our civilization, and on what paths do we want it to proceed? This last issue I leave for the concluding part of this chapter. My first object is to establish the extraordinary efficacy and depth of Foucault's critique of Western thought as a discipline of power and only after that to treat the implications of his thought for a new politics.

Turning then to More's *Utopia*, we see clearly that certain aspects of its organization conform straightforwardly to Foucault's pre-Enlightenment paradigm of princely power and horrific punishment. In this category appears the marking of the bondsmen. Despite the witty narrational emphasis on the Utopians' wondrous devaluation of gold, which decorates the bodies of criminals, the discipline of the state is still advertised on the convicts' bodies. As Hythloday puts it, "criminals who are to bear through life the mark of some disgraceful act are forced to wear golden rings on their ears, golden bands on their fingers, golden chains around their necks, and even golden crowns on their heads" (51).[5] The very institution of slavery emphasizes the power of the Utopian state. These practices are confirmed by the Polyerites, a people praised for their charity and public spirit, who require their convicts/slaves "to wear a special badge" upon penalty of death and also to suffer the tip of the ear to be cut off or "cropped," the better to prevent conspiracies or escape (19). The purpose of such discipline of the body is made explicit when Hythloday concludes that in Utopia "slaves . . . are permanent and visible reminders that crime does not pay" (67).

In these several ways More's dialogue exhibits the ideology of pre-Enlightenment penal systems. Nevertheless, for Utopia's citizens, mainstays of the society and its principal work force, this crude sixteenth-century model of repression does not apply. Hythloday's denunciation of hanging in the debate at Cardinal Morton's clearly shows that his subsequent account of Utopian customs in Book Two is set forth in *opposition* to the repressive regime of punishment endorsed by the lawyer. These same liberal values govern the entire book, and for this reason the prevailing techniques of discipline among the Utopian citizenry belong to an Enlightenment model of discipline. The point is significant. In Foucault's history, it was only from the eighteenth century, after the development of techniques of continuous supervision along with precise computations of the efficacy of human labor, and the deployment of a "network of relations from top to bottom" in an "'integrated' system" (176) that comprehensive disciplinary prevention became imaginable or practicable. *Utopia* reveals, however, that More had fully conceived of an "'integrated' system" of social control and had comprehensively represented it in the early sixteenth century. Indeed, by 1650 Gerrard Winstanley was actually attempting to implement a "utopian institutionalism" based on a regimen of discipline in his communistic Digger settlement (Kenyon 193–224). From a slightly different perspective, John Archer argues that "the techniques of surveillance were firmly rooted in the court politics of the pre-Enlightenment state ruled by a personal sovereign" and that "sovereignty and surveillance are [were] more continuous than Foucault's dichotomous periodization suggests" (6). This continuity between early modern and Enlightenment thought suggests that the major distinguishing feature of the eighteenth century may be only its superior technology of control.

Such continuity is worth exploring further. At issue is how pervasive the use of rationality was as an instrumentality in Western social organization and planning. Using *Utopia,* we look for the rational application of techniques, tactics, strategies, and disciplines, and what we find, to begin with, is movement tightly controlled. To visit another city or even the countryside requires the permission of the syphogrant as well as a letter from the prince. Even moving in one's own district requires the permission of the father and for married people the spouse. Such discipline ensures an adequate supply of human labor by organizing bodies into functional economic units. Wherever a person goes, he or she gets no food until a half day's work has been completed. As Hythloday sums up the situation, "There is no chance to loaf or kill time, no pretext for evading work; no taverns, or alehouses, or brothels; no chances for corruption; no hiding places; no spots for secret meetings. Because they live in the full view of all, they are bound to be either working at their usual trades, or enjoying their leisure in a respectable way" (49). This is a straightforward example of the Foucaultian paradigm of the "disciplined" body as "a useful force only if it is both a productive body and a subjected body" (Sheridan 139).

As Hythloday depicts it, Utopia turns out to be but a version of Bentham's panopticon as Foucault theorized it (195–228). In Foucault's formulation, the panopticon is effective not because the supervisor views every prisoner at every moment but because he *might* do so and therefore the prisoners introject this all-seeing eye, behaving *as if* they were being watched at all times (201). Once the Argus-eyed mechanism of social control is internalized, "docile" bodies are produced and "mechanized" for the workplace and the "souls" within them efficiently fashioned to work hard and willingly. It is this latter, sophisticated state of subjection, working at the level of subjectivity itself, we find, that also prevails in Utopia.

We are not prepared for this kind of modernity. It is not just the panoply of external controls that makes *Utopia* a "mastering" Western text; it is the organizational practices that "make" Utopian citizens into subjects. The partitioning of city districts into fourths with a market at the center of each, the regularization of city size by imposing a six-thousand-household limit, and the prescription of ten to sixteen adults in individual households are not to be explained benignly as the product of the Utopians' devotion to mathematical precision and love of reason. Rather, these are preconditions of Utopian surveillance, a form of control most completely exhibited in Utopia's planned cities. In cities people can be counted, accounted for, and assessed in numerous ways. For example, the repeated surveys in Utopia of the citizens' requirements and of the economic output of each district ("surpluses" and "shortages") depend upon modern organizational controls, controls that Foucault identifies with the "drawing up of 'tables'" to satisfy a "scientific, political and economic technology in the eighteenth century" (148). Although Hythloday reports (responding in effect to England's economic plight) that all Utopians spend part of their time working on farms, the children are first trained at school in the theory of farm work, then gradually introduced to nearby farms through field trips. Clearly, the farms More imagines in Utopia are organized on the model of the cities. Of course, the supervision of the crafts, although located within families, adumbrates the training for the modern factory and the schools (that other modern factory). So does the discipline of wearing uniforms. Whereas open-air activities occurring over large expanses of land make continuous supervision impractical or at least labor-intensive, enclosed dwellings are much more conducive to effective control. More's society *was* substantially agrarian—but the geographical imagery of Utopia belongs to the towns, the cities, and the workplace.

The invisibility of the king in Utopia (unlike Machiavelli's prince or the prince cited in Foucault's delineation of sixteenth-century discipline) discloses a basic truth about Utopia—its strategies of control are comprehensively institutional, not personal. Functionally, Utopia's prince is no more than the chief executive officer in a bureaucratic machine. This we see in the Utopians' hierarchical organization, with its strict proportional representation of thirty households by a phylarchs, its denomination of a head phylarch position for each ten phylarchs, and, finally, its nameless prince, who is selected by the phylarchy. The structure, not the person, ensures the regularizing authority essential to the Utopian apparatus of control. And while the election of officials is supposed to demonstrate that Utopians enjoy superior political freedoms, that very mechanism produces and legitimates a self-perpetuating, static, and unquestioned social-political structure.

Equally crucial in this disciplinary integration is the educational system; it mints subjects. Hythloday presents this point unflinchingly. While the children are "still young and tender," the priests instill "principles which will be useful to preserve the commonwealth. What is planted in the minds of children lives on in the minds of adults, and is of great value in strengthening the state: the decline of a state can always be traced to vices which arise from wrong attitudes" (84). Through the priestly class's administration of virtue and its monopoly over educational functions, religion too becomes an instrument for the fashioning of Utopian "souls." The military, a relatively minor force in *Utopia,* also functions by controlling interpersonal relations, not by physical coercion. Spouses and children accompany their men to the front, ensuring that the husband-father-soldier, with the image of his dearest ones constantly before his eyes, will fight courageously to the end.

The care of families at church is symptomatic of the regulating discipline of bodies throughout the entire system. The parishioners "take their seats so that the males of each household are placed in front of the head of that household, while the womenfolk are directly in front of the mother of the family. In this way they insure that everyone's behavior in public is supervised by the same person whose authority and discipline direct him at home" (86). Similarly, family life is organized to promote intellectual pursuits that are strictly prescribed through the game of the virtues. A regimen of domestic supervision, with its rigorous system of rewards and deterrence, fashions the conditioned subject. Even the Utopian philosophy of epicureanism, innocent as it seems, works ideologically to engender a docile tranquillity. As Frank E. Manuel puts it, in Utopia "tranquillity is the highest good" ("Psychological History" 75). All of these features characterize what Alan Sheridan calls "a normalizing society"—that is, a society which is "the historical effect of a technology of power centered on the body as mechanism and organism" (193). They are part and parcel of what we call today human resource management. But these effects, we must recognize, are not generated by *mere* oppressiveness. To the contrary, they are made possible by an ideal of learning based on the Greek and Roman classics, the championing of the oppressed, and the insistence on neutralizing the inequalities of class and property. A liberal humanist analysis is powerless to account for these contradictions except by appeals to paradox and irony. A Foucaultian critique reveals that such a humanistic ideal, with its elevation of rationality as an instrument for the reconstruction of society, necessarily engenders its own dark side. Put more dramatically, humanism's dark side is that it seeks to remake the self under the name of virtue.[6]

The special care for precise proportional representation in Utopian society is too important to be missed, for it discloses a homology with Enlightenment accounts of the mathematical principles on which, say, the political nation was redistricted in revolutionary France. However anachronistically articulated, these principles establish the genus to which More's Utopia, conceived as a feasible, improved society, belongs. In *Reflections on the Revolution in France,* Edmund Burke described—hostilely—the practical principles of the French: "The French builders, . . . forming everything into an exact level, propose to rest the whole locale and general legislature on three bases of three different kinds: one geometrical, one arithmetical, and the third financial. . . . For the accomplishment of the first of these purposes they divide the area of their country into eighty-three pieces, regularly square, of eighteen leagues by eighteen. These large divisions are called *Departments.* These they portion, proceeding by square measurement, into seventeen hundred and twenty districts called *Communes.* These again they subdivide, still proceeding by square measurement, into smaller districts called *Cantons,* making in all 6400" (152). These calibrations, performed in the name of revolutionary equity, may be viewed as an end product of France's theorizing philosophes, who attempted to rationalize the process of social organization while simultaneously creating a new field of political science (with the emphasis on "science").[7] In both respects More's *Utopia* is a template. To compare these Enlightenment schemes with More's gives us insight into the rational organization not just of Utopian society but of rational organization itself as it has developed in the West.

This conclusion indicates that the Enlightenment discourse of disciplinary supervision was actually more of a summation and consolidation of an ongoing rationalizing process than the beginning of rational, modern history. If this is so, as I think it is, then another explanation of the development of the disciplinary powers is required. Such an explanation might take the following form: the imagining of a fully disciplined society must be dated at least from that time when political thinkers and philosophers could conceive of society as the product of social forces and believed that systematized alternatives were not only imaginable but feasible and indeed practicable.

Alternatively, one might argue that More's *Utopia* derives (in what I would describe as a flattened history-of-ideas approach) from Plato's *Republic.* But in its final form, with Book One (written after Book Two) on England's deplorable economic condition placed before Hythloday's account of his travels in Book Two, More's *Utopia* cannot be said to belong to that tradition of thought. Plato's ideal commonwealth is a philosophic treatise quite removed from concrete circumstances because it seeks to universalize, not historicize, its arguments. Thus its ten books are organized around the idea of Justice as an ideal form and the Good as an end of government. Justice is developed in terms of the "soul" of the ruler who balances reason, appetite, and spirit (Bk. 4) and then in terms of the ruler's recognition (knowledge) of "reality" as an Idea behind appearances (Bk. 5). Even specific ideas pertaining to the training of rulers and the state's communitarian organization, in which children belong to the whole rather than to any one set of parents, are presented as philosophic consequences of the original conception. There is no concrete or particular political context.

` *Utopia,* by contrast, broke that mold for Western culture when More contextualized his already specific account of Utopia's social and political organization by placing his narrative, quasi-dramatic account of England's economic crisis, composed a year later in 1515, in front of the former as Book One (Dolan 26). Once More did that, he created for the West a new paradigm for the operation of "reason." No longer functioning as an abstract, transcendental exposition of truth, reason—as applied to matters of government and social organization—is redeployed in its comprehensive, system-creating features so that it results in concrete practices and recommendations applied to real-life societal problems. On this analysis, *Utopia* may be viewed as an effect of the realization that society is driven by human-made economic and political forces (cf. Machiavelli's *Prince*), whose evils human beings may attenuate by substituting practicable, alternative forms of social organization through reason's systematizing authority. To the early sixteenth century belongs, then, not the discovery of a platonic archetype but the appearance of a distinctive discourse.

This reading of More's historical moment may explain why outpourings of narrative on the ideal commonwealth erupted in the sixteenth century. Clearly, the impetus for such intellectual activity was accelerated by the discovery of the New World, which was itself made possible by the explosive growth of trade under nascent capitalism.[8] New world narratives brought Renaissance writers face-to-face with strange accounts of novel social organizations, as we see in Montaigne's essay on the Cannibals, further stimulating the imaginative construction of alternative worlds. This momentum to conceive and then elaborate upon optimal, rationalized, feasible forms of social organization continued to be felt into the next century in such narratives as Campanella's *City of the Sun* (1623), Bacon's *New Atlantis* (ca. 1624), and the anonymous *Histoire du grand ét admirable royaume d'Antangil* (1616)—and from the seventeenth well into the eighteenth century.

To illustrate how these utopias function within the same disciplinary discourse as More's, we may look to Campanella's treatise, whose emphasis falls on educational and medical systems. Again the restrictive rule of reason is immediately acknowledged in the prescription that arts and honors are held in common "in such a manner that no one can appropriate anything to himself" (166). The regimen of order is apparent in the subtle, pervasive ways that Foucault has elucidated in his works. For example, institutional control is achieved by developing licensed professional classes who operate for the common good. Thus, "the medical officers . . . tell the cooks what repasts shall be prepared on each day, and what food for the old, what for the young, and what for the sick" (173). Elsewhere we learn that women breast-feed their babies "for two years or more as the physician orders" (175). This is close to what Foucault calls the "medicalization" of the female body, which must be overseen by experts (*History of Sexuality* 1:120). In the interests of organizational efficiency the labor force is deployed so that certain men, objectified as "weak in intellect," are sent to do farming work, and if they become more proficient "*some of them* are received into the state" (175, emphasis mine). This interventionism by the state in the name of reason even extends to the naming of children, who at birth receive one name and later in life, after they have developed special skills, receive another. In this modernist turn, the power to organize the formation of identity is routinely delegated to an official who, in the name of a state good, inscribes the "I" of selfhood.

The raison d'être of the City of the Sun is wholly communitarian because "the race is managed for the good of the commonwealth and not of private individuals, and the magistrates must be obeyed" (176). To achieve this goal, the principal mechanism of control is not horrific punishment (although talionic justice is permitted in cases of grave injury) but discipline through "deprivation of the common table," "exile," and "exclusion from the church and the company of women" (195). The aim is not to terrorize through spectacle but to induce permanent and complete identification with the society. Under such a (modern) regimen, it follows, as Foucault reasons, that crime can only be viewed as a "misfortune" because the social process of education has failed and a "ceremony of mourning" must ensue (*Discipline* 112). This perspective is exactly what we find when Campanella declares that whenever a citizen is made subject to the death penalty, "the whole nation laments . . . that it should as it were have to cut off a rotten member of the state" (196). Clearly, Campanella's treatise belongs to a concrete discourse of control enacted in the name of humanism. Even more important, its author refused to grant that his utopia was not possible to implement (Manuel and Manuel, *Utopian Thought*, 278).

Much more selective in its purposes and vision, Bacon's *New Atlantis* (ca. 1624) propounds the virtues and possibilities of science as a bureaucratic instrument of technological progress and longevity. The programmatic character of the imagined good society is especially evident in the institutionalization of knowledge. Science has become a governmental function. Knowledge is reduced to an economy, a taxonomy of crafts organized both longitudinally and vertically for the benefit of all. In describing the "Merchants of Light," who collect knowledge, and then the bevy of experimenters equipped with appropriate technical names such as "Compilers," "Inoculators," and "Interpreters of Nature" (5:410–11),[9] Bacon clearly envisions nothing less than the bureaucratization of research for the production of knowledge and then of goods. This kind of knowledge is a power that reduces learning to a governmental economy, which in turn generates economic wealth, social allegiance, and ultimately, political stability. The wonder is that knowledge for Bacon is conceived of abstractly, as Foucault does (albeit in opposition), as an instrument of social control for the comprehensive ends of the "modern" state.

The institutionalization of medical knowledge is part of this discipline of power, for the Stranger's House, which combines the functions of hospital and prison in Bacon's narrative, ensures health by surveillance. Indeed, it must be so. Medicine is unthinkable, then as now, without subjecting each patient (and the would-be patient, hence everyone) to careful observation, record-keeping, and restraint, all tending toward an analysis of the patient as object of study and ending with prescriptions of diet, behavior modification, physical isolation, bodily surgery, and the like. Surveillance and modern medicine, as *The Birth of the Clinic* contends, go hand in glove. Archer's argument that "social organization and social surveillance are inseparable from the achievements of science" (146) is particularly apt to *The New Atlantis* because his insight leads to a larger generalization: any scientific approach to eradicating problems of health becomes under this regimen inseparably tied to the dark side, where darkness inheres in the coerciveness of a systematic logic applied to people as a condition of solving human problems. Modern science can proceed only by analyzing its objects of study—here human beings—and ultimately testing its hypotheses on their bodies, which it groups, organizes, treats, and otherwise subjects as a condition of freeing its patients from the scourge of disease. This utopian coerciveness is implicit in the promise of science itself, before whose laws, it is demanded, human beings submit. This oxymoronic condition wherein utopian freedom is predicated on human submission to the "laws" and "methods" of science is actually given voice by Bacon in the *Novum Organon* (1620), where the logic of science is invoked as *the* means of repairing the effects of the Fall and restoring man's "dominion over creation," methodically extracting from nature its hidden knowledge, "educing axioms, and from established axioms again new experiments" (8:115, 350).

The rigorous application of systematized practices to the ordering of human behavior underlies all these sober, early modern utopias. It cannot be stressed too much that this appears to be a precondition of serious utopian thinking, at least in the West. The principle is summed up in the *Royaume D'Antangil,* which states that "The Confusion of All the Provinces of This Empire" and the disorder they bring in war can be overcome by instituting a rational order of government that commands the support of the citizenry (37–38). In this context, "rational" again means logical, consistent, and replicable, as against disorderly, inconsistent, and haphazard. One hundred years later, the Abbé de Saint Pierre was still employing these methods in proffering his *Projet pour rendre la paix perpetuelle en Europe* (1713). From the early sixteenth through the eighteenth centuries, these utopian narratives are all predicated on embracing reason's system-building powers as humanity's only realistic hope of making (ordering) a better world. The warrant for the continued production of such utopias, it may be noticed, proceeds from the liberal principle that such remade societies must function under the gentle sway of discipline (the dark side being largely veiled), inducing and positively promoting a subjectivity that is as closely identified as possible with the prevailing rule of reason. The very ideals of the roundly able Renaissance courtier and the good citizen draw their strength from humanism's ideal of producing a reconstituted social self—"like man new made" (*Measure for Measure* 2.2.79)—but the other side of this wonder is that the humanistic project of personal transformation (self-fashioning) is predicated on the application of social, political, and educational discipline for the purposes of inculcation. Since the self is not autonomous, as we have come to learn from so many theorists and practitioners,[10] the very identity of the educated or cultured person is fashioned by those humanistic institutions that ironically proclaim that self to be an autonomous agent—and actually credit their own humanistic pedagogy for constituting that "free" self. In this way freedom and servitude are confounded in Western discourse.

Foucault's project exposes the concealed authoritarianism of modern, liberal-democratic culture, raising a disturbing question: what kind of social organization in the West could conceivably elude such constraints? A passage from the Abbé de Saint-Pierre's *Projet pour rendre la paix perpétuelle* enables us to focus the issue. This utopian narrative proposes to penetrate into the origins of war to discover "whether It was so inseparable from the Nature of Sovereignties and Sovereigns, as to be absolutely without Remedy" (83). The ontological idea underlying this investigation, it will be noted, is not fixed on the essential nature of human beings but on their government and by extension the social organization of sovereignties. Apprehended in this way, the inquiry clearly belongs to the same class as that which motivates Foucault's own project. As such, it can be appropriated to address a problem in all new-historicist inquiries touched by Foucault's methods and outlook. In brief, Is the omnipresence of the disciplines so inseparable from the operations of modern society as to be absolutely without remedy? Significantly, whereas the Abbé holds that war *is* separable from the operation of society and that by curing "the Causes of the Disease" of war Europe may be reorganized into "some permanent society" of peace (84–85), Foucault envisions no alternative political organization or society. Nonetheless, Foucault's critique of modern society is unremitting. How can this be? Surely the prospect of an improved, realizable society underlies Foucault's project.[11]

Two considerations illuminate this problem. The first is that the very notion of a feasible alternative society, not to say an ideal one, is problematic. Greenblatt has pointed out that More's *Utopia* is a paradoxical construct that at once expresses its author's own disciplined "self-fashioning" and his "self-cancellation" to realize the values of "communal solidarity" (*Renaissance Self-Fashioning* 57, 69). Virtually every comprehensive social scheme arouses our basic fears of dystopia no less than our hopes for reformation. That is why More and many who succeeded him delineated each new utopian scheme with a patina of irony. The profound ambivalence with which the scientist-creator is presented in science fiction exemplifies similar apprehensions. However benign the original intentions, grand scientific schemes, like utopian ones, can—and usually do, the genre tells us—make Hydes of Jekylls when the attempt is made to implement them. From a systemic standpoint, the utopian vision almost always faces its antiutopian dark side. And when apprehensions about the power of reason to reconstitute society grow portentous enough, the dystopic anxiety produces the counter-critique of the *Brave New World*s and *1984*s that supplants the utopian vision. If Foucault were to delineate a seriously conceived, alternative society, it too would have to face its utopian dark side. The fact that he does not is an aporia that leaves us wondering how a less repressive society could be constituted and what it could plausibly look like. As Jane Flax reminds us, although postmodernist thought points in a general way to the "liberating potential of freeing differences and refusing totalities," beyond this "it is not clear that postmodernism has or could offer a positive vision(s) of justice or the good life. . . . Nor do most postmodernists have much to say about the concrete practices and knowledges that could replace the current ones" (233). This is as true of Foucault as of any other postmodern theorist.

The second consideration follows from the first. It is that the price one pays for any seriously conceived, alternative society—the dark side as I have called it—is an unavoidable condition of any systematically applied rational scheme rather than the result of an eighteenth-century technology of power, as Foucault held. This can be shown on the prima facie ground that rules involve prohibitions and limits; they circumscribe behavior. But can we live without them? This possibility of rejecting real-life social limitations actually has its own literary history, and it is located, significantly, just at the juncture where utopian thought takes serious hold.

This second type of utopian narrative, which may be called the "counterlogical utopian vignette," consists of narratives begotten in disillusion with real-world conditions and posited in reaction to organized social life. Their salient features are, variously, a rigorously observed lack of system, an insistence on contradictory freedoms, haphazardly deployed, and assertions on nonsystem as *the* ideal system. Gonzalo's ideal commonwealth in *The Tempest* is the best-known case in point:

> I' th' commonwealth I would, by contraries,
> Execute all things; for no kind of traffic
> Would I admit; no name of magistrate;
> Letters should not be known, riches, poverty,
> And use of service, none; contract, succession,
> Bourn, bound of land, tilth, vineyard, none;
> No use of metal, corn, or wine, or oil;
> No occupation, all men idle, all;
> And women too, but innocent and pure;
> No sovereignty— (2.1.148–57)

The identifying element of Gonzalo's utopia is its complete playfulness, its utter rejection of property, service, law, supervision, sovereignty itself. The other side of this vision is its primitivist nostalgia for a world made perfect without effort and its (ironically) systematic rejection of system—reason's forbidding, sober side. Preposterously, the sovereign himself, Western-born assuredly, must rule in nonrule to ensure such free play. This is why Gonzalo's state can exist only by "contraries" in a reason beyond reason, beyond the bourne of consistency, constraint, and realizability. Gonzalo's is a genuine "ou-topia" or "no-place" because it supposes as Golden Age myths do "that Noplace does indeed represent the best state of a common-wealth, that negation equals perfection" (Helgerson, "Inventing Noplace" 103). Under this regimen Gonzalo's perfect world is a reaction against a dreary, demanding present without a plausible vision of the future. But it cannot be implemented.

Inasmuch as Gonzalo's new world commonwealth functions as a primi-tivist fantasy (cf. Montaigne's Golden Age quasi-fantasy account, "Of Can-nibals") it is reactive, gaily dancing away from the rude world on which applied reason builds, because its author knows that such reason, the demanding mother of systems, is of necessity a maker of tasks and an enemy of the sweetest nostrums.

Rabelais's "Abbey of Thélème" operates by similar (non-) principles. The playful avoidance of consistency and of the entire system of controls that appears to be the condition of any seriously imagined Western society is one of its distinguishing marks. In contrast to the drab earnestness of More's precisely imagined new world, these display an irrepressible "jouis-sance," which overleaps the regulatory prescriptions of "sober-faced offi-cialdom" to posit in a grand "uncrowning," as Mikhail Bakhtin calls it, the free play of body and spirit (73–96). Rabelais's genteel inhabitants of Thélème break all bondage "to vile constraints" and live according to one rule only: "DO WHAT THOU WILT" (124). This dictum permits the people of Thélème to spend their lives "not ordered and governed by laws and statutes and rules, but according to their own free will" (124). Doing what they will in a world without clocks, they are yet all punctual and agree completely on harmonious, complementary manners of dress, as well as on all their daily group activities. Interpersonal conflict is not even a category of possibility.

The very contrariness of these anti-organizational organizations that are hailed as utopias illustrates the hold that an applied rationality, or appre-hension of it, was already exerting on Western high culture. As counterdiscourses, these exuberant utopias all oppose the restrictions of European life and work to dispel the phantasm of rationally "improved," disciplined new worlds.[12] Recoiling from the restraints of reason and social-scientific regulation that are preconditions for implementing such dreams in the world, they indulge in free play. That is also why they are so brief, so contradictory.

Ironically, these texts point reflexively to the unacknowledged ground underlying Foucault's systematic critique in *Discipline and Punish.* Foucault never gives himself up to the fantasy of describing his optimal world. Rather, his discourse is circumscribed by a rule of reason—his genealogical criticism—critiquing the course of technology/power in the West. This rule of reason refrains from venturing on unfamiliar seas to map a "nowhere" with a name, a place, and a social structure. In this absence we discover a Foucault far less playful than Rabelais or Shakespeare and yet more utopian than More. In declining to present his fantasy-in-reason, Foucault nods toward an alternative world that in a concrete political sense is "noplace." From the sixteenth to the eighteenth centuries and beyond, the concretely imagined, utopian narrative permits a calculation of the social price that must be paid for the benefits of a proposed new world. Each frankly prescribes the means that will be employed to secure the sought-for ends.

This circumstance prompts us to ask the same question of Foucault's *Discipline and Punish* and of new-historicist criticism generally. If the systems of discipline are to be resisted, because despicable, what mechanisms of control are to replace them? Beneath Foucault's anatomizing construction of modern institutions is what alternative social foundation, what system, what preferred body politic? This is what we do not know and what new historicists must determine if a politics is to emerge from critical practice. Of course, it may be contended that Foucault's critique of the disciplines ought not to be required to produce the kind of systematizing it relentlessly exposes and resists. In "Foucault's Body-Language," Nancy Fraser surmises that Foucault does not elaborate any "substantive, normative alternatives to humanism" because he views such efforts as "implicitly totalitarian because totalizing . . . [and] normalizing because normative" (56, 58). But this very refusal is ensnaring. A concrete politics cannot meaningfully be proposed without a notion of a possible future, which is to say a concept of what ought to be, or a sense of the feasible alternatives. Foucault's *rhetoric* of revulsion for the production of docile bodies intimates a position of implacable opposition, but it does not provide a corresponding politics or an alternative, postmodern value system. Crucially, it declines to offer an account of the ways that such a society, ought—indeed must (if it is to be a society)—*legitimately* deploy its coercive powers. By the same token, new historicism's predilection, along with poststructuralist thought generally, for treating "power" as if were something ever to be resisted must be redirected (as Greenblatt has begun to do, at least theoretically, in *Learning to Curse,* chap. 9) toward those expressions of power that are to be preferred over other, less productive ones.

In the absence of a concrete vision of our better place and an account of how any future society will underwrite its own authority, it is hard to establish as a matter of political commitment to what purpose the modern disciplines of power should be resisted. James Holstun complains, "One searches Foucault's writings in vain for a detailed analysis of the dynamics of resistance" (201); Lentriccia discovers the same pessimism ("Foucault's Legacy" 234, 240), and Gerald Graff finds that what resistance there is "turns out to be only another of the faces of power, another means by which power reproduces, distributes, and extends itself" (169). For new historicists this produces a bind. Foucault's legacy provides practitioners with a deconstructive orientation that always intimates resistance to what Foucault saw as the nightmare of the modern disciplines but no means of discerning how positive social transformation is to take place.

Foucault's social thought thus leaves new historicists with an unimagined future society that must be described both as a "good place" and a "no place." His methods afford practitioners vivid representations of the totalizing progress of the Western world and with the impulse to resist but, philosophically, with no independent oppositional space and, consequently, no political program. The means by which (post)modern pilgrims are to progress to *our* New World thus remains uncharted territory and Foucault, along with the new historicists who owe so much to him, are taxed with a defeatist, totalizing conception of culture.

This set of circumstances brings new historicists to an apparent cul-de-sac. Escape may be had in at least two ways, however. The first can be had by drawing out the implications of Foucault's later thought. Certainly Foucault "denounced with passionate ambivalence"—Fredric Jameson's felicitous phrase—the rhetoric of liberation (in Lyotard xix), rejecting humanism's self-critiquing counterdiscourse because he believed it obscured the modes of social domination operating in the very thought processes and conceptual systems by which resistance expresses itself. He also held, it is true, that the idea of inalienable individual rights presupposes an (illusory) category of selfhood that parades as a transhistorical reality. Nevertheless, Foucault engaged the notion of emancipation by speaking, however vaguely, of "subjugated knowledges" and the recovery of half-forgotten discourses, "local knowledges," which constitute as he called them, "genealogies" of opposition.[13]

Second, new-historicist practitioners might recognize that even as Foucault rejected the notion of a subject position for intellectuals outside power he also rejected the intellectual's objectification in the discourse of power/knowledge.[14] While always operating from within power, the intellectual, he argued, has traditionally sought to testify "in the name of those who were forbidden to speak the truth: he was conscience, consciousness, and eloquence" (*Language* 207). The role of today's intellectual, he contended, must be to struggle against the objectifying forms of power in "local and regional" settings (208). This struggle against the disciplines must be "aimed at revealing and undermining power where it is most invisible and insidious" by sapping power and taking power (208). In "Power and Strategies," Foucault invoked the concepts of class struggle and multiple resistances from within as appropriate responses to the ideology of power/truth (*Power/Knowledge* 142). In this way, Foucault saw intellectuals resisting not the fact of the disciplines of power but specific social practices within them. It is unfortunate that practitioners have as yet neglected to incorporate these insights of Foucault into the new-historicist project.

Another possibility is that new historicists renounce part of their Foucaultian inheritance. As psychoanalytic critic Jane Flax observes, "It is incomprehensible that such [local and suppressed] discourses [as Foucault endorses] could persist despite the 'disciplinary and surveillance' aspects of power without the existence of some form of 'self.' Something must exist within and among persons that is not merely an effect of the dominating discourse" (231). If new historicists were to follow these insights they could still freely accept the Foucaultian commonplace that power/knowledge is omnipresent in culture but clearly not the notion it is always facelessly, "selflessly," the same.

To recapitulate, then, this chapter argues that the regulatory disciplines of power, which Foucault located in the eighteenth century, actually have a much longer history, since they were already being formulated in detail in More's *Utopia*. Most important, the organized disciplines of power are best understood as proceeding from the application of systematizing rational thought to the concrete problems of group life in the West. These several findings suggest our need to produce, not just hypostatize, dynamic, diachronic readings of culture. On this evidence as well, Foucault's volcanic conception of erupting epistemes, metamorphically periodized as they are, ought to give way to a method that can also accommodate the concept of transitions in cultural development, for all aspects of cultural processes help to determine outcomes.

A practice built on this recognition would demand that the category "power" be revised so that kinds of power/knowledge within power may be distinguished and assessed—some positively. On this point, we do well to hear Anthony Giddens's analysis in *Central Problems of Social Theory* that the "structural properties of social systems are both the medium and the outcome of the practices that constitute those systems. . . . *Structure thus is not to be conceptualised as a barrier to action, but as essentially involved in its production*" (69–70). This ineluctability of power, as well as the positive potential inherent in all systems, may be further refined by drawing out the submerged values in Foucault's discourse. Undertaking this task, Nancy Fraser finds Foucault's own rhetoric to be predicated not on a set of trans-formative, postmodern values but on antitotalitarian values rooted, ironi-cally for Foucault, in humanistic discourse, in a commitment "around the humanistic notions of autonomy, reciprocity, mutual recognition, dignity and human rights" ("Foucault's Body-Language" 58).

These revisitings of Foucaultian theory, it must be acknowledged, do not leave us with a concrete politics—but neither do they leave us unarmed for cultural critique. The "eu-topia" implicit in Foucault's thought is not equivalent to a concrete politics, but the values that underlie his method prepare a ground for the spadework that generates a politics. For this reason Foucault's analysis of the disciplinary regimes of modern life has a real political significance today. Along with new historicism, whose meth-ods owe so much to his perspective, Foucault alters our understanding of the world, our understanding of the covert operations of power. He thereby implicitly moves us to an alternative politics. The question I have posed with recourse to More's *Utopia* is, What might the mature practice of such a politics look like? I have suggested that our practical criticism must ac-knowledge our own commitments to the disciplines of power. Such a recognition is a precondition to the practice of an effective, concrete poli-tics.

In the chapters that follow, I build on the perspectives of this one. Still focusing on the expressions of disciplinary power in early English culture, I probe for the fissures produced from within. Toward this end, chapter 3 examines the effects of disciplinary surveillance as they are registered on the consciousness of literate Elizabethan and Jacobean subjects. In particu-lar, this chapter presents a method by which subjects can be heard to rehearse their own subject positions, and from that interior vantage point it is possible to explore the ways that they recursively receive and resist the waxen impress of power.

3

Tropes of Surveillance in Jonson's and Shakespeare's Poetry

Decentering Traditional Historicism

In *Utopia* one of the principal methods of fostering conformity among citizens, as we saw in Chapter 2, is the use of extensive procedures of surveillance. Such surveillance is presented half-fancifully as a construct, a voyage of More's imagination. But beneath this flight of fancy lurks the question of how much the imaginative framing of Utopia is predicated on or inspired by the informing practices of Henrican England. In other words, what exactly is the relationship between the disciplining imagination in *Utopia* and the disciplining culture of early modern England?

To answer this question, I propose to examine the relationship between imaginative discourses on surveillance—in this chapter limited to a select number of poetic texts—and the production of historical understanding. In the following chapter, I will examine a wider, more representative range of textual responses to surveillance in an effort to define the scope of that inquiry we designate as "historical." As a limiting disciplinary term, "being historical" can signify the making of a narrative of past events based on documentary evidence and using cause-and-effect reasoning as the mode of explanation. According to Dominick La Capra, "The predominance of a documentary approach in historiography is one crucial reason why complex texts—especially 'literary' texts—are either excluded from the relevant historical record or read in an extremely limited way. Within intellectual history, reduction takes the form of synoptic content analysis in the more narrative method and the form of an unproblematic identification of objects or entities of historical interest" (33). Even when the mode of inquiry shifts to the social history of ideas, "it too may take ideas, structures of consciousness, or 'mentalities' as relatively unproblematic entities," failing to "raise the question of how they function in texts or actual uses of language—looking instead into the causes or origins of ideas and their impact or effect in history. In brief, social history often adjusts a history of ideas to a causal framework and a conception of the social matrix without critically investigating what is being caused or having an impact" (34).

An important example of a traditional historiography is that of the eminent Tudor historian G. R. Elton. In *The Practice of History*, Elton propounds the view that history is a discipline-specific, documentary enterprise; it is also autonomous and distinct in its object from all other disciplines (8–12). "History," he argues further, concerns itself solely with change—event-based and particular (10). "Description"—which I would call "descriptive history"—is relegated to the discipline of "archaeology" (9). This conception of history, which itself may be understood historically as coeval with the emergence of departmental disciplines in the academy over the last century, is too restrictive to accommodate a postmodernist understanding of what historical study is and must be. Even apart from this issue of the scope appropriate to the discipline of history, the notions "historical understanding" and "history" itself ought to encompass our inescapably present relationship to the past in the production of knowledge. As we saw in Chapter 1, the relationships between object, sign, and interpretant are constitutive features of historical understanding and must be acknowledged lest we fall prey to an objectivist positivism. Moreover, the discipline of history cannot be narrowly restricted to a binary concept ("change" = history) that refuses to acknowledge the alterity on which it depends ("description" = archaeology). This binary refuses other possibilities, including the idea that descriptions of ongoing processes, within institutions and among institutions and people, for example, do not by any means exclude the notion of change and thus blur the distinction Elton is making.[1] To reverse this emphasis, if *historical understanding* is a disciplinary term, then disciplinary boundaries must be broken so that history is made to engage new-historicist concerns with synchrony and the constructedness of events. To these must be added the need to cultivate the broader charter of a cultural historicism capable of treating cultural processes both synchronically *and* diachronically.

Extending this purview to Elizabethan and early Stuart culture, the present chapter will treat the limitations of the dominant tradition of documentary history as defined by La Capra (32–36). As a way of overcoming these limitations, I will present an account of the effects of surveillance as they are registered metaphorically in imaginative texts whose surface content is not explicitly about surveillance at all. These will provide insight into the construction of the self and the representation of conscience in Tudor-Stuart England. By so breaking down the boundaries between poetic discourse and a restrictive conception of empirical evidence, I intend to provide by example a form of historiography that extends beyond documentary history and that nevertheless contributes to our historical understanding.

My starting point is the standard study of surveillance published in 1972 by the eminent Tudor historian G. R. Elton, *Policy and Police: The Enforcement of the Reformation in the Age of Thomas Cromwell*. Meticulously researched using original documents and papers of the regime of surveillance organized by Cromwell, Henry VIII's Lord of the Privy Seal (1536) and Lord Chancellor (1539), Elton's study refutes an argument prevalent among Whig historians that Cromwell created a cadre of intelligencers who enforced the English Reformation through a "reign of terror" (374). As revisionist history, Elton's study was one piece of an argument shaped over many years challenging the Whiggish view that there was an inevitable road to civil war brought on by Tudor-Stuart absolutism. In particular, Elton rejected F. W. Maitland's claim that Cromwell sponsored a royal absolutism based on Roman law and opposed the "immemorial" liberties of English subjects. Instead, Elton held that Cromwell was a superb administrator who in effect created a new monarchy founded on Parliament and bureaucratic institutions which took on a life of their own. As for the charge that Cromwell employed totalitarian methods and initiated a terror, Elton concluded in memorable sentences that this argument is false:

If there was terror it existed in the mind only, and the evidence for this is thin and circumstantial. Cromwell's terror did not mean the indiscriminate extermination of those against whom accusations were brought; it did not mean the organised supervision of people's thoughts, words and deeds; it did not mean the use of *agents provocateurs* or necessarily even that all England became a happy hunting ground for informers. His control involved the enforcement of the law as it stood, by the age's lawful methods of trial and investigation; such success as it obtained it owed not to the creation of new machinery or the introduction of new principles, but to the energy with which the normal interaction of local event and central authority was exploited, and to the vigorous encouragement, by exhortation as much as by threats, of the loyal cooperation of all sorts of Englishmen on which Tudor government depended at all times. If this necessarily resulted in encouragement for private malice and grudges, it is also plain that great care was taken to establish the truth before the power of the law was brought into action. (374–75)

In this view Cromwell, far from introducing hitherto unknown totalitarian methods of surveillance, merely modernized the irregular, existing machinery of government by making its bureaucratized parts work more effectively. This analysis of Cromwell's regime, amplified by the testimony of people who worked within or were affected by the system he enforced, is calculated to demonstrate that the Lord Chancellor operated within the traditional limits of English law enforcement procedure. The argument functions as a liberal defense of Tudor government on the ground that it was generally moderate and avoided the wanton use of brutal measures. And if this defense is then projected beyond the mid-1500s into the Elizabethan and Jacobean periods, a commendatory evaluation of the moderateness of early English law enforcement emerges.

What I find most intriguing about Elton's assessment is not the status of its evidence—although historians are far from accepting the Elton thesis of "The Tudor Revolution" (Williams and Harriss 8–58; Russell 110–11)—but rather its manner of constituting the historical in that dismissive sentence introducing the rhetorical conclusion—"If there was terror it existed in the mind only." In the economy of knowledge that comprises Elton's historiography, the mind and perceptions generally (as distinct from "hard facts") appear to lie outside history and certainly outside Elton's view of the retrievable facts of history. For those of us who believe that such an empirical conception of knowledge is based on an inadequate idea of what knowledge is, Elton's offhanded qualifier raises the challenge to produce a cultural historicism based on alternative or reconstituted methods of historiography.[2]

To be sure, Elton's documentary brand of history cannot be taken as wholly representative of the history profession. The contributions of such cultural historians whose work is gathered under the banner of mentalité criticism have been under way for a generation; the symbolic cultural histories produced by Roger Chartier (sometimes called representational history [9]) is another trend, and so are the intellectual and narrational histories of La Capra and Hayden White, whose theoretical critique of empiricist histories informs my own work. Nonetheless, Elton's approach, particularly its underlying epistemology, remains the dominant one among historians. Its prevalence is epitomized by the title phrase of J. H. Hexter's 1971 collection of essays, unproblematically called *Doing History*.[3] More important, many students of literature think Elton's kind of documentary history is what historians do. So the dominance of Elton's historical method remains a challenge to any cultural historicism.

As Dominick La Capra frames the problem, "The predominance of a documentary approach in historiography is one crucial reason why complex texts—especially 'literary' texts—are either excluded from the relevant historical record or read in an extremely limited way" (33). When Elton describes the evidence for terror as "thin and circumstantial," he means that few documents or reports can be adduced to support such a contention. When he denies that Cromwell supervised in any "organised" way "people's thoughts, words and deeds," his analysis is implicitly causal, and it takes the papers of a ruling-class official for its raw materials because its underlying concept is that history is created (i.e., "caused") by those who make critical administrative or legislative decisions. Under the same rationale, Elton's use of the term *organized terror* underscores his working assumption that if there was a terror, people would initiate it, and the records of their activities would constitute the documents or traces we call empirical evidence.

For these reasons, Elton's historical method makes no attempt to conceptualize the unofficial and circumstantial ways in which "people's thoughts, words and deeds" were (are) indeed organized. Such organization, it might be said, is precisely what distinguishes one culture from another. A more promising approach would be to view official surveillance as an instantiation of a network of cultural practices, only some of which are officially sanctioned. This approach reverses the historical method for which Elton's work stands and treats the legally constituted Tudor-Stuart system of surveillance as a cultural effect. In brief, a society that employs surveillance extensively in unofficial ways is likely to legitimize such functions in official ways as well.

To think seriously about surveillance as a cultural phenomenon rather than a legally sanctioned policing system is to realize that it was virtually ubiquitous. It underlay ceremonial occasions, as when marriage banns were proclaimed with the request to know if anyone possessed knowledge that might impede the joining of the engaged couple in holy matrimony. It appeared in communal supervision of heterodox spousal behavior, as in the practice of the skimmington and in the observations (and sometimes the voyeurism) of husbandmen, householders, farmers, shepherds, constables, and other community members who discovered illicit sexual behavior.[4] More mundanely, such oversight operated in the parental supervision of children, husbands' supervision of wives, and householders' supervision of servants, not to mention guildmasters' superintendency of apprentices and pastors' stewardship of parishioners.

Wherever discipline existed or exists, it begins with oversight.[5] Christian communities enshrined such cultural practices by constituting them as reflections of spiritual reality. God's all-seeing eye, homilists reminded their charges, observes every human event and divines every thought. The idea was reproduced in the engraving on the frontispiece of Sir Walter Raleigh's *History of the World* (see frontispiece of this book); it circulated as a commonplace in the motto "Dominus vivit et videt" ("The Lord lives and sees"), and it was further disseminated in the emblem of the fallen Adam crouching behind a tree, attempting to hide his face even as heaven's brilliant light blazes upon him (fig. 1). The epigram beneath reads, "Oh foole, no corners seeke, thoughe thou a sinner bee; / For none but God can thee forgiue, who all thy waies doth see" (Whitney 229; Daly et al. 335). The belief also circulated in popular dramas, for example, in *The Revenger's Tragedy* when Vindice, imagining a midnight world of "Drunken procreation" and incest in which the offenders put "their mask on" in the morning, warns that there is yet "that eternal eye / That sees through flesh and all" (1.3.58–67).[6] From God's all-piercing gaze there followed the apocalyptic truth of the Last Judgment, in which the virtuous and the wicked are separated according to their deeds. This spiritual reckoning shows surveillance to be inscribed in what was thought to be the very nature of things. So pervasive was this discourse of surveillance that it finally took the form of conscience. Secular and religious discourses from plays, poems, and epigrams to homilies, treatises, and histories tirelessly promoted such subjectification and all without depending on explicitly institutionalized forms of surveillance.

This delineation of a culture of supervision enlarges the ground on which surveillance in prerevolutionary England can profitably be examined. Was this supervisory culture effective enough from the sixteenth century to insinuate itself into the subjectivity of ordinary English citizens and how, if it did, could access to such knowledge be gained? One answer appears in the private diaries of such middling-rank persons as Ralph

Fig. 1. The Emblem of God's All-Seeing Eye.
"Dominus vivit et videt" ("The Lord lives and
Sees"). From Whitney, *A Choice of Emblemes*,
1586. Courtesy of the University of Illinois.

Josselin, where expressions of pangs of conscience over failings of character are recorded as a datum and are thereby open to a traditional historiography (MacFarlane, *Diary* 114). Another less obvious one may be found in
literary and especially dramatic texts whose tropological properties can
play a significant role in the interpretation of culture.

In particular, tropological representations of subjectivity in imaginative
literature open the way to a new historical understanding. The reasons for
this are compelling. Because imaginative literature functions with *implicit*
reference to the linguistic reality seemingly outside it and to which its own
language is inextricably tied, imaginative and "fact-based" historical writing are (in this sense) part of a common discourse. Also, because metonymy and synedoche connect ideas associatively, they reveal aspects of
cultural similitude that might otherwise remain concealed.[7] Such study
becomes significant not because metaphors can be construed as *referring* to
a local or topical reality (a form of documentary history) but because the
seemingly inexplicable imaginative connections they make to "the world
outside" show the character of prior inscriptions that underlie creativity. In
this sense metaphors write the writer. Whether authors consciously fash-

ion such constructions is less important than the cultural fact that they are represented in the first place.[8] Both the casual, embedded trope and the self-conscious, strategically placed trope are legitimate objects of study, a species of anthropological "thick description," or what Clifford Geertz calls "deep play"—the play of culture that includes agency and intention but far exceeds them because culture is a symbolic web of significations (*Interpretation of Cultures* 3–30).

For this kind of study, I turn to Jonson and Shakespeare, not merely because their poetry is densely tropic but also because it exhibits a high degree of interiority—of subjective self-examination. In particular, their poetry allows us to see most clearly the play of surveillance as an internally produced pattern of culture. Their tropes give us access, in a word, to those prior cultural inscriptions that underlie creativity. The point, of course, is not that cultural analysis demands the reading of canonical texts but quite to the contrary that there are occasions, which must be specified, when canonical texts such as Shakespeare's become the appropriate object of new-historicist inquiry.[9]

Jonson's Epigram to his Bookseller, which begins with the poet asking the seller, "Bee thou my Bookes intelligencer, [and] note / What each man sayes of it, and of what coat / His judgement is" (*Underwood* No. 58, 3–5), offers a subtle entree.[10] The announced topic of concern is who will or will not approve Jonson's new book. Jonson's behest to the bookseller is at once businesslike and playful, yet the sustained trope energizing it reproduces seventeenth-century surveillance practices. Like the intelligencer, the bookseller "wilt heare all censures" because unto him "All mouthes are open, and all stomacks [i.e., thoughts] free" (1–2). The poet instructs the seller to "Thanke him" who is "wise, and praise[s]" the book, but for those dolts who fail to praise it, "a Cram-ring [i.e., like a bull] / Will be reward enough" (8–9)—the last phrase alluding to the rewards given for "useful" information.

The obvious set of economic relations (seller to entrepreneurial author) is not what defines the transaction between the two men; rather, the conceit reveals, it is a quasi-juridical relationship. Implicitly, the poet designates his book as a kind of sovereign and his bookseller as an eavesdropping agent assigned to "note" (3) those who dare censure the book. As late twentieth-century readers, we are roused by the strangeness of this early Stuart text that records a fairly mundane merchandising event as a set of power relations in which the poet designates his bookseller as his personal

intelligencer. The epigram is reinscribing contemporary surveillance practices in the otherwise unrecorded imagination of everyday life.

And there is something a little more ominous. Jonson not only imagines
his book to be presiding like a monarch over the shop that presents him; he
arrogates to himself princely powers of enforcement, displaying not the
least scruple about employing this wished-for authority to make the bookseller his servant, his good agent. So in the seemingly innocuous climactic
couplet—"If they goe on, and that [i.e., if] thou lov'st a-life [i.e., dearly] /
Their perfum'd judgments, let them kisse thy Wife" (13–14)—the poet
places himself in the monarchical position of superiority. As a reward for
those whose judgments he approves, Jonson proffers the titillation of an
illicit kiss. The bookseller-as-intelligencer is relegated to an inferior social
position and becomes an object of humor, while the poet, the dispenser of
the "reward," urges the seller to become a wittol of sorts. All the while,
Jonson assumes a triumphant posture, suspending the cultural prohibitions that forbid one person access to another's sexual body.

In this manner, Jonson's slender epigram reveals the way in which
hegemonic relations are reinscribed in the soul of the poet, who longs to
reproduce in his own sphere the sovereign's power of intelligencing. Phrased
with somewhat different emphasis, the power accorded the informer in
culture begets Jonson's desire to appropriate it for himself. But the point, of
course, is less the kind of person Jonson is revealed to be but that the trope
underlying his epigram reveals the cultural power belonging to those who
employ intelligencers. It also discloses something about the way power
insinuates itself into subjectivity, quietly revealing the poet's desire to
assume the role of the informer's employer, rewarding some and controlling or punishing those who oppose his will.

The embeddedness of surveillance in the representation of everyday life
is just as apparent in Shakespeare's *Hamlet,* whose Elsinor Francis Barker
identified as "a place of spies and actors, actual and metaphorical, where
scenes are played out to acknowledged and unacknowledged audiences"
(26). But leaving aside the manifest examples of surveillance, I turn to a
casual trope—hardly a full-fledged metaphor—from one of Hamlet's so-
liloquies. In it, Hamlet, denounces his own inaction, envies Fortinbras's
celerity in retaking Norway's lost land, and laments, "How all occasions do
inform against me" (*Hamlet* 4.4.32). The *OED* records that the operative
verb *inform* means "to take shape" or "to take on a form," but Evans glosses
the primary meaning as all occasions do "denounce" or "accuse" the prince
(4.4.32n). Events, embodied as a ubiquitous informer, "take shape" against

Hamlet. However, it is not that Hamlet feels betrayed by these informing events, that they are evil; to the contrary, these occasions are represented to Hamlet's mind as the telltale testimony of an inner truth he must confess to himself—that he is lily-livered and lacks gall. Untrue to his vow of revenge, he cannot fulfill his own ethical injunction and thus judges himself as deserving to be informed upon.

The form of this self-reproach, in which the subjected ethical self anxiously voices its belief that every event has been recorded to accuse him to himself, discloses something important about the relationship, as Shakespeare represents it, between conscience and the disciplinary practices of surveillance. Hamlet's informer trope, appearing in a context that has nothing palpable to do with informing, points to the encompassing social-political field through which the conscience recognizes itself and holds itself morally accountable. Surveillance intrudes into the field of perception and channels seemingly unrelated life events into the supervisory field of vision. More than just another social practice, surveillance shows itself to be a medium of exchange that converts an array of otherwise dissimilar units of thought into a common currency.[11]

In Shakespeare's poetry the most prevalent denomination in which the trope of surveillance is exchanged is not social but psychocultural coin. *Venus and Adonis* offers an apt illustration for it reveals that the psychology of seduction is actualized by metaphors showing the internalization of Elizabethan surveillance practices. Venus describes the inward kingdom of love as disturbed by "Jealousy"—that is, suspicion—which "Gives false alarms" as "Affection's sentinel" (649–51). In this role, suspicion, the accusing aspect of the inner self, is derided as "This sour informer, this bate-breeding spy, / . . . / This carry-tale, dissentious Jealousy, / That sometime true news, sometime false doth bring" (655–58). The metonymic exchange by which "contiguous entities can be *reduced* to the status of functions of one another" (White, *Tropics of Discourse* 253)—that is, Jealousy converted into the informer/spy of Elizabethan culture—does not appear to be a quirk of thought; it circulates more widely. The same metonymic operation appears again in Sonnet 125, when the narrator monitors his own jealousy after being denied the opportunity to carry an honorific canopy for his beloved. Having vented these negative feelings, the narrator then rejects them, declaring, "Hence, thou suborn'd informer, a true soul / When most impeach'd stands least in thy control" (13–14).

Although the purported subject of both passages is love, it is the self-evaluating operations of the mind that are foregrounded. These operations, all part of an internalized discourse, are represented to the reader as well as to the speaking self in terms of an external, highly visible, social-political apparatus established to produce truth.[12] The inner self that monitors the transgressing self (falsely informing "Jealousy") is metonymically exposed in a startling transference of world into self as lying and perfidious, just as the stereotypical informer was. Depicted as an inextricable part of the self, the informing mechanism is exposed as venal, untrue to another part of the self that is felt to possess integrity. Here the social perturbations produced by the Tudor-Stuart disciplinary powers are reenacted to exhibit a fracturing from within so that the self can no longer be sure of the quality of its information. The very testimony upon which the will is supposed to choose has been impugned. This view is considerably more complex than that in Jonson's epigram or Hamlet's soliloquy. The very process that internalizes the Tudor-Stuart system of surveillance does not fully believe in its authority, calls it into question, and then denounces it.

It is of course crucial to ask in what sense this tropological display is culturally significant. Judith Butler's position is that the critical question on subjectivity "is not *how* did that identity become *internalized*? as if internalization were a process or a mechanism that might be descriptively reconstructed. Rather, the question is: From what strategic position in public discourse and for what reasons has the trope of interiority and the disjunctive binary of inner/outer taken hold?" (134). The evidence suggests our having been able to reconstruct descriptively the internalization of that part of identity we call conscience, and this illuminates Butler's second, social question. Indeed, the repeated use of the informer trope to represent, paradoxically, both conscience and self-betrayal shows the disciplinary structures of society being transported into the internal mechanisms of control. Such tension-filled representations provide insight into the ambivalence with which the Elizabethan juridical system, reliant as it was on informers, was regarded and, at the same time, the ways that individuals could represent their own inadequate, self-defeating behavior to themselves.

The conceited representations of the informer-as-deceiver in both *Venus and Adonis* and Sonnet 125 reveal a culturally persisting way of understanding divisions within the self. Probing further to corroborate the hypothesis, we come upon Jonson's "Epode #11" from *The Forest*. There the operations of the mind are self-consciously described in explicitly juridical terms through a master conceit representing the psychology of cognition, including, most notably, a hypostatization of the mind's structures. This epode's rhetorical bravura and elaborately developed informer-sovereign conceit corroborate the inference that the trope of the internalized spy or informer was culturally persistent:

> Not to know vice at all, and keepe true state,
> Is vertue, and not *Fate:*
> Next, to that vertue, is to know vice well,
> And her blacke spight expell.
> Which to effect (since no brest is so sure,
> Or safe, but shee'll procure
> Some way of entrance) we must plant a guard
> Of thoughts to watch, and ward
> At th'eye and eare (the ports vnto the minde)
> That no strange, or vnkinde
> Obiect arriue there, but the heart (our spie)
> Giue knowledge instantly,
> To wakefull reason, our affections king:
> Who (in th'examining)
> Will quickly taste the treason, and commit
> Close, the close cause of it.
> 'Tis the securest policie we haue,
> To make our sense our slaue.
> . . . .
> [But often our affections do rebel]
> Or some great thought doth keepe
> Back the intelligence, and falsely sweares,
> Th'are base, and idle feares
> Whereof the loyall conscience so complaines.
> Thus, by these subtle traines,
> Doe seuerall passions still inuade the minde,
> And strike our reason blinde. (8:ll.1–30)

The conventionality of the topos in which affection's course is depicted as a rebellion against reason argues for (not against) the cultural significance of the master conceit. Especially significant is the correspondence it establishes between the wardens of the law and the psyche. In fact, the structure of the psyche actually recapitulates and then sanctions as natural the social hierarchies belonging to monarchy. By the same logic it sanctions the information-gathering mechanisms of control. In this way, the self-censorship that Elizabethans-Jacobeans were taught to exercise in suppressing unapproved sensations (the "guard / Of thoughts") becomes the equivalent of a legal examination in which "the heart (our spie)," the good intelligencer, reports to the examiner, "affections king." The poem thus conjoins the juridical system of political justice (with its notion of transgression) to the concept of a virtuous self, with its pronounced emphasis on self-examination.

Clearly, all these tropic iterations of surveillance are evidence of the efficacy with which Elizabethan culture succeeds in producing a self-evaluating subjectivity that explains the self to the self by means of the legally sanctioned mechanisms of external control. But this internalized judicial system again brings forth mixed consequences. When the self discovers that it cannot live up to its ideal of rational self-control, it records this failure as perjured testimony that deludes the sovereign reason into believing its seemingly treasonous informations are but "base, and idle feares." By this tropological association, the subversion of personal virtue is made not only analogous to but the functional equivalent of the informer's defamations, which subvert justice and beget unjust verdicts.

Since the tropes of surveillance assume a prominent place in representations of the mind's understanding of itself, a reasonable expectation would be that such prominence should appear in the drama as well. Characters, stage props, and dramatic leitmotifs also ought to function like tropes and toward the same ends. And they do. In *Othello*, my prime example from Shakespeare's plays, the trope of the informer as (false) conscience takes dramatic life in the relationship between Iago and Othello. Iago depicts his relationship to Othello not as that of friend to friend but as servant to master. The kind of service he offers is conveyed in juridical metaphors. Though "bound to every act of duty," he ought not utter his dark thoughts, he protests, for "Who has that breast so pure / But some uncleanly apprehensions / Keep leets and law-days and in sessions sit / With meditations lawful?" (3.3.134–41). Initially presenting himself as the scrupulous informer (and would-be judge) who fears his own damaging, possibly false testimony, Iago paints himself out, as the scene wears on, as the hired informer or spy who would only disclose indisputable truths. The activity of spying into abuses, however, is ambivalently presented as difficult and unwanted but necessary:

> (As I confess it is my nature's plague
> To spy into abuses, and oft my jealousy
> Shapes faults that are not), that your wisdom then,
> From one that so imperfectly conjects,

Would take no notice, nor build yourself a trouble
Out of his scattering and unsure observance.
It were not for your quiet nor your good,
Nor for my manhood, honesty, and wisdom,
To let you know my thoughts. (3.3.146–54)

The passage effectively illustrates the way in which a person who merely observes another's doings—here Othello's lieutenant—becomes translated into (or sees himself as) the informer of imagination. Although the scene may surely be read literally as showing one person deceiving another, it may be interpreted with greater resonance if Iago is viewed as an encoded idea, a corrupted informer. The medieval tradition of the psychomachia and the play's very emphasis on the operations of Iago's mind impressing themselves on Othello's encourages readers to behold the action as a symbolic projection of Othello's internal spiritual conflict.[13] From this vantage point, Iago is both the jealous false informer he pretends to be (the external sign) and an unrecognized alien part of Othello's inner being (the internalized sign).

The form of this betrayal, we notice, precisely recapitulates that of Jonson's Epode, in which the rebelling affections "keepe / Backe the intelligence, and falsely sweares" to "strike our reason blinde." In other words, in the sign system of the tragedy, Iago is both informer and spiritual tempter— the self-deceiving voice of Othello's own mind and the externalization of Othello's skewed manner of processing "informations" revealed to him. In addition to being the cunning devil who pours the leprous distillment of his false "informing" observations into the citadel of his master's mind, Iago is already Othello's overthrown reason, the deceiving informer within. The betrayal is at once outward and inward, mutually constitutive.

This tropological understanding of surveillance that dissolves the binary construction between inner and outer truth can be extended to a still larger field of observation for *our* criticism is a form of cultural surveillance as well. In *Sejanus,* the play that furnishes the most sensational of examples in the Jonson canon, the colloquy of conscience is projected outward on the world. More important, the tropes of surveillance are at once embedded and objectified in the regime of Tiberius and his prying agents so that the issue may be held up to examination:

Silius: For your state
Is wayted on by enuies, as by eyes;

And euery second ghest your tables take,
Is a fee'd spie, t'obserue who goes, who comes,
What conference you haue, with whom, where, when,
What the discourse is, what the lookes, the thoughts
Of ev'ry person there, they doe extract,
And make into a substance.
Agrippina: Heare me, SILIVS,
Were all TIBERIVS body stuck with eyes,
And ev'ry wall, and hanging in my house
Transparent, as this lawne I weare, or ayre;
Yea, had SEJVNES [Tiberius's agent] both his eares as long
      As to my in-most closet: I would hate
To whisper any thought, or change an act,
To be made IUNO's riuall. (2.442–56)

This passage, with its images of piercing eyes and telltale ears and its emphasis on the fearsome tribe of Tiberius's paid spies, reveals a world where "observation is clearly out of control—or rather, it has itself become a form of control," revealing "a state under surveillance."[14] But there is a different, crucial significance to the passage. That significance inheres in the representation of a subjectivity that is in the process of being constituted by a regime of surveillance. The "what," "with whom," "where," and "when" of Silius's speech convey a sense of unrelieved menace. Even "lookes" and "thoughts" are to be interpreted—to who knows what ends—and this state of affairs is to become the lot of "ev'ry person." The effects of a surveillance so complete that one's innermost chamber ("closet") is unsafe from prying ears does more than destroy the desire for privacy (rendered in our time as privacy rights)—it initiates a process of self-censorship.

Epitomizing the point are the metaphors of Argus-eyed surveillance that disclose a repression that pervades the mental world of Rome's citizens. In psychoanalytic terms, a generalized paranoia becomes free-floating anxiety. So certain is Agrippina that her every word is being overheard that she "would hate / To whisper any thought." Such a set of circumstances becomes the most efficacious form of surveillance because, as Foucault discerns, it polices itself and makes unsanctioned thoughts fearsome (*Discipline and Punish* 200–201). To be sure, this order of poetic narrative differs from the embedded tropes previously described: the site of surveillance is no longer the divided self but a divided polity in which frightened citizens look out upon the world as if it were a nightmare. This politicization of surveillance is made possible by externalizing it, making it an object of historical examination, thereby constituting it as an object of attack. Ironically, the objectification of surveillance as political oppression leads back to the cultural process whereby that surveillance is again internalized, as in Agrippina's fear "To whisper any thought."

The exposition has come full circle. Jonson's play creates, not in hard "fact" but in metaphor and imagination, the nightmare vision, the "terror," that Elton dismissively describes as existing, if at all, "in the mind only." This is precisely the process at work in "Inviting a Friend to Supper," except that the latter poem, far from being distanced by a historicized Roman setting or the imaginative new world setting of Utopia, is grounded in the circumstances of contemporary English life, in a kind of empirical "fact" after all. Speaking in his own voice, Jonson celebrates the joys of a "free" supper, which he defines both with respect to the plenitude of fowl he and his guest will enjoy and the liberty of reading Virgil, Tacitus, and Livy, discussing whatever they please without fear of informers standing about—"we will haue no *Pooly*,' or *Parrot* by" ("Epigrammes" No. CI ll. 35–36).

These names, we observe, are no fanciful "literary" allusions. As Charles Nicoll has shown, "Pooly" (or Poley) and Parrot were professional informers who in 1597 worked at Jonson's haunt, the Mermaid tavern, and were part of the network of spies in which Jonson too became enmeshed.[15] Jonson even speaks of this power to harm others when he reflects that neither he nor his friend need fear making "any guiltie men" by words spoken in "our cups" (37). He then celebrates their meeting as a purification: "at our parting, we will be, as when / We innocently met. No simple word, / That shall be vtter'd at our mirthfull boord, / Shall make vs sad next morning: or affright / The libertie, that wee'll enioy to night" (38–42). Paradoxically, this celebration of freedom—a situation precisely the obverse of that in *Sejanus*—is in fact hemmed in by the ghosts of informers. The informers, with their prying ears, indeed constitute the event celebrated, as absent presences. This point may be pressed to say that these absent presences are ineradicable. Richard Burt argues, for example, that the experience of "freedom" is illusory "because he [Jonson] and his friend have already internalized censorship" (47). But even if this point is resisted, what must be granted is that "Inviting a Friend to Supper" is like *Sejanus* and all the colloquies of conscience previously considered; they all make explicit and therefore subject to evaluation the processes of surveillance that appear as a tortuous undercurrent in the tropological discourse of Shakespeare's and Jonson's poetry.

The foregoing analysis prepares us to return to the original issues of this chapter. Beginning with the hypothesis that More's *Utopia*, a text designated by its author as a voyage of the imagination, might actually be rooted in Henrican intelligencing practices, which later English sovereigns developed further, I sought to examine the relationship between later "imaginative" poetry in the Elizabethan and Jacobean periods and the material practices of surveillance at that time. The resulting portrait of surveillance as a series of cultural practices is quite different from that obtained under Elton's method of documentary history. Whereas Elton, whose purview was Tudor surveillance, treated its programmatic implementation under Thomas Cromwell and concluded that the process was socially and politically reasonable, the present analysis has sought to demonstrate the enormous disciplinary power of surveillance. It has attempted to do so by showing its pervasiveness and insinuation into subjectivity. Jonson's and Shakespeare's recurring representations of internalized moral debate as an informer's testimony highlight the regulatory functions of surveillance and illuminate the process whereby that conscience-filled debate is made understandable to the self.

The process that establishes a similitude between self and world, this evidence shows, is dynamic and operates with greater potential for resistance than the Foucault of *Discipline and Punish* allows. The self, in the paradigm just presented, must be viewed as a meaningful unit of study possessed of agency. It is not merely mechanically reproduced, not merely cloned. As applied to hegemonic formations, this means, following Raymond Williams, that though hegemony is often treated as a totalizing abstraction, it is a *process* that in practice "can never be singular" (112).[16] In a word, hegemony, to be meaningful, must mean dominance over something else. Applying the concept to the internalization of surveillance, we see that the same process whereby the sanctions of law are introjected to become conscience also critiques and impugns the system of surveillance in which conscience recognizes itself.

The permeability between self and world in these tropic representations of the informer shows that the authoritarian fantasy underlying More's utopianism is no mere fictive construct; its basis is the material reality of Tudor England. Put slightly differently, the internalized voices in the poetry of Jonson and Shakespeare show the permeability of the seemingly disparate categories of the material and the imaginative. And there is a genuine exchange between them. The brooding accounts of self-betrayal and seduction in this poetry disclose a subjectification that is nonetheless capable of denouncing the entire system of institutionalized surveillance.

Such a set of conclusions casts a glaring light on Elton's dismissive thought that the terrors of surveillance, if they existed at all, could be found "in the mind only." Even if Elton's evidence were drawn from the Elizabethan and Jacobean periods, which it is not, Elton's historical method cannot absorb the kind of psychocultural data this chapter adduces because it insists on the reality of the boundary between inner and outer and adheres to a restrictive conception of history—of what it conceives as evidence (the materials of the knowable). So long as the discipline of history is restricted, as Elton affirms, to "the investigation of things that happen and not things as they are" (*Practice of History* 10–11), there can be no way of negotiating the reciprocal relationships between "things as they are" (such as mental processes) and event-based change.[17] The very category of "things as they are" beguilingly propounds a static truth that conceals the recursive activity that makes things—and most especially human beings—"as they are."

By Elton's precepts, imaginative literature is accorded a peripheral role in shaping historical understanding. Except where literary texts treat factual matters via topical allusion or allegory, documentary history is unable to countenance as data the "fictional" evidence of poetry. For ourselves, the determination to cross disciplinary boundaries and to take as a legitimate object of inquiry the cultural embeddedness of tropological discourse holds the prospect—and not just the possibility—of generating a new cultural historicism.

4
———————

The Informer in Popular Culture

A Critique of the Anecdotal Method

The resolution to achieve a new cultural historicism is quite different from actually producing one. To recall the evidence that the informer in Jonson's and Shakespeare's poetry appears not only as a symbol of authority but of failed authority and betrayal is tantalizing. So is the notion that the self, as constituted in their poetic tropes of surveillance, questions the very structures of authority to which in some sense it assents. But a critical question arises. What is the relationship between the symbolic representation of authority in texts and the social-political structures themselves? Alternatively put, do the surveillance tropes in Jonson's and Shakespeare's poetry disclose a state of mind that obtained among a limited group or class—for example, the literati—or, much more pervasively, across classes? And how could we know? Similarly, if the tropes of surveillance reveal at once an acceptance of and resistance to the juridical functions of the informer, does that state of mind emerge in the world in discernible social-political forms? And again, how might we gauge this interrelationship?

To approach these questions new methods are required. Having sought in the previous chapter to urge the limitations of documentary history, I propose in the present one to begin with a fashionably new-historicist treatment of surveillance and to turn the method back upon itself before proceeding to press the claims of what I called in the first chapter a new cultural historicism. The idea is to expose points of weakness in current new-historicist practice by showing how the evidence of a more traditional historiography may usefully be brought to bear upon it. My purpose, of course, is not to repudiate the methods of the last chapter, and certainly not its insights, but by turning the method around and around again, a little like a whirling dervish, to create multiple perspectives that encourage an appreciation for, even wonder at, the difficulty of producing an adequate new cultural historicism.

In the Marble Hall at Hatfield House, to the right of the carved fireplace hang two portraits of Queen Elizabeth. The one nearer the hearth, attributed to Marcus Gheeraerts and known as the Rainbow Portrait (ca. 1600), exhibits the queen sumptuously appareled in oranges and browns (see fig. 2). On her left sleeve appears a serpent in its benign aspect, the symbol of wisdom; in her right hand she holds a rainbow, the symbol of peace. The motto nearby, "Non Sine Sole Iris" ("No rainbow with the sun"), refers to Elizabeth's regal self. Like Nicholas Hilliard's Ermine Portrait, hanging to the right of this one, with its live ermine as a symbol of virginity on the left sleeve and the sword of state at hand, the Rainbow Portrait reveals the queen accoutered with the appurtenances of her office. There is, however, an extraordinary feature of the portrait: the queen's orange-lined dress is embroidered with little eyes and ears whose images are hardly noticeable except upon perusal. These indicate that the queen sees and hears all.

As a symbolic statement, it begets wonder. Is this regalia a haberdasher's hyperbole preserved in painter's oil, or is there a substantive basis for this symbolic vaunt? Surveillance, the previous chapter indicates, seems to have been sewn into the seams of everyday life and was (im)pressed on the minds of poets, whose work reveals its presence even when their subject had nothing to do with surveillance per se. But in the Rainbow Portrait surveillance is frankly represented and approvingly depicted as an attribute of sovereignty. The queen is, as it were, the nerve center of the realm to whom all intelligence returns. This principle of power is highlighted by the thematic emblem of the rainbow, betokening the covenant, which Elizabeth's rule assures, linking God to humankind. Rainbowlike, Elizabeth's government symbolizes harmony and peace. These are effects guaranteed only by a rule of knowledge. If God's "all-seeing eye," as represented on the frontispiece to Raleigh's *History of the World* and in plays and emblem books, apprehends all things ubiquitously (see frontispiece), Elizabeth achieves almost the same end through the multitude of human eyes and ears that deliver all knowledge to her. The nexus between all-seeing divine sight and the queen's, which may be inferred on analogic grounds, is made explicit in John Davies's anagrammatic poem (spelling out ELISA) in *Hymns of Astraea:* "E ye of that mind most quicke and cleare, / L ike Heav'ns eye,

Fig. 2.. "Elizabeth I" ("The Rainbow Portrait"). Attributed to Marcus Gheer-aerts, ca. 1600. Hatfield House. Courtesy of the Marquess of Salisbury.

which from his spheare / I nto all things prieth; / S ees through all things everywhere, / A nd all their natures trieth" (xv ll. 1–5). By virtue of her comprehensive secret intelligence, Elizabeth as a God-appointed sovereign is celebrated, without irony, as the judge and arbiter of truth. At one point Davies avows that Elizabeth's heart is a "cleare true mirror, / H er *looking glasse*, wherein she spies / A ll forms of Truth and Error" (xxii ll. 1, 8–10). In the Rainbow Portrait this cloak of knowledge/power uses real gold, is represented as golden, and is decorated with orange and crimson glazes (Strong, *Gloriana* 158). Elizabeth's rule, then, is at once irresistible and beautiful; it bespeaks no terror and entirely becomes the queen's symbolic person.[1] Iconographically, Elizabeth's munificent use of knowledge/power is vouchsafed by the coiled serpent on her sleeve, the symbol of wisdom, which holds in its mouth a golden chain with a heart-shaped ruby pendant, tokens of goodness and good counsel (Strong, *Gloriana* 159). This emblem of benign all-seeing authority circulates in less pretentious ways in the popular drama in the disguised-duke plays. Not only Shakespeare's Vincentio but John Marston's Altofronto in *The Malcontent* and Duke Hercules in *The Fawn,* Middleton's the Phoenix after James I in the play of the same name, and Edward Sharpham's deposed duke eponymously called "the Fleer," all use the cloak of disguise—the sign of a princely secret knowledge and power—for the reformation of society and the maintenance or restoration of royalty. All such texts are predicated on the freely circulating idea that princes must see and know to be effective.

Nevertheless, a regime of power is being extolled representationally. Servants must be the sovereign's eyes and ears. This principle is made clear in Ripa's *Iconologia.* There the emblem of the "Ragione di stato" presents the state bedecked in a garment of ears and eyes (Strong, *Gloriana* 158). The practical implications of this principle are ratified, as it were, in Henry Peacham's *Minerva Brittana* (1612), which builds on this iconographic tradition: "Be seru'd with eies, and listening eares of those, / Who from all partes can giue intelligence / To gall his foe, or timely to prevent / At home his malice, and intendiment" (22). Even as the English monarchy was displaced by Cromwell and Parliament in the civil war years, the iconography persisted on the loyalist side. On the front page of a broadside entitled "A Spie, Sent out of the Tower-Chamber" in the Fleet Prison, a spy is shown carrying a lantern and a lighted faggot. His body, approvingly described as a "Diogenes-like Argus," is shown covered with a hundred eyes (fig. 3). Published in "the seventeenth year of the Author's Oppression," the illustration shows the spy promising, "No rest I'le give to feet, nor eyes, till I / Have done the duty of a watchful Spy." The sheet also bears the boastful advertisement, "If any one there be / that wants my Spies, / Let him repair to me, / I'le spare him Eyes."

To judge from the constellation of symbolic representations in paintings, poems, plays, emblem books, and broadsides, the monarch's rule of eyes and ears, made possible by a network of informers and spies, was not

Fig. 3. "A Spie, Sent out of the Tower-Chamber in the Fleet." 1648, E 428(i). By permission of The British Library.

only acceptable but laudable. Indeed, it would be easy to read the disciplining order of Elizabethan and early Stuart high culture as an apotheosis that also expresses itself concretely—as Jonathan Goldberg, Graham Parry, Stephen Orgel, and Roy Strong have shown—in the Rubens ceiling at Whitehall, the arches of triumph at James's coronation, and even in the royal currency. The study of representation as exhibitions of power in coins, wonder cabinets, cameos, festivals, witchcraft rituals, maps, and paintings—exhibitions that are read alongside literary texts—has, of course, become characteristic of the new historicism. Not statutory, police, or institutional power nakedly wielded but power inscribed in cultural practices, in work and entertainments and above all in the words and images of the theater—this has been the province of what many call the "representational" school of new historicism. Clifford Geertz, from whom new historicists have learned to read culture symbolically, epitomizes the case in respect to Elizabeth: she was "the center of the center"; "it was allegory that lent her magic, and allegory repeated that sustained it" (*Local Knowledge* 129).

Attractive as it has proven to be, such a manner of reading is not without its problems. Over the last several years, the scrutiny has become intense, particularly over the practice of reading only *two* texts across the culture. In "Are We Being Historical Yet?" Carolyn Porter has pointed to the analogical reasoning underlying this new-historicist methodology as a fundamental weakness. The point of contention is whether the conclusions reached by new-historicist methods are valid. Using several essays by Greenblatt, Porter shows that the generalizability of arguments based on the juxtaposing of evidence from two texts in which "A is to B as C is to D" (Porter 762) is neither established nor disproved by the similitude discovered. The cultural and historical claims made in such essays must be argued, not assumed prima facie. In similar fashion, Walter Cohen's critique of Greenblatt's essays contends that the cultural conclusions reached are contradictory. The strategy is not, strictly speaking, a matter of argument by analogy but of assuming, Cohen observes, that "any one aspect of a society is related to any other" (34). In "Invisible Bullets" Greenblatt argues that the monarchy "involves as its positive condition the constant production of its own radical subversion and the powerful containment of that subversion" (30), but in "Murdering Peasants" the subversion of the lower classes, in the form of the Peasants' War in Germany, is produced for its own sake not for that of the aristocracy. Taking the most accessible path, through Greenblatt, Cohen takes the measure of the new historicism in a memorable phrase that threatens to stick: the new historicism is committed to "arbitrary connectedness" (34). Brook Thomas's painstaking review of this critique begins by paying homage to Greenblatt's dazzling ingenuity and insightfulness but treats Cohen's analysis very seriously, showing that it illustrates the persisting problem of the "text/context opposition" that new historicism has not overcome (40). Because new historicism attempts to read social practices cross-culturally without a predetermining social context or ground, Cohen's argument alerts us to the predetermining selection process by which one text or artifact is set beside another, exposing the fact that a ground is implicitly present despite the synchronic treatment.

Nonetheless, new-historicist criticism has not generally been given to random readings of Renaissance culture. To the contrary, it has shown a pronounced tendency to read it in totalizing ways from the royal center outward. Goldberg's *James I and the Politics of Literature,* Tennenhouse's *Power on Display,* and Greenblatt's early version of "Invisible Bullets" all illustrate the point. Greenblatt's revision of that essay and his later protestations against totalizing arguments in *Learning to Curse* (164–66) and elsewhere is a promising development. But, given this legacy, new historicists feel the obligation, increasingly, to *produce* a more complicated picture of the cultural landscape. Social forces must be seen to do something more than contend only to be contained. In fact, the whole subversion-containment binary needs to be set aside for a more supple terminology.

There is no inherent reason why any cultural historicism should read Renaissance culture in a totalizing way or why, in a weaker construction, it should insist that the only effective powers are hegemonic. There are, however, telling reasons for new historicism's having done so. The application to literary study of the anthropological methods of Clifford Geertz, Victor Turner, and others leads, first, to a steady-state description of culture. Because the aim of such field investigation is not so much to learn how culture changes as how it works, the concern for synchrony has tended to generate studies emphasizing the reproduction of culture, wherein the subtle effects of the dominant ideology are shown to insinuate themselves throughout the society.[2] Foucault's critique of discourse as a power system is a second, perhaps more central influence. Generally eschewing particular sites of contestation in favor of the pervasive systems of disciplining thought, it offers no place for discerning the distinctive voices of women or those of the dispossessed, for example. Greenblatt's use of the term *invisible bullets* incorporates this Foucaultian sense of language's power. The phrase, taken from Thomas Harriot's journal, records that the American Indians perceived that disease and death selectively struck them down wherever the English went (while the English remained healthy). The Indians could not tell whether the white men were "gods or men" but came to believe the colonists' story that it was "the special work of God" because "for love of us [He] did make the people to die . . . by shooting invisible bullets into them" (36). In this way, Harriot established among his English readers a colonialist discourse which—like invisible bullets—first voices the Indians' skeptical reception of the power of Christ and then shows how that skepticism was overcome. Greenblatt's conclusion, "This recording of alien voices, their preservation in Harriot's text, is part of the process whereby Indian culture is constituted as a culture and thus brought into the light for study, discipline, correction, transformation" (37), strikes a Foucaultian note. It modifies the dynamics of Foucault's totalizing account of culture (in one reading of his work) and makes it more theatrical by reading into it new voices, but it does not alter the ultimate result.

The sweeping overview that we see in the above argument also expresses itself in the analogic method new historicism has made current. The strength of the method is that it "sees through" power's more obvious manifestations (its empirical expressions) to underlying constitutive forms.

Cultural practices, discursive formations, seemingly innocuous artifacts, all hold the power to reveal the culture's underlying codes. By relegating the notion of specific agency to the margins, the critic is prompted to discover (uncover) the suffusive, indeterminate sources of power that engulf institutional power and are antecedent to it. This is a worthy object of study, but it brings forth at least two signal weaknesses.

The first is the problem of verifying the claims made. On what grounds, for example, can Greenblatt's conclusion, "There is subversion, no end of subversion, only not for us" (65), be sustained when it rests entirely on an anecdotal comparison adduced from Shakespeare's second Henriad and Harriot's journal? Substituting the term *poetics* (cultural or otherwise) for *new historicism* fails to remove the problem because the claims made are not merely literary but historical as well. The second problem is that the procedure is preemptive. A linguistic model of culture that sees power indeterminately inscribed everywhere is able to discover only similitude in culture, and this is what the paradigmatic or anecdotal method results in. Whenever it is rigorously employed change will not be a category of explanation.

Obviously, new historicism must be open to evidence of difference *and* to the possibility of change. Some new historicists are. One of the pleasures of reading Montrose's "'Shaping Fantasies'" essay on *A Midsummer Night's Dream* is that it is so open to the play of difference and contradiction that literal representations are completely subverted. In Montrose's analysis, "the ostensible project of elaborating Queen Elizabeth's personal mythology inexorably subverts itself" because it "generates ironies, contradictions, resistances which undo the royal magic" (84). This manner of reading shows the suppleness of new-historicist practice—all things are possible.

But even in this reading, we come to the problem of undecidability. How could we know whether the royal magic of Elizabeth's dazzling gown of eyes and ears convinces all, whether it undoes itself, or whether it is merely an ineffective boast? Unless critical readings are solely a game, there must come a moment when the relationship between words and institutions is engaged. Texts must be seen as participating in practices and practices recognized as constitutive expressions of institutional processes. Discourse may be viewed as a primary, constitutive power—but not as power's only manifestation. Examining secondary and tertiary expressions of power ought not be excluded from the project of being historical. By secondary, I mean the obvious power-bearing structures of society that traditional criticism takes as its major or fundamental object of analysis—the activities of the sovereign, of parliament, the church, educational institutions, and the like. By tertiary, I mean such institutions as the theater, which are invested with no formal authority and which traditional criticism slights as merely reflecting history because it does not credit the power inherent in representation. To recognize these secondary and tertiary sites as fit subjects for study without neglecting the constitutive primacy of language is to provide a means of securing a fuller, more integrative cultural historicism. More specifically, such recognition provides a means of evaluating, assessing, the paradigmatic conceptions of monarchical power to which new-historicist practice has been prone.

The Rainbow Portrait, with its daunting message that the queen's eyes and ears see and hear everything, is my focal point for both method and subject. Two primary questions concern me: What basis was there for the sovereign's extraordinary claim to the knowledge of her kingdom? and To what degree can it be said that the state, embodied in its sovereign, was able to contain or deflect challenges to its powers of surveillance? These questions do accord a role to a documentary historiography but under an altered field of vision in which representation assumes a prominent role in interpretation.

To begin, the same emblem that appears in the Rainbow Portrait may be set beside the passage from Jonson's *Sejanus* in which Agrippina warns Silius of the emperor's cadre of spies:

> Heare me, SILIVS,
> Were all TIBERIVS body stuck with eyes,
> And eu'ry wall, and hanging in my house
> Transparent, as this lawne I weare, or ayre;
> Yea, had [Tiberius's agent] SEIANVS both his eares as long
> As to my in-most closet: I would hate
> To whisper any thought, or change an act,
> To be made IVNO's riuall. (2.449–56)

In representational analysis, the choice of the parallel or exemplary text is decisive in determining meaning. So too here. The same image used to describe Elizabeth as a sea of eyes and ears is applied to Tiberius, bearer of the Roman imperial power from which English sovereigns traced their lineage. Both corroborate a mythology in which the imperial body is clothed in an ineluctable secret knowledge. But in *Sejanus* the emblem is filled with menace. Far from eliciting a uniform response, the same emblem of absolutist omnipotence begets in Jonson's rendering the fear of repression, of being informed upon. Voyeuristic, grotesque, and strangely impersonal, Jonson's world of eyes intimates unrelieved personal violation and heralds what John Archer describes as "a state under surveillance" (105). Not fully a representation of the modern state because Tiberius's control, a virtually unseen mastery from the center, is still depicted as a personal style of rule, Jonson's disturbing tragedy nonetheless adumbrates the apprehensions of a modern sensibility.

Within this common field of representation, new possibilities of resistance are thus disclosed, but the evidence is limiting. The efficacy of a single iconic representation cannot be evaluated apart from counter-representations of the same and the relationship of such representations to actual informing practices. In a word, the interactive relationships between representations and practices must be investigated. This is what I propose now to do.

The general term *intelligencer* meant simply information-gatherer. It included both the spy, one hired, especially by the government, to keep persons under close observation, secretly, for the purpose of obtaining information, and the "common informer" (*OED*). The business of the latter was to present information (that is, to "lay informations") against those who violated the penal laws and so by their evidence to win in court a portion of the financial penalty assessed. Although the use of surveillance procedures did not entail the concept of crime prevention, the administrative bureaucracy did attempt to establish an effective information-gathering network to garner the legal evidence necessary for the efficient functioning of a modern judicial system (Foucault's knowledge/power).

The deployment of the common informer, recorded in the reign of Henry VII, became part of a regular process of law enforcement under Henry VIII, who tried to secure religious conformity by encouraging ordinary citizens, not just professional informers, to report the utterance of treasonous opinions (*Select Cases* 16:xcix-c; Elton, *Policy* 337–39; cf. 271–72). Working through local magistrates and sheriffs, senior officials such as Thomas Cromwell attempted to forge a nation of public-spirited servants (Elton, *Policy* 332–34, 344). There was also a fiscal motive. Acting as localities do today when they nab traffic offenders to generate revenues, officials used informations to discover ordinary infractions of the civil statutes for which the statutory penalty was usually a fine.[3]

Tudor-Stuart authorities began by merely reinvoking practices begun in the Middle Ages and encouraging the public at large to enforce the statutes "by giving any member the right to sue for the penalty imposed, and for their breach" (Holdsworth 4:355, 2:453; Elton, "Informing" 150). But when these traditional measures proved ineffective in deterring crime, the Tudors moved to create a tier of professional informers. During Elizabeth's reign especially, the prerogative powers of informers were vastly increased. Not only could these designees sue for the penalties imposed on behalf of the crown, keeping as much as half the proceeds, but they could personally compound (negotiate) with offenders. They could even set aside the observance of the statutes.[4] In her proclamations, Elizabeth promised informers handsome rewards to enforce the customs laws, regulate commerce, suppress dangerous printed matter, and protect her title from libel.[5] By virtue of their special commissions, these agents, like monopolists with their letters patent, came into their own as a quasi-professional class. For a country lacking a regular police force, a file-keeping bureaucracy, and salaried officials, informers became the principal means of English law enforcement (M. Davies 23–32; Hirst 65). Along with ordinary citizens who might occasionally report someone for the violation of a statute, intelligencers detected offenses ranging from infractions of the intricate customs regulations on imports and exports, wool dealing, the marketing of goods, and the onerous poor laws, to the violation of the Lenten proscriptions against the consumption of meat, and to the laws regulating apprenticeship, usury, guns, archery, and horses (Beresford 222–28).

If our principal source of information about informers came from the centers of power, for example Whitehall or London's officials, we might expect that the activities of intelligencers, officially sanctioned as they were, would generally be approved. We might further expect that the government's supervisory mechanisms would succeed in curbing negative representations from the particular individuals who had personally felt the informer's sting. As it turns out, these presuppositions will not serve. The high-cultural representations we have of informers are not uniformly approving; in fact their popular representations in the form of pamphlets, essays, poems, plays, and social histories, disclose an unstintingly derogatory critique. Better put, the composers of these texts all *participated* in this public and highly visible critique. Even more surprising is that the common informer tainted the legal process itself, for he was the figure most closely associated with its operation.

A concrete example of this phenomenon is Francis Beaumont's *Woman Hater* (1606). Presenting a topical burlesque of two garden-variety informers, Beaumont shows them ensconcing themselves as they overhear conversations while recording their scattered, misinformed observations on table books. The mimicry in this representation of contemporary practices is evident from a Star Chamber deposition of 1540 that records a professional informer's "dylygent labour to take and note yn wrytyng the defautes of persones offendyng the sayd statute," despite his being called a "promoter and false knave" (*Select Cases* 25:220). In Beaumont's play the community's judgment against the informers awaits no fifth-act revelation but is pronounced at the outset by their employer himself, Count Valore: "This fellow is a kind of Informer [who] . . . brings me informations, pick'd out of broken wordes, in mens common talke, which with his malicious misapplication, hee hopes will seeme dangerous" (1.3.169–76). The body of the play satirizes the informers' botched investigative techniques, poor judgment, cupidity, and the farcical illogic of their "discoveries" of sedition.

Extreme as Beaumont's representation is, it can be shown to function normatively as a theatrical stereotype. Sustaining both the stereotype and the critique is the allegation that informers maliciously misconstrue innocent conversations. Desiring personal profit, they are viewed as undermining the integrity of the legal system they serve. For example, the keen-witted English citizens in *A Chaste Maid in Cheapside* (1613) have no difficulty distinguishing between the laws made for the common good and the "corruption of promoters, / And other poisonous officers that infect / And with a venomous breath taint every goodness" (2.1.115–17).

Against this assessment, a documentary historical method might try to show how the informations system "really worked." Thus, for example, Margaret Davies presents evidence that the informers' reputation for extortion was exaggerated (60–61). As Davies's work reminds us, the traditional historian considers objective (meaning "official") data such as the number of arrests informers made, the percentage of convictions achieved, and the precise penalties exacted to be the most valuable data to be garnered. From one perspective, this is important information; I am resorting to it myself. In this documentary view the intelligencing network as a piece of the judicial system is what "makes" history. But in the pages below, I attempt a cultural argument that discloses the antecedent values operating beneath the system.

That informers aroused an odd combination of mirth and contempt tells us something important about their reputation for misconstruing evidence and, as many saw it, their feeble detective work. This is, however, only the beginning of the critique. Every bit as significant is the development of a cultural critique of the informer. By comparison, the legalistic critique seems narrow. For example, the allegations just mentioned pale before the contemporary ridicule directed at the low social standing of informers. Because few enjoyed a patrimony or a reputable profession before their licensing, informers were commonly viewed as seedy types, "lewd" (meaning unlearned or vulgar). Middleton depicts one as "promis'd faithfully" to "a kind gentlewoman in Turnbull Street" (*Chaste Maid*, 2.2.110, 112), a notorious haunt of prostitutes. Informers seem to have enjoyed little of the mystique attached to undercover agents in American culture; they were usually ordinary members of local communities with poor reputations. When the Husband in *A Yorkshire Tragedy* contemplates the loss of his lands, he imagines that "My second son must be a promoter [informer] and my third a thief, or an underputter [procurer], a slave pander. O, beggary, beggary, To what base uses dost thou put a man" (2.48–51). Bosola makes a similar point when he derogates court officers as so craven that they would have "Made their first born intelligencers" (*Duchess of Malfi*, 3.2.232–33). These citations underline the chasm dividing the gentry from licensed informers. In the first quote, moreover, the Husband's conjoining of the professions of promoter and procurer suggests that respectable people viewed both as shamelessly exploitive, the one befouling people's bodies, the other their good name.

The informers' woefully inadequate powers of deduction must be viewed as inseparable from their inferior class identity as highlighted on the public stage. The critique of the judicial system's operative deficiencies is thus constituted by this double set of conditions. The drama routinely portrays informers as uneducated and stupid. *A Chaste Maid in Cheapside,* a comedy celebrated for its social realism, shows Allwit successfully determining to "baffle 'em gallantly" and, afterward, dismissing them with an obscene gesture—"a foutra for promoters" (2.2.69, 94). Jonson's *Poetaster* makes its intelligencer the epitome of gullibility and avarice. Described as "that goat-footed enuious slaue; hee's turn'd fawne now, an informer, the rogue," the informer answers to the name of "Assinius Lupus" (4.7.8–9), thereby spelling out a satirical assessment of his professional life through his name.

Coterminous with the informer's inferior caste was his lack of learning or, in the root sense, "lewdness" as Goodlove Freeman's dialogue on "A Character of an Informer" suggests in its subtitle—"his lewd practises layed open." From a juridical standpoint, the professional informer's feeble capacities are captured through a word association that likens him to "ignoramus"—the technical term for an indictment petition dismissed by a grand jury for lack of evidence (*OED*). Made famous by George Ruggle's *Ignoramus* (1615), a dramatic satire on lawyers, the title word was routinely applied to persons associated with the law courts, including informers. Beaumont so applies it in his poem the "Vertue of Sack," describing those "silly *Ignoramus[es]*, such as think / There's powder-treason in all Spanish drink" (207). The satiric hit echoes in the over-eager celebrations of two informers in *The Woman Hater* who declare with anachronistic reference to the Gunpowder Conspiracy, "the plots discovered, fire, steele, and poison, burne the Palace, kill the Duke, and poison his privie Counsell" (3.2.105–7). Powder plots are not to be found in every nook and cranny, and these ignoramuses lack the sense to know that their absurd allegations would be rendered "ignoramus" in a court of law.

There was another contemporary standard of evaluation that depended upon an aristocratic code of honor. Penetrating several strata of society below the gentry, this code supported a social construction of the reputation and dignity of individuals that countered the culture of surveillance and is still very much alive today. As the legal scholar Robert C. Post has pointed out, defamation suits repeatedly cite, almost obligatorily, the speech from *Othello* (3.3.155–61) that defines "good name" as the "'immediate jewel' of the soul," so far above wealth (a notable status marker) that the theft of one's "purse" is by comparison mere "trash" ("Defamation Law" 692, 699, 712). As a social role accorded on the basis of one's position or status in society, honor is closely associated with the notion of integrity— the individual's sense of self-worth—and is thus constitutive of one's social identity (700). Furthermore, because honor has been construed from the Renaissance as "'a public good and not merely a private possession'" (702), injuries to reputation have to be seen as damaging to society itself since society invests so much in the process of esteeming individuals differentially.

From another perspective, reputation can be construed as dignity, a notion distinct from rank by which individuals both enjoy and mutually affirm their participation in society. This concept of dignity has both public and private functions, mutually constitutive and self-reinforcing. Drawing upon concepts from symbolic anthropology and Erving Goffman's role-playing psychology, Post argues that societies find ways of affirming the importance of the members of the community through what he calls "rules of civility" (709; "Privacy" 957–1010), the means by which persons act out their respect for one another in socially prescribed ways. By following these rules, which, Post urges, deserve protection, "individuals both confirm the social order in which they live and constitute 'ritual' and 'sacred' aspects of their own identity" ("Defamation Law" 709).

Because these cultural codes are so important to individual identity and the public good, normatively construed, it becomes easier to understand why the activities of legally created informers could be anathema: cultural codes cut deeper than legal prescriptions. In seventeenth-century England, the vilifying representation of informers unerringly illuminates the threat they posed to the larger community. By community standards, the trade of intelligencing was written as beyond the pale. Because the informer was routinely believed to "misapply" what he heard, his "word" was obviously meaningless—he followed no code of honor, had no integrity to lose—and could thus be written off as an affront to society and to the Christian religion.

The promulgation of these codes of respect and dignity is especially evident in the theater, whose paying audiences had a stake in society to protect. *Hamlet* provides an excellent example. When Polonius charges Reynaldo to procure information about Laertes in Paris by laying a "bait of falsehood" such as "'I saw him enter such a house of sale,' / *Videlicet*, a brothel" (2.1.58–60), the sly minister shows himself oblivious to the sanctity of his paternal relationship. By "laying these slight sallies" on his son (2.1.39), Polonius uses the intelligencing trade to get information, but only by cutting away a primary familial bond. Moreover, because all such intelligence-mongering presumes the taint it proposes to discover, it must perforce, as Reynaldo protests, "dishonor" (2.1.27) the person observed.

From this cultural perspective, the intelligencer must be seen as breaking an unwritten covenant ("the rules of civility," Post would say) in which friendly discourse for its own sake is converted into a commodity whose contents can be marketed for lucre. When as a member of a town or village, an intelligencer undermines that communitarian identity, agent and subject alike are impoverished. We hear it in Hamlet's disillusioned reproof to his former friends-turned-intelligencers, Rosencranz and Guildenstern, who play on him like a flute seeking to pluck out the heart of his mystery to sell it for "a king's remembrance" (2.2.26), and we hear it half a century later in Edward Bourne's testimony against those "who make it their work to inform against their neighbours for meeting together peaceably in the fear of the Lord" (title page).

Bourne's reference to the "neighbours" of informers indicates that the latter were not the anonymous, shadowy figures we imagine today but recognized members of a local community who violated its deeply held value of mutual respect and thus undermined its solidarity. Although aristocratic codes clearly come into play here (as we have seen), all members of society were seen to be threatened by the informer's work. On just this point William Harrison's *Description of England* (1587) offers powerful anecdotal evidence.

> Certes it is a lamentable case to see furthermore how a number of poor men are daily abused and utterly undone by sundry varlets that go about the country as promoters or brokers between the pettifoggers of the law and the common people, only to kindle and espy coals of contention whereby the one side may reap commodity and the other spend and be put to travail. . . . John of Ludlow, *alias* Mason, . . . did bring one man (among many elsewhere in other places) almost to extreme misery (if beggary be the uttermost), that before he had the shaving of his beard was valued at 200 pounds . . . and also to satisfy that greedy ravener, which still called upon him for new fees, he went to bed and within four days made an end to his woeful life. . . . (175–76)

John Stephens's character sketch "The Informer" (1615) sneeringly defines its title character as "*a protected Cheater,* or *a Knaue in authoritie, licensed by authority*" and denounces the informer's victimization of his prey through a process of legalized blackmail that enables him to collect charges as "he harkens readily to a composition."[6] The sketch concludes with the sober assessment that the informer "takes away the relation betwixt a lawyer and his Client; and he makes it generally extend to the Clearks in Offices; under whose safeguard hee hath his License seal'd to trauaile" (287–88). In the last instance, then, Stephens's critique of the informer falls as much upon the threat he poses to the network of social relationships as upon the illegality of his endeavor. For similar reasons the composer of *The Wasp* (ca. 1638) eschews the popular stereotype of the informer as a bumbler, portraying the functionally named "Huntit" as a sharpster who takes hundred-pound bribes "of vintners & vitlers for dressing & vending flesh vpon fasting dayes," and yet "had wit to take the money & pollicy to betray them to a brother of [. . .] who sued the statut vpon e'm. recoverd & sharde the dividint" (ll. 1268–71).[7] By his own admission, Huntit promotes "quarrells causes suits & actions" because "our faith is wholy Included in the penall statutes & our Relligion grownded vpon writts of Error, . . . & if we chance to vndo, two or thre Lords of the soile, yow must not think it envy but want of good mannors: one trick we borow too from the knights oth poast to have our heareings when our ears are lost" (ll. 843–49). This highlighting of the technicalities of the legal process and the abuses perpetrated by informers and knights of the post satirizes the operation of the judicial system itself. Yet the force of the satire is ultimately social. Huntit's neologic description of himself as a "deformer" (l. 841) captures this value. The *in*former who should be a *re*former becomes society's *de*former.

Because informers generally lived and operated in their local community but were paid by a removed central authority, it is not difficult to see how they could be viewed as "Judases," betraying that Christian community for money. A process of objectification actually identified the breed typologically with Christ's betrayer. In this vein Thomas Nashe speaks of "the hellish detested *Iudas* name of an Intelligencer" (*Saffron-Walden* 3:105). The author of *The Informers Looking-Glass* actually codified the equivalence between the two, saying, "*Judas* was covetous, so the Informer; *Judas* knew the place, so the Informer; . . . *Judas* betrayed Christ, Informers betray true Christians: he is worse than *Judas*" (2). Again it is the community as a whole, not merely the abused individual, that is seen to be victimized.

This set of circumstances strongly suggests that local communities had identified the informer as the agent of an impersonal, "rationalized" production of knowledge. Indeed, the value of the rational production of knowledge, we come to see in the informer himself, is being contested by those affirming the countervalues of affiliation and mutual respect. This cultural conflict reveals the intelligencer to be an amphibolous figure, a modern personality type in the making, for by licensing the informer and giving him legal authority his performative self assumed an equivocal identity, constituted by a necessarily ambivalent relationship to members of his community and his own problematic place within it.

To underline the social process in the production of identity, it is important to see that the defining of intelligencers as persons operating outside the bounds of civilized society (that is, the uncodified "rules of civility") meant that by a further analogical equation they could be identified with every other detested social group, including usurers, lawyers, and flatterers. This reification indicates that the identity of informers was simultaneously constituted by government officials who licensed them and by the local communities in which they lived and worked. Nashe brought the damning result of this confluence into powerful alignment when he wrote, "To bee an Intelligencer is to haue oathes at will, and thinke God nere regards them; to frame his religion and alleageance to his Prince according to euerie companie he comes in. A Iew he is, that but for spoile Ioues no man; a curre, that flatters & fawns vpon euerie one, low crowching by the ground like a tumbler, till hee may spie an aduantage, and pluck out his throate" (*Saffron-Walden* 3:106). The light oath making is a marker of atheism, the chameleonlike allegiance a marker of dishonorableness, the fawning of inferior class, the Jew of Christian betrayal, and the throat-plucking of ruthless robbery. Nashe's diatribe, a satiric, communal exorcism, is a remarkable example of the tropic felicity with which the intelligencer was converted into every other despised social type. In all these passages, the repetitive pattern I have cited conforms precisely to Giddens's structural analysis showing that as a practice "surveillance . . . becomes a key mechanism furthering a breaking away of system from social integration" (*Constitution* 183–84). Furthermore, the counterdiscourse of the informer as a groveler and satanic deceiver was itself the product of a recursive process that simultaneously produced institutional knowledge and the informer's "satanic" identity. By this means the informer became, at once, part of and separated from the community in which—and off which—he lived.

The values that constituted the informer as an alien other, we begin to understand, were deeply inscribed. He was stigmatized not merely for the activities he undertook but for the kind of person he was deemed to be. Statutes and proclamations made him powerful, but his own problematic intelligence-gathering activities exposed him as self-motivated, and the codes of communal solidarity, which he necessarily violated, routinely vilified him. Through their prolific, derogatory representations, fiction writers, pamphleteers, and especially dramatists helped to fix the intelligencer's identity in the public imagination as an untrustworthy amphibole.

When placed in this broader context of cultural contestation, the gulf between the benignant iconographic representation of Elizabeth as the seer and hearer of all and the denigrating popular representations of her agents is astonishing. Even royal proclamations and parliamentary regulations disclose the government's acknowledgment of the public outrage against its surveillance agents. For example, Elizabeth's pronouncement of November 10, 1566, alludes to the "divers light and evil-disposed persons who in great routs and companies have assembled themselves together against such as be informers" and have "beaten and very evil treated divers of the same informers" (*Tudor Proclamations* No. 547). The proclamation demands on pain of the whip, the pillory, and imprisonment that those who abuse informers desist. That the same proclamation was reissued in 1595 (No. 767) shows that the need for informers was enduring. When a bill to restrict their use was introduced in 1571, William Cecil objected, declaring that it "'forgets the Queen's prerogative, customs etc.'" and "weaken[s] the execution of good laws which as *pater patriae* the monarch had the duty to see enforced" (Beresford 233). We know that under Cecil's ministry payments to intelligencers were a recognized budget item totaling 1,195 pounds from July 1597 to July 1599 and 1,302 pounds from March 1597 to June 1598 (*Calendar of State Papers* 5:275). Repeated parliamentary proposals presented in 1580–81 and 1589–90 under Elizabeth and in 1604, 1621, and 1624 under James seeking to regulate the activities of informers (M. Davies 65–66, 71; S. White 52, 65–69) underscore both the importance of informers in English law enforcement practice and their troublesome position within the commonwealth.

In the midst of England's recurring attempts to reform the intelligencing system, a significant discursive phenomenon begins to appear. The attitudes expressed in popular literature of the informer insinuate themselves into the language of the government's own ministers, whose ambivalence is expressed as much in personal as in juridical terms. In the reign of Henry VIII and the early years of Elizabeth's reign, *Journals of the House of Commons* record bills "touching Informations upon Penal Statutes" (October 4, 1563, p. 73). As the years pass, the bills begin to be couched in terms describing the person rather than the activity, and these become more personal and descriptive. Thus the bills of April 3, 1571, and March 1, 1575, are "for Reformation of Promoters" and "against common Promoters" (85, 109). The early Jacobean bill of May 25, 1604, is entitled "For Reformation of Abuses of Informers upon penal Statutes" (225), and the extensive legislation of 1621 was presented as "a great Grievance by way to Informers" and their "abuses" (575). The King's Learned Council acknowledges that as "The Title sheweth," the bill speaks directly of the "Troublesome Persons, called Informers"; and modified versions of the bill are elsewhere referred to as endeavoring to "Ease the Subject" to reform the legal activities of informers whose activities are "Snares to the People" (678, 584–87). The striking tension between this culturally reconfigured identity and the functionally prescribed, legalistic one is aptly illustrated by Cecil's own admission near the end of Elizabeth's reign that the queen "'naturally likes them [informers] as little as concealments or monopolies'" (Beresford 233). Ironically, the majesterial Sir Edward Coke, speaking the language of the common people, in eloquent vituperation describes "vexatious informers" as "viperous Vermin, which endeavored to have eaten out the sides of the Church and Common-wealth" (194).

A consequence of the inability of even government officials to identify the activities of informers with the normative execution of justice was a diminished confidence in the Tudor-Stuart system of justice. Some juries refused to convict defendants when the case rested on an informer's testimony (Elton, "Informing" 165–66). The situation reached the point that a Star Chamber recorder denounced informers as among "the meaner and worst kind of people," and James himself publicly depicted the breed as "troublesome and restlesse spirits" who had brought "great damage and disquiet" to his subjects.[8] This litany and the widespread personal distaste that endues it show clearly how even government officials occupy overlapping, even contradictory subject positions: even for them informers were a grievance because they programmatically violated the norms of civility and were therefore an affront to community solidarity. Without attempting to assign precise effects to causes, we may observe that in the Parliament of 1624 Sir Edward Coke successfully campaigned to hold informers accountable to their local communities (which generally hated them) and not to Westminster. The language of the statute severely restricted the crown's use of informers, restrained their testimony in the courts at Westminster, and put them at the mercy of local ones (Russell 298; S. White 68). A decade later, Charles I issued his "Proclamation for prevention of abuses of Informers" (2: No. 204), signaling a reoriented official view.[9]

The royal edict returns us to our starting point—the informer as a grievance in Tudor-Stuart law enforcement. But the perspective has been reversed. The juridical grievance is now the last point to notice, not the first. If government leaders altered the laws pertaining to informers, restricting their powers and severely limiting their locale of operation, these actions are best interpreted as illustrating the law tardily adjusting itself to popular representations, not the reverse.

Obviously, these representations are limited. They do not give us access to other possible sources of popular discontent for which we do not have texts—village grumbling and defiance of particular informers among England's nonliterate classes, for example. Possibly, these other expressions of what Annabel Patterson calls "the popular voice" were equally or more instrumental in bringing about legislative reform, but we have what we have. And apart from our not being able to know the effects of unrecorded speech, the evidence adduced here turns on its head the traditional notion that the lawmaking bodies of English society make history while popular literature passively reflects it. Far from mimicking the official position, popular vilification of the informer was rooted in a deeper, antecedent cultural logic, in which king, ministers, and Parliament, each in their subject positions, actively participated.

Such evidence opens to our surveilling gaze the utter inadequacy of the tired, new-historicist binary of "subversion" and "containment."[10] Under the terms of such analysis the only change that counts is so narrowly conceived and arbitrary that it can be represented only by a predesignated political value, subversion. This manner of framing the issue obscures a basic concern of historicist criticism, processual change. For we are interested not only in whether literature has the power to subvert but the kinds of cultural power it possesses in all its potent and fruitful possibilities. If *containment* is taken to mean that resistance appears only as a safety valve, as hot air venting, then this study of popular representations of the informer cannot be contained in the term *containment*. Our examination of the unofficial, stigmatizing representations of the informer reveals the generation of something in between subversion and containment, a something best described as a social process in which the informer is endowed with an official power that is then recursively limited and redefined. In the interplay between official and popular representations, a pattern of culture is disclosed by which the informer was judged to be an integral part of the judicial system yet separate from the operation of justice itself, suspended between official authority and the community, denounced on both sides.

Returning for a final time to the Rainbow Portrait, we realize that our own oversight of Elizabeth's gown of eyes and ears allows us to decry its resplendent brag of England's comprehensive network of surveillance as embarrassingly overstated, ludicrous, in fact. The conclusion is methodological and historical. The tables of our historical recollections disclose that the promiscuous counterrepresentations of real-life intelligencers exhibited an unheralded cultural power. The sheer fact of a singular royal representation cannot be equated, prima facie, with the efficacious exercise of power. Shorthand asseverations of representation's power are likely to be overstated. The cultural historicist must still survey the multiple, competing discourses within culture. In a word, few anecdotes can be made to stand for the whole. That very concept of the whole is itself a totalizing abstraction—a black hole we may enter but never fully comprehend.

So, in our attempt to understand, it is useful perspectives that we seek. Toward this end, in the chapters that follow I examine the subject of surveillance in its gendered forms, through the cultural oversight of the sexual body. Of particular interest to me is the reproduction and disruption of normalizing patterns of sexual control as displayed in Elizabethan and Jacobean theaters. These plays reveal the drama in a progressive mode, interrogating the problematic construction of sexual codes, the realm where cultural oversight is most pronounced. In examining this subject, I propose to show how a new cultural historicism—one that extends beyond new-historicist categories—can reconstitute aesthetic criticism by illuminating the cultural work such plays perform.

Part Two

The Sexual Body

5

The Cultural Foundations of Shakespeare's Problem Plays

Monitoring Sexuality

Part One of this book treated the discipline of surveillance in terms of producing a new cultural historicism, but it devoted only cursory attention to the distinctive subject position of women. In an attempt to continue producing pertinent, modern perspectives on the past, I have devoted Part Two to examining early modern surveillance in England, no longer on surveillance as an organized discipline of government but rather as a cultural process whereby behavior—specifically, sexual behavior—is shaped through normalization. No other form of behavior was so carefully monitored, so fully subject to gendered oversight, and yet, as we shall see, so difficult to bring under complete control and so open to counter-interrogations.

Describing Western culture up to the end of the eighteenth century, Foucault asserted that "the marriage relation was the most intense focus of constraints; it was spoken of more than anything else; more than any other relation, it was required to give a detailed accounting of itself. It was under constant surveillance" (*History of Sexuality* 1:37). There is much evidence to support such a critique, especially in Elizabethan-Jacobean drama. *Measure for Measure*, for example, vividly represents ordinary citizens capitalizing on the Elizabethan law that stipulated, among many other prohibitions, "All unlawful games, drunkenness, whoredom, incontinency in private families [are] to be reported" to the local authorities (M. Davies 233). Thus when the Provost accuses Mistress Overdone to Escalus as "A bawd of eleven years' continuance," Overdone complains, "My lord, this is one

Lucio's information against me" (3.2.196–99). The same kind of oversight brings Claudio and Julietta to be apprehended by the authorities. Indeed, Julietta's body betrays her to them because the "stealth" of her "most mutual entertainment / With character too gross is writ" upon her belly (1.2.154–55). Clearly, an examination of the external apparatus of surveillance and informations might be extended in this way to the sexual body.

My purpose in Part Two, however, is to examine the subtler ways that sexual conduct is constrained in culture. In particular, I am interested in studying those forms of control that become effective when the individual subject comes to choose the desired behavior on principle. This process whereby the familial, religious, and civil surveillance of sexual conduct is internalized, whereby identities are shaped and the ideals and expectations of the culture transmitted as duty or conscience, may be viewed as the most complete form of surveillance, and it is to this kind of oversight of the sexual body that I now turn.

Even this subject, which might properly reach into a myriad number of social practices, is limited here to the cultural functions of Elizabethan-Jacobean theater because that is one of the most prominent places where the sexual body is reproduced within a public order of virtue. It is also a site where a certain kind of play—the problem play—characteristically interrogates the utility and ethical basis for such normalization. That is, the rehearsal of appropriate (or idealized) sexual conduct in Elizabethan and Jacobean theaters was not equivalent to the mechanical reproduction of those values: the recursive process whereby theater presents society to itself at once embodies and re-creates, as Anthony Giddens has theorized, both order and processual change.[1] In particular, the problem-play drama stages the gendered, class-ridden asymmetries of power that underlie sexual relations. It also interrogates the procedures of oversight and surveillance by which the society transmits its values. A way to put this is that the recursive features of problem-play drama hold up to relentless critique the contradictions and impasses within English culture. Ironically, the surveillance of sexuality and the symbolic ideals it is asked to sustain are themselves put under surveillance.

To appreciate the problem play as a genre in the complex terms just described, it is necessary to examine the genre historically, as the product of a significant discourse embedded in our recent past—specifically, the Victorian-Edwardian periods. Such historicizing tells us a good deal more than an examination of the so-called problem-play genre examined as an autonomous object of study.

As applied to Shakespearean drama, the term was coined in 1896 by Frederick S. Boas, who spoke of "Shakspere's problem-plays."[2] The late date reminds us that the problem play was not a recognized genre in 1600. Our continued use of the term illustrates straightforwardly that categorical understanding is produced by communities of readers. The fact, moreover, that this notion of a special category of Shakespearean drama has been continually explicated and revised but never discarded suggests, indeed, that it continues to perform meaningful cultural functions. But to identify those functions requires an archaeological dig of sorts.

Both formalists and literary historians have been disposed to "solve" the problem of the problem plays. Because the project of formalist criticism was to validate Shakespeare's art, critics were driven to discover the hidden integrity of the problem plays, or as a last resort the contradictions and confusions that mar them. When criticism has taken the latter course, the anxiety that the plays fail to yield a coherent meaning has been projected onto the works themselves, as if the category of the Shakespearean problem play has an empirical existence "out there." Early testaments to this formalistic construction appeared in Walter Raleigh's designation of "the later and darker comedies" (162), E. K. Chambers's of "the three bitter and cynical pseudo-comedies" ("Shakespeare" 785), and E. M. W. Tillyard's distinction between the structurally flawed plays of *Measure for Measure* and *All's Well That Ends Well*—the "genuinely abnormal" problem children, as he called them—and *Hamlet* and *Troilus and Cressida*, problem children because they present interesting problems of interpretation ("Problem Plays" 2). Northrop Frye's attempt to dissolve the category of the "problem comedies" by appealing to the spirit of the magical in romance and the folk origins of the "myth of deliverance" (61) is a late twentieth-century example of the same transhistorical impulse applied to *All's Well That Ends Well* and *Measure for Measure*.[3] The problem with such formalisms, as Jean Howard has put it, is that "criticism of the[se] comedies has not sufficiently acknowledged their problematic dimensions, that is, the presence within them of conflicting generic codes and cultural norms that resist easy harmonization" ("Difficulties of Closure" 114).

But producing an adequate historicized account of the problem play is not easy. It requires looking at the Edwardian-Victorian culture that produced this category in the first place. Put with somewhat different emphasis, if the category of the Shakespearean problem play is to be understood in its historical embeddedness it is necessary to establish a genealogy in Foucault's sense, to show how the plays within the category were constituted as a new class of drama.[4] This is what I intend to do in the following section.

When Boas introduced the notion of the Shakespearean problem play, he was not discovering a concept sui generis but was transposing to a new theater of operations, as it were, a then fashionable term referring to the resurgent social drama of Henrik Ibsen and George Bernard Shaw. Although Boas never said he was engaged in bridge making, the affective language of his definition shows that his preoccupation with late nineteenth-century social drama suffuses his "discovery" of Shakespeare's problem plays. At the time Boas was composing his own critical histories, contemporary drama in his native England, and in fact throughout Europe, was in constructive upheaval as new forms of drama were being presented. In England, the dominant figure was George Bernard Shaw, who began to compose his "Plays Unpleasant" under the influence of Ibsen's *Ghosts* (1881) and *A Doll's House* (1879). These included the little-known *Philanderer* (publ. 1898), as well as *Widowers' Houses* (1892), which treated the "social horrors" of slum housing, and *Mrs. Warren's Profession* (publ. 1898), a thesis drama exploring the taboo subject of prostitution.[5] Following him, many others from Henry Arthur Jones and Arthur Wing Pinero to Harley Granville-Barker continued to develop this vital social drama throughout the Edwardian period. Cutting through the urbane surface of the long-lived comedy of manners, they treated abrasive and perplexing social issues that were decidedly uncomic by normal standards, and they frequently presented plays with an open-endedness of form as wide as the door Nora Torvold walked through when she left her husband and children to discover her own identity.[6]

Easy as it is to distinguish between Shakespeare's problem plays and those of the later age, which were *pièces à thèses* for polite society, both were shaped to address disquieting contemporary issues and often deliberately avoided formal resolution. In fact, the very notion of a problem-play genre was already in vogue when Boas was writing. In 1895, for example, Shaw reviewed a new Pinero play as "an intellectual drama, of social problem [*sic*]," and at the turn of the century J. T. Grein described *Mrs. Warren's Profession* as "a 'problem play' in the fullest sense of the word" (Rowell, *Victorian Criticism* 240, 311). This nexus in terminology signals that the constitutive features of the problem-play discourse of Boas's age were immanent in the "discovery" of the new Shakespeare genre.

To reconstruct those immanent features it is useful to recall the specific language Boas employed in his own account of this "new" Shakespearean form:

> All these dramas introduce us into highly artificial societies, whose civilisation is ripe unto rottenness. Amidst such media abnormal conditions of brain and of emotion are generated, and intricate cases of conscience demand a solution by unprecedented methods. Thus throughout these plays we move along dim untrodden paths, and at the close our feeling is neither of simple joy nor pain; we are excited, fascinated, perplexed, for the issues raised preclude a completely satisfactory outcome, even when, as in *All's Well* and *Measure for Measure*, the complications are outwardly adjusted in the fifth act. In *Troilus and Cressida* and *Hamlet* no such partial settlement of difficulties takes place, and we are left to interpret their enigmas as best we may. Dramas so singular in theme and temper cannot be strictly called comedies or tragedies. We may therefore borrow a convenient phrase from the theater of to-day and class them together as Shakespere's problem-plays. (345)

Scrutiny of Boas's definition shows it to be actuated by two principal ideas—that problem plays depict societies "ripe unto rottenness" and that they "preclude a completely satisfactory outcome." This positing of an unpleasant atmosphere leads directly to the "plays unpleasant" of Boas's time that treated prostitution, syphilis, and social hypocrisy. The very idea that society was "rotting" was current in Edwardian theatrical circles (Trewin 49). For example, Henry Jones's *Hypocrites* (1906) uses dialogue that virtually reproduces Boas's own: "Civilisation is rotten at the core, especially in a rotten little place like this."[7] Years later Boas described retroactively the revolution in Victorian domestic drama as a turning toward depictions of the "seamier," "uglier side of sexual relationships" (*Richardson to Pinero* 257–58). The circulation of such metaphors illustrates a cultural exchange between the Victorian-Edwardian age and Shakespeare's, one that discovered in Shakespeare a contemporary preoccupation with perturbing, even taboo issues.

Shaw's own declaration that all drama was either noninstitutional or institutional, timeless or temporal, "permanent and universal" or (by doing "work in the world") "intensely utilitarian,"[8] further contextualizes the problem-play concept. If the former treats perennial subjects of love and death, the latter, which Shaw championed, treats contemporary social, economic, and political conditions. This late Victorian turn toward social drama yields a fundamental point: when Boas fixed on societies "ripe unto rottenness" he in effect dissociated a group of Shakespeare's plays from the category of the timeless, highlighting instead their social realism and issue-oriented character. In other words, the Shakespearean problem play was originally constituted as a social category, not a formalist one.

Boas's second basic element, the absence of "a completely satisfactory outcome,"[9] points to the same social concerns, although they are framed within the category of the aesthetic. The invocation of this critical category signifies that despite Boas's immersion in the new drama, his criterion, originating in the normalizing expectation that good plays are lucid and well-made (*pièces bien fait*), is formalist: lack of resolution betokens a problem in dramatic construction. Nonetheless, Boas, along with many other theater critics and socially minded Edwardian theatergoers, clearly found something valuable in the irresolutions, let us say, of *A Doll's House*, in the discursive open-endedness of Granville-Barker's exploration of the sexual double standard in *The Madras House* (1910), and in the plainly unsatisfactory "solution" in Pinero's *Mid-Channel* (1909), where Zoe commits suicide in response to the sexual double standard. *Mrs. Warren's Profession*, August Strindberg's *Miss Julie* (1888), Pinero's *The Second Mrs. Tanqueray* (1893), and Henry Arthur Jones's *Mrs. Dane's Defense* (1900) also stand out for their exploration of the "woman problem" and the sexual double standard in the Victorian period, as do Jones's *Hypocrites* (1906), Pinero's *Mid-Channel,* and Granville-Barker's *Madras House* in the Edwardian.

As modern readers we recognize that the tendency toward irresolution and open-endedness in these plays is a consequence of dramatizing painful, unresolved conflicts and contradictions within culture. "Happy endings nice and tidy," as Bertolt Brecht tells us in *The Threepenny Opera*, "are the rule." They are also products of a worldview in which coincidence and fortune affirm a providential order. By contrast, nineteenth-century problem plays open a space for a drama that probes and challenges the values and worldview of its audience (Simon 6, 49–51). W. W. Lawrence put it well when he discerned that the special function of *Shakespeare*'s problem plays is "to probe the complicated interrelations of character and action, in a situation admitting of different ethical interpretations" (21). This ambiguous set of relations, he argued, in turn gives rise to a "'problem' mood [that] must not only be prominent in the action; it must dominate it."[10] If these insights are compelling, they can only mean that the problematic form of problem-play drama reproduces its substance.

The emphasis on women's sexuality and their asymmetrical marital position—or, as the Victorians called it, the "woman problem"—is crucial to our cultural reconstruction of the problem-play concept in early modern English drama. Broadly construed, sexual conduct and the cultural significance ascribed to that conduct is the single most distinctive feature of the Shakespearean problem play. A. P. Rossiter nods at this when he says that Shakespeare's problem plays are profoundly concerned with "the bad reality beneath the fair appearances of things" and "with seeming and being: and this can cover both sex and human worth" (126, 128). Especially significant in this regard is Boas's inclusion of *Hamlet* among the original three problem "comedies." His reason is not that *Hamlet* portrays the politics of regicide and hypocrisy or raises problematic questions about the ethics of suicide but that it depicts the scurviness of sexual appetite and hypocrisy.[11] This latter thematic is what underlies the rottenness in Denmark and becomes the metaphor for everything else wrong in the world of *Hamlet*.

This last observation points to another feature of the problem-play mode. It is not just that sexuality, or even its gendered asymmetry, is central to the problematic dramatic representation, but that the cultural construction of sexuality is symbolically laden.[12] The irresolution and over-ripe atmosphere Boas discerned can be recontextualized as part of a coded discourse in which issues of sexual conduct are treated inconclusively in relation to a spectrum of social expectations and ideals. Through this metonymic process, the well-being of the entire society and not just sexual behavior per se becomes the subject of dramatic reflection and debate. The recursivity of this process ends by questioning the appropriateness of the ideals themselves and not just the sexual behavior of those under examination. A further result is a surveilling of the authorities who surveil and an interrogation or judgment of those who interrogate or judge the sexual conduct of others.

The concluding statements of the previous paragraph on the symbolic representation of sexual conduct introduce a criterion not previously applied to problem-play criticism. To epitomize the point: the central sexual issues in problem-play drama call into question, metonymically, and almost always through the symbolic bodies of women, the broader ideals and expectations of English culture. Such a symbolic production of meaning, it is important to understand, must be sharply distinguished from the symbolic feminization of the external world. Annette Kolodny's study of

seventeenth-century America as a virgin territory to be explored and con-
quered in *The Lay of the Land* is one example, and so are Carole Fabricant's
and James Turner's economic and political analyses of the sexually fraught
topology of eighteenth-century English and Italian gardens. Fabricant, in
particular, shows how the landscape and its flora are observed with a
"faintly voyeuristic" appreciation of the naked female form and its secret
parts (110). Both the framing of nature's "parts" and the "*containing*" of her
are represented in terms of the female body (112). In these several studies,
the identity ascribed to woman is *projected* onto a part of the world's
landscape with the additional consequence that this projection redounds
upon women themselves, reinscribing attitudes toward them.

The procedure I propose in respect to the problem play reverses this
approach: it shows the well-being of the entire culture being read into
women's sexual bodies. But to read the female sexual body is difficult, if
not perilous, for as a symbolic signified it is remarkable for its instability
and the multiplicity of values, often conflicting, it embodies.

This complexity bears illustration because it enseams itself into the
culture even before the problem play appears. On the one hand, there is the
figure of "Magistra Vitae," a bare-breasted female who, as exhibited on the
frontispiece of Raleigh's *History of the World* (1614), holds up the world
(Figure 1). Flanking her is the ample female figure of Truth, represented in
a laudatory nakedness, along with the aged figure of Experience, modestly
clothed. With similar positivity, the Allegory of Tudor Succession shows
the womanly figures of Peace and Plenty being ushered in by Elizabeth
(Kotker 51). On the other hand, this same iconographic tradition normally
depicts the figure of Inconstancy as a mature, helmeted, able-bodied female so powerful that crowned kings sit naked and bound behind her
(Daly et al. 23). Deception in general is represented as female, as in the
emblem depicting Isis as the false god whom men worship (Daly 97). In
this same vein, England's nemesis, the papacy, was figured as the salacious
and bold Whore of Babylon, who brings about the confusion of kings on
earth (Daly 25). Too numerous to cite is the plethora of poets and iconogra-
phers who depict woman as Satan's accomplice because, as the tradition
has it, she is the weaker vessel, full of vanity and lust, easily given to
temptation, and prone to witchcraft. The material consequences of these
identifications are evident from trials of accused witches such as Margaret
Ferneseede, whose alleged activities, including prostitution, illustrate the
constellation of sins associated with women. More important, they illustrate the metonymic transpositions by which defilement in one area is read

as tantamount to defilement in other areas, so that adultery, for example, also signals a disposition to disobedience, whoredom, and treason.[13]

With equal but opposite symbolic effect the powers of chastity exhibited by women through the example of the Virgin Mary were celebrated as repelling the devil's temptations (de Bruyn 37–38). By this victory, women symbolically demonstrated their victory over their own sexuality, defeated the guileful eternal seducer, and were seen to engender a social-spiritual harmony throughout the community. Even after the Tudor suppression of Marian worship, Elizabeth replaced the Virgin as the inspirational, fetishized icon, Diana/Gloriana. And by another act of displacement the chaste Tudor gentlewoman was elevated in status and extravagantly praised in the new secular order as a prime bearer of household virtue.[14] Often celebrated as part of the emancipation of women, this shift witnessed gentry wives enacting multiple roles as managers of the household, practitioners of husbandry, entertainers of guests, child rearers, and teachers of piety and religion. But the shift was uncertain, for living women enacted their roles as icons and were thus forced to confront the cynicism, not to say misogyny, that follows hard upon such pedestal-raising.

This multivalent discourse illustrates the constitutive relationship between representation and social practice. So too, the issue of symbolic sexuality cannot be restricted to its iconographic, court-centered, and religious representations. Those representations, themselves a product of social history, penetrate into (are already part of) the social order and manifest themselves as social practices. But what messages underlie these representations and practices? From the variety of examples described above, it is apparent that no unifying identity places woman in the symbolic order except that her positive functions are commonly associated with the restraint or suppression of her sexuality.

Sexual restraint in general was a virtue. In the spiritual universe of early modern England both male chastity and female virginity were prized. Both were virtual preconditions for sanctity inasmuch as bodily purity and spiritual transcendence were held to be integral.[15] This idea is clearly revealed in *All's Well That Ends Well,* where Bertram's considerable princely deficiencies are read in terms of his ruttish behavior, and in *Measure for Measure,* where Angelo's fitness to rule is made to hinge on his ability to sustain his own uncompromising standard of chastity. Still, it was women's purity—such as we see in Shakespeare's Isabella—that became the mystified object of adoration. The reason for this symbolism, Caroline Walker Bynum theorizes, was not solely that women were seen as the weaker vessel, more prone to succumb to bodily passion, but far more complexly that women's bodies were also reified as *em*bodying the physical, tangible humanity of Christ: in marriage, in childbirth, and in their caregiving powers, including breast-feeding, they sustained the human community (Bynum 148–52). England's Christian inheritance from the early Middle Ages, however, celebrates with paradoxical self-awareness the mystery of the fruitfulness, bodily and spiritual, of the sexually abstinent woman. The Virgin Mary's unique power proceeds, of course, from a miraculous condition in which she brings forth the Son of God and nurtures him as a loving mother while being spared the contamination of a human insemination.[16] The devolution of such mythic values in the Renaissance is obvious in the iconographic depictions of Elizabeth I as Diana, whose purity ironically identifies the virgin queen as the undefiled mother of her kingdom. Her bodily purity becomes the symbolic guarantor of the virtue and well-being of English society generally.

This evidence shows vividly the symbolic power of sexuality, and, in particular, it reveals woman's power as symbolically creative and destructive. Like Inconstancy herself—like Eve, like Pandora, like Elizabeth— woman has the power to engender either a beneficent or an inhospitable social order. In her reproductive powers above all, she is the unstable signified upon whom the well-being of society precariously depends.

There is a dark side to all this. The symbolic powers of the female sexual body give rise to a voyeuristic fascination with the secrets it harbors. If read as sexually active and uncontrollably free, that body is invested with a fearsome significance because it inscribes and reinscribes (sometimes despite itself) the social identity of lover, husband, or children, or all three. This anxiety is a recurring feature of problem-play drama. To know his own identity, even the nature of his being, the male exhibits a compulsive desire to unlock the inaccessible sexual truth harbored by the body of spouse or mother. Such male desire takes the form of a febrile fascination/ inquiry: the status of the female sexual body in question must be authenticated, guaranteed. The suspicion that the world's falsity and deceptiveness are encased in women's bodies appears prominently in Hamlet's distrust of Ophelia's honesty as well as in his suspicions about the impropriety and excessiveness of Gertrude's sexual appetite, where the issue takes on ontological dimensions. The same compulsion takes on global proportions in Troilus's surveillance of Cressida's fidelity. Both revering and fearing the mystified power of the female body and the secret knowledge it possesses, the male responds with his insatiable desire to control, to expose, and even to destroy. As a group, Shakespeare's problem plays record these cultural apprehensions, and they do something more as well. They take us into another dark recess because they recursively call into question the social or spiritual foundation of the authority that passes judgment on those whose sexual conduct it surveils.

These hallmarks of the problem-play pattern merit illustration. Problem plays are plays of trial. Always, it is the probity of one or more person's sexual conduct that is the subject of the trial or testing. Bertram's honor and, by extension, his manliness and royal pedigree are put into question by rumors of his sexual incontinence. Consequently, trial is made of Bertram, the would-be adulterer, first by the symbolically dressed Helena, his pilgrim-disguised wife, and then in a further testing by Bertram's miraculously cured, wise, aged father, the king of France. Cressida's fidelity, upon which a universal order is viewed as depending, is put into question and tested by a snooping Troilus, as well as by the generals of the Greek camp who attempt to observe "every joint an motive of her body" to "wide unclasp the tables of her thoughts" (*Troilus and Cressida* 4.5.57). Cressida's mind, which controls the secret portals of her body, must be interpreted by the public movements of that body as if it were a book of tables, even such as informers use to write down what they see. The entire question of Cressida's worth is then refracted in the comprehensive question of the value of the Greek enterprise itself. In parallel fashion, that enterprise is read in and measured by the worth of Helen's body, the issue being whether she is really a goddess or a whore. The gendered identities of both Helen and Cressida, it becomes clear, are shaped not by some unitary absolute within the self but relationally, between the self in the world and the interpreters of that self's identity (Collins, *Cosmos* 58–60). In consequence, the "truth" about Helen, Cressida, womanhood, human endeavor itself can be read only through the dominant overseers, the assessors of value, whose perceptions endow the world with meaning.

More spectacularly, Duke Vincentio adopts the role of surveiller by disguising himself as a friar and hearing other people's confessions. Through this disguise, he in effect also answers Angelo's wish that "more test [be] made of my mettle" and explicitly tests the deputy's uprighteousness and chastity to "see / If power change purpose: what our seemers be" (*Measure for Measure* 1.1.48, 1.3.54). Furthermore, as Jonathan Dollimore points out, "the Duke's choice of *religious* disguise" underscores the proposition that sovereigns work as "political devisers" to work upon the inward as well as the outward self ("Transgression" 81). Before we are done, Julietta's state of mind has been examined in respect to her lost chastity and Isabella's chastity as a novitiate has undergone the Duke's probing inquiries, and the sexual probity of Claudio, Lucio, Pompey, and, in an important turn, even the Duke have been put in question.

Hamlet, that problem play of problem plays, is above all a contention of people making endless trial of one another, uncovering motive against motive, deed against dark deed. And underlying the covert act of regicide is the polluting and mind-disturbing sexual deed of darkness. It lies at the center of Claudius's guilt over his marriage, and it appears in Gertrude's own guilty awareness of her o'erhasty marriage. So too, with evident prurience, Polonius charges Reynaldo to gather informations on Laertes's sexual peccadilloes, and he sets himself behind an arras to observe Hamlet's amorous proclivities. Claudius conspires with Polonius to discern the same and even hires Rosencrantz and Guildenstern "to gather [of Hamlet] / So much as from occasion you may glean," who in turn agree to sift him (2.2.15–16). "Madness in great ones," as Claudius says, "must not unwatch'd go" (3.1.188).

The result in each case is surveillance. The surveyor becomes the truth-seeker, often disguised, always lurking in the shadows. And beneath these overseeings, the laxity or probity of sexual appetite becomes a trope for assessing the well-being and values of the entire culture.[17] In *Hamlet* Claudius's and Gertrude's dexterous posting to "incestuous sheets" makes the young prince experience "all the uses of this world" as "weary, stale, flat, and unprofitable" (1.2.157, 133–34). In *Troilus and Cressida* Helen, and implicitly Cressida, become the subject of a wider inquiry into (among other things) the nature of value in a society. As Troilus puts it, "What's aught but as 'tis valued?" (2.2.52). And in *Measure for Measure* the Duke's seeing of dark deeds as "a looker-on here in Vienna" begets the general assessment of Vienna—England—as a place "Where I have seen corruption boil and bubble, / Till it o'errun the stew; laws for all faults, / But faults so countenanc'd, that the strong statutes / Stand like the forfeits in a barber's shop, / As much in mock as mark (5.1.317–21).

It is not just the rectitude of the tested persons that falls subject to surveillance, however. Distinctively, the problem play turns back upon itself, reflexively. The dramatic pattern thus takes the form of the surveyor surveilled. This reflexivity ensures that those who do all the testing and would hand out the sanctions will themselves be subjected to searching oversight. Thus Troilus's belief in the absolute and transcendent value of love is put under question by the raisonneur Thersites, who undercuts Troilus as "that same young Trojan ass, that loves the whore there" and who, indeed, views the whole chivalric, Trojan enterprise of war and lovemaking as "All the argument is a whore and a cuckold" (5.4.5–6, 2.3.72–73). The progress of the play in fact gradually turns Troilus's fearful scrutiny of Cressida into an interrogation of the very value system by which Troilus himself evaluates his beloved. In the end, Troilus is made to recognize the "Bi-fold authority, where reason can revolt / Without perdition, and loss assume all reason / Without revolt" (5.2.144–46). Similarly, Angelo, as the severe but impeccable deputy who sentences others, is put to the test under the Duke's own sure-sighted surveillance, but then even the latter's motives are put under pressure by the shadowing Lucio, who marks the absent Vincentio as "the old fantastical Duke of dark corners" who "would have dark deeds darkly answer'd" (*Measure for Measure* 4.3.155–56, 3.2.177). So too, Hamlet, relentlessly put under surveillance by Claudius's lackeys, puts on his own antic disposition to play upon Rosencrantz and Guildenstern, who play upon him, and then his play-within-the-play, his mousetrap, to "catch the conscience of the King!" (2.2.605).

This movement toward counterjudgment, crucial to the problem-play mode, is, of course, closely tied to the play of surveillance itself. Among the most reflexive of plays, *Hamlet* puts under question every authority figure it represents, from Old Hamlet, who demands that his son take revenge on Claudius while leaving to heaven the sexually incontinent wife, to Hamlet himself, whose inaction and motives for revenge are both put into question at every turn. Even the veracity of the majestic Ghost, source of the play's guilt-ridden knowledge of Claudius's and Gertrude's adultery, is put into question so that the very basis of the play, the injunction to revenge, becomes problematic. Such dazzling circularity as we see in these plays is part and parcel of the metatheatrical features of the problem play. Theater's capacity to present itself as theater, self-consciously to present the putting on and taking off of roles, is a built-in means for scrutinizing the authority or warrant for all assumed roles. When the justification for those judging the sexual transgressions of others is problematically called in question, the authority of the dominant culture itself is impugned. When this happens, we are in the presence of problem-play drama.

Pervasive as this discourse of symbolic sexuality is, the case must not be overstated. Especially in view of the new-historicist tendency to make sweeping judgments about the all-pervasive powers of specific representations, we should hesitate to assume that the anxious discourse underlying the problem-play mode penetrated every stratum of society. From the available evidence, it appears that the lower strata were little touched by the kinds of high-cultural representations examined above. Those from the overwhelmingly uneducated classes, it is true, have left few traces in their voices, but they can be heard. Ironically, the official records of surveillance upon their activities give us access to a sexual discourse shorn of the symbolic elements cited above.

G. R. Quaife's study of the depositions presented at the Quarter Sessions of the county of Somerset offers extended anecdotes by ordinary, largely illiterate people on the illicit sexual behavior they encountered. These Quarter Sessions, with their bureaucratic organization, clerkish depositions, and records of punishments, are testaments to an endless, unsuccessful surveillance over ordinary citizens who were unresponsive to the restrictions on sexual behavior imposed by the dominant culture. To cite the kind of behavior brought to judgment, record is made, for instance, of two churchgoing informants who, suspecting a girl of promiscuity, climbed a tree to observe her lovemaking. When that proved unsuccessful, the informants confronted the girl, who retorted that if they had only remained in their perch a little longer, they "might have seen more than they did."[18] In Quaife's assessment, "Few girls in this sample raised any moral or religious objection to the suggestion of sexual intercourse" (64). Some consented to pre-marital intercourse with a beau in the belief that "if she were with child by him she might put it to [accuse] her master"; others actively sought out sexual contact, as when one servant girl came to the bed shared by two males, "And supposing this informant to be asleep came into the bed that side where . . . John Stevens, lay with her clothes not taken off. And desired . . . John to put his legs in between her legs. . . . [John did] get upon Sarah . . . [and] did pull away a part of the clothes."[19] The sheer volume of the offenses brought forward suggests their ordinariness. In Essex County alone, the spiritual courts summoned more than fifteen thousand persons in an adult population of thirty-five thousand during Elizabeth's reign (Emmison 1, cf. Stone 519). And although the ribald rhymes, satires, and "Bawdy Court" depositions that Martin Ingram reproduces in his study of the church courts in Wiltshire, Cambridgeshire, Leicestershire, and West Sussex do reveal (despite the religious venue) "a degree of popular intolerance of blatant immorality," their prurience, lighthearted mockery, and pornographic element suggest that they also "served as a proxy form of sexual indulgence" (165). This evidence, in short, does not support the hypothesis that sexual behavior among these cohorts was experienced as shameful or that it was invested with transcendent significance of any kind. In fact, the depositions of accused persons, female as well as male, reveal a counterdiscourse of indulgence and plain fun.

Obviously, this eminently literal discourse of sexual conduct is the precise counterpoint of a symbolic discourse of sexuality. Nevertheless, such open, literal accounts of sexual indulgence make their way into problem-play comedy, introduced there as yet another counterpoint to the high-minded, anxious symbolic discourse that otherwise dominates. Thus the counterpoint to Troilus's idealizing sentiments about Cressida is Pandarus's go-to-it, celebratory indulgence. More sensationally, the low-life characters of *Measure for Measure,* in opposition to the strictures of the law, live out a complaisant, imperturbable indulgence that ranges from the vegetable existence of the dissolute Barnardine to the blithe amoralism of Mistress Overdone and Pompey the bawd, the last of whom believes simply that prostitution would be a lawful trade "If the law would allow it" (2.1.227). Ironically, then, this very discourse that fails to absorb the symbolic sexuality of the dominant culture *is* absorbed into the problem-play mode, complicating the issues and revealing a fuller range of problematic perspectives.

In sum, the tropic, iconographic, and dialogic modes of early modern drama in England especially equip it to represent *both* the social tensions manifest in more monologic texts—sermons, conduct books, and proclamations—and the conflicts inherent in the codes that underwrite the gendered, symbolic construction of sexuality. For this reason, all of the plays we call problem plays should be read not merely for the social and sexual issues they patently treat but, following a more anthropological impulse, for the symbolic codes that underlie their problem-filled representations of sexuality.[20]

These insights pertaining to the cultural construction of the problem play mode force a critical question that also serves as a segue to the next chapter. If a group of Shakespeare's plays seizes upon the representation of sexual behavior to exhibit a web of cultural tensions and contradictions, what reason have we to believe that Shakespeare's drama alone functions in this manner? What warrant is there for continuing to designate the problem play as a category of Shakespeare's mental development without examining the possibility of its larger expression in the Jacobean drama generally? The answer is that there is no warrant at all except the authority of tradition.[21] Already, we have seen that the problem-play discourse of the

Victorian-Edwardian period provides the rationale for undertaking a cultural-historicist study of the problem play as a diachronic, not a merely Shakespearean, phenomenon. So too, by recontextualizing the criteria of Shakespearean problem-play scholarship, the broader set of criteria we have adduced is available for application to the Jacobean drama itself. To apply these principles where they have not been applied before and to test the power of this cultural-historicist method, I turn now to the *Jacobean*[22] problem play.

6

The *Jacobean* Problem Play

Sexuality, Surveillance, and the Critique of Culture

I seek in this chapter to extend the inquiry on the surveillance of sexuality beyond its appearances in Shakespeare's problem plays. Still focused on the thematic of surveillance as normalization, I will apply the historicized and reconfigured concept of the Shakespearean problem play (as developed in Chapter 5) to a group of Jacobean plays. My aim is to demonstrate how these Jacobean problem plays generate a discourse that works to reproduce and also to modify the culture of sexual surveillance in early modern England, holding it up to examination and interrogating it.

Two of the plays I will discuss in depth are comedies—George Chapman's *Widow's Tears* (1604) and John Marston's *Dutch Courtesan* (1603/4). The third is Chapman's *Tragedy of Bussy D'Ambois* (1604). Limitations of space do not permit me to treat plays such as Thomas Dekker's *Honest Whore* (1604), John Heywood's *Woman Killed with Kindness* (1603), and Marston and William Barksted's *Insatiate Countess* (ca. 1610), each of which exhibits in more limited ways the social-sexual features belonging to this Jacobean problem-play grouping. My object in any case is not to offer an exhaustive exegesis on all the Jacobean plays that might be read in whole or in part as problem plays, but to demonstrate the productivity of the concept and the cultural suppositions that underwrite it. In so doing, I will lavish on these problem plays the same intensive analysis commonly accorded to Shakespeare's own, arguing that, like Shakespeare's, each presents a distinctive atmosphere of rank sexuality, frames a crucial debate involving a trial of sexual conduct in which the would-be examiner is put under examination, and, consequently, reaches a conclusion that calls into question its own resolution. Cutting across all these categories and implicit in these just mentioned is another—the representation of sexual conduct as a symbolic trope posing crucial questions of English social organization and justice.

Sexuality and Social Disintegration

The presence of an atmosphere of a "civilization . . . ripe unto rotten-ness" (Boas 345) and even of a diseased sexuality is easy to demonstrate in the Jacobean problem play. More difficult and important to show is that this atmosphere betokens conflicting attitudes toward sexual behavior that lead to the problematic representation of major issues pertaining to social organization and justice. Violations of and challenges to the ideals of chas-tity and virginity are the prime matter of the problem plays because these concerns circulate dynamically as a metonym for legitimacy of rule,[1] the sanctity of received values, and the well-being of the entire society. Phrased slightly differently, the problem play, by virtue of its tropic, dialogic, and plot-making features, employs its sexual matter to air more general cul-tural anxieties that may themselves be subjects of debate.[2]

The ambience of diseased sexuality in *The Widow's Tears* is first exhibited in the depiction of the widowed Eudora's effete suitor Lord Rebus who, armed with letters of introduction from his kinsman, "his Altitude" the Viceroy (1.2.20), promises a duchess-ship.[3] This class puffery is quickly punctured by observations as caustic as Thersites's tongue. He is "A lean lord, dubb'd with the lard of others! A diseased lord, too, that [has] . . . as many aches in's bones as there are ouches in's skin" (1.2.112–15). The contrast between Rebus's venerable ancestry and the crude fact that "he has been long wedded" to "the venerean disease" (1.2.32–33) establishes a characteristic problem-play feature that Rossiter identifies as "a refusal wholly to credit the dignity of man" (116).

This terminology, with its liberal emphasis on individual dignity and its submersion of female identity in the encompassing term *man*, now has a slightly old-fashioned ring that bespeaks the need for greater awareness of gender and class in problem-play analysis. Chapman's refusal to credit the dignity of man is for the most part focused in fact on woman. The tropes of venereal devaluation quickly spread to the exalted female protagonists and become prime matter for the play's inquiry into the legitimacy of the social order. First, Eudora's celebrated chastity as the deceased governor's widow is challenged by the buoyant cynicism of Tharsalio, who believes that the "angry heats" from "strait-lac'd ladies are but as symptoms of a lustful fever that boils within them" (2.3.25–27). Then Eudora's privileged social position comes under scrutiny through tart sexual innuendo. Hearing how Tharsalio has "nine in a night made mad with his love," Eudora begins to compromise her chaste pretensions with the ironic double entendres of Arsace, who begs the countess "for virtue's sake" to "fix your whole womanhood against him [Tharsalio]" and "urge his unreasonable manhood to the full" (2.2.85–86, 94–95, 101–2). Eudora's shocked response— "let me see this reformation you pretend continued" (112–13)—is enveloped in an ambivalent rhetoric of hypocrisy and self-betrayal. So are her sexually tinged protestations, reminiscent of Isabella's—"I abhor his thought," and "I abhor him"—with the scarce-concealed pun on "whore" (2.2.76, 87; cf. 3.1.116). In this way, traditional ideas of female concupiscence clash with newer Tudor ideas of gentry women's chastity and privileged place.

To the same effect, a loftier but equally equivocal language infuses the sexually charged speeches surrounding Cynthia, the play's second paragon, whose power—like Eudora's, like Isabella's—lies so much in her chastity that "the Paphian widows" (as Tharsalio mockingly imagines it) will erect an altar in her honor (4.1.117–18). Like Isabella, this woman too "abhors" to think that Eudora, "So great and vow'd a pattern of our sex / Should take into her thoughts, nay, to her bed / (O stain to womanhood), a second love" (3.1.117–19). The equivocal ribaldry that undercuts the protestations of both these women, revealing their chastity as venery, exhibits just that "emphasis (comic, derisive, satiric) on human short-comings" (116) that Rossiter reserves for the problem-play mode.

In *The Dutch Courtesan* this atmosphere of diseased sexuality is endued with suggestions of contamination of the male through illicit sexual contact with the female. But this reading is itself unstable. The issue is joined by the contention between the hapless Malheureux, an abstinent "man of snow" (2.1.82) and "psychological virgin" (Adelman, "Bed Tricks" 151), who, like Shakespeare's Angelo, believes "The sight of vice augments the hate of sin" (1.1.153), and Freevill, his more experienced friend, who contends that the bawdy house is a harmless outlet for the natural passions.[4] Presented at the outset as an indeterminate signified, the brothel setting becomes the site for a reexamination of the social regulations of sexual activity.

Concealed in this problematic representation are issues of status and rank that the comedy is not frank in owning up to. Compared to *Measure for Measure*, the bawdy house of *The Dutch Courtesan* is more elevated than

Mistress Overdone's salty stews in which Pompey plays the tapster. It attracts a more exclusive clientele and is peopled by accomplished courtesans such as Franceschina, who can play a musical instrument, sing, conduct polite conversation, and solicit the gentler affections as well as the passions. This surface attractiveness, initially a kind of argument in favor of the brothel, has as its counterpoint a repugnant web of sexual images that begins to assert itself once Malheureux falls headlong for Franceschina. Freevill's newly denigrating descriptions of the courtesan as "an arrant strumpet; and a strumpet is a serpigo [creeping skin disease], venom'd gonorrhy to man" (2.1.130–31) mix with Cocledemoy's scampish street speech to depict Franceschina as a beguiling "Frank Frailty, a punk, an honest polecat, of a clean instep, sound leg, smooth thigh, and the nimble devil in her buttock" (2.1.151–52).

Such language does indeed constitute the atmosphere characteristic of the problem play. But the more important consideration, as I have urged, is the end served by this representation.[5] The terms *venom'd gonorrhy, serpigo, devil in her buttock* and, elsewhere, *glister-pipe* and *suppository* (1.2.12, 99), exhibit more than an exuberant vocabulary of denigration. Beneath the high-spirited mockery of Franceschina and the profession of the prostitute (*Franceschina* means prostitute) is a prior discourse anthropologists recognize as a fear of contamination for verboten activity. The glister and suppository function like defiled phalluses that intrude into the forbidden vaginal passage—here re-presented as the dirty buggery hole—bringing pollution and punishment upon the perpetrator. The forms of that pollution are social as well as sexual, for the male risks loss of status for his unlicensed, out-of-class copulations. This apprehension, ritualistically expressed in an obsessive, misogynistic language of sexual vilification, contends with a counterdiscourse of sexual congress as natural.

The notion that the entitlements of rank may be gauged by assessing the sexual activities of those in great place is resonantly dramatized in *The Tragedy of Bussy D'Ambois.* As a contemporary historical tragedy depicting the faction-ridden court of Henry III of France, the play is extraordinary for its depiction of an aristocratic court mired in promiscuity and sexual hypocrisy. Prominently on display is the politics of sexual desire, wherein the ladies of the French court talk uninhibited bawdry and make midnight trysts with secret lovers. The king's conspiratorial brother Monsieur woos the Countess of Montsurry, Tamyra, with a rhetoric of libertinism mixed with subtle threat. To these advances the countess's uxorious but politic husband, Montsurry, casuistically counsels permissiveness, while he himself later proves to be "busy about" the Guise's wife (3.2.221).[6] Tamyra herself, despite refusing Monsieur's enticing chain of pearls, has enjoyed a clandestine lover, and after finding herself overwhelmed with passion for Bussy chooses the way of hypocrisy to gratify her desires.

But the tragedy problematizes Tamyra's female desire. The same woman who can for public consumption affirm, "Mine honour's in mine own hands, spite of Kings" (2.2.59), also employs a graphic sexual language in private chambers to express her passion, exclaiming, "What shall weak Dames do, when th' whole work of Nature / Hath a strong finger in each one us?" (3.1.47–48). The distance between Tamyra's formulaic protestations of chastity and her intimate confessions of strong, unsought-for feelings of sexual arousal exhibits just that kind of perturbation characteristic of the problem-play mode.

Bussy's sexuality too is ambivalently represented both as a politics and an independent expression of self-assertion. Thus Bussy fearlessly courts the greatest ladies of the French court, countering their ribaldry with his own, remarking that it is "leap-year" and thus "very good to enter a Courtier" and that he can sing "prick-song" at first sight and would gladly "take entrance" under the Duchess's princely colors (1.2.79–87). Even as Bussy's bawdy underscores his heroic confidence, it also undermines the orthodox Christian virtue that he originally commends in his "green retreat," where he affirms, "We must to Virtue for her guide resort, / Or we shall shipwrack in our safest Port" (1.1.32–33) and resolves to "bring up a new fashion, / And rise in Court with virtue" (1.1.125–26). Alternatively stated, the tragedy works both to establish and challenge the normalization of virtue.

The same double perspective is inextricably tied to Bussy's sexual conduct. When Monsieur, having become Bussy's mortal enemy after his protégé allies himself with the king, conducts a prurient investigation into his opponent's secret love life, he begins by comparing Bussy to "the most royal beast of chase, the Hart" (3.2.152). Because the hart cannot be brought down by the arrow, Monsieur appears to ennoble his opponent. But this view is quickly undermined by the assertion that the stag can yet be taken in his "venery," "behind some queich" where he "breaks his gall, and rutteth with his hind" (3.2.155–57). The entire oration is infused with smuttily expressed insights about catching the "upstart" in "a loose downfall" because great women's "falls / Are th' ends of all men's rising" and they "Still hold men's candles: they direct and know / All things amiss in them" (143–49). To Monsieur and his cohorts the viewpoint is like that of *The*

Dutch Courtesan—women's sexuality contaminates men; it brings them down. The discovery itself, celebrated with a leering humor in which the Guise characterizes their informant as one who must have "swallowed a porcupine, she casts pricks from her tongue so" (3.2.232–33), throws the affair into an obscene light that stands in glaring, irreconcilable contrast to Bussy's own chivalric devotion to Tamyra.[7]

This atmosphere of rank sexuality that links *Bussy D'Ambois, The Dutch Courtesan,* and *The Widow's Tears* to Shakespeare's problem plays does not just happen to be pervasive; it is a necessary condition of the problem-play mode, whose obsessive concern is to read sexual conduct as a marker of the society's core values—its sense of justice, its privileging of the privileged, its hierarchical organization. To recast the emphasis of Boas's phrase, in the problem play the atmosphere of "rank sexuality" is really a vehicle for interrogating "rank" itself.

The Debate Mode

The ambivalent double vision that constitutes the atmosphere of the problem plays is part of a larger debate structure. All Jacobean problem plays exhibit a crucial scene of debate, which, as Vivian Thomas observes referring to Shakespeare's problem comedies, "focuses sharply on the central themes" (15). We may say further that the problem-play mode interrogates cultural ideals by scrutinizing sexual conduct. But it focuses less on lowly incorrigibles than on the virtuous and highly placed, and this is because the sexual behavior of the privileged classes is invested with symbolic significance and so subject to public scrutiny.

The hallmark of *The Widow's Tears* is that every one of its debate scenes elaborates the meaning of women's virtue until the whole culture is implicated. This process becomes evident when Cynthia declares that the well-traveled Tharsalio's cynical evaluation of women's chastity is the product of miseducation. "I fear me in your travel you have drunk too much of that Italian air, that hath infected the whole mass of your ingenuous nature, . . . poison'd the very essence of your soul, and so polluted your senses that whatsoever enters there takes from them contagion" (1.1.125–30). Although critical tradition has it that Tharsalio has been debauched by a Machiavellian atheism, the issue is primarily social rather than political. The operative terms in Cynthia's assessment are *infection, pollution, poison,* and *contagion.* The aristocratic culture for which Cynthia speaks holds Tharsalio's thinking to be polluted because it declines to mystify gentry women as the symbolic guarantors of the entitlements of class and property. Tharsalio, in short, challenges the cultural inscriptions that underlie the valorization— and cultural enforcement—of women's chastity: he challenges the entire process of normalizing class distinctions.

As against the received creed, Tharsalio champions an empirical counter-doctrine rooted in experience, which "hath refin'd my senses, and made me see with clear eyes, and to judge of objects as they truly are, not as they seem, and through their mask to discern the true face of things" (1.1.132– 34). Underlying these polar allegiances are two radically different politics, two ideologies, two competing worldviews. And the concrete subjects on which all these issues are made to depend are the exalted bodies of Eudora and Cynthia.

The problem-play mode demands a testing, and so a cohort of self-appointed male intelligencers monitor the behavior of these exalted wives and in so doing inspect the foundations of hierarchy and privilege. The mutating trope in which this investigation is depicted is "reformation," and the pivotal subject of scrutiny is the chastity of the exalted female body. When Eudora warns the pander Arsace to "let me see this reforma-tion you pretend continued" (2.2.112–13), her intended usage is conven-tional, but the inadvertent double entendre undermines her moralistic stance. By contrast, "reformation" in Tharsalio's lexicon means the satiric exposure of hypocrisy. When Tharsalio determines to storm Eudora's chaste defenses, saying, "Well, I see this house needs reformation" (2.4.102), he is acting out his precept that the appearance of saintly virtue is a mere cloak for concupiscence. Implicit in his daring reconception of "reformation" is that the act of making a society honest again entails turning the social hierarchies on their head. Under such circumstances, truth will prevail— but the removal of vice with a firm purpose of amendment there will not be.

In the onion-scaling logic of *The Widow's Tears* not just women's virtue but the pretensions of society itself are stripped away. Reformation be-comes indistinguishable from metamorphosis. When in the moments be-fore succumbing to Tharsalio's brash wooing, Eudora boasts, "destiny must have another mold" before he can "transform me to another shape" (2.2.88–90), she unearths the Rosetta stone that enables us to translate the discourse on chastity into every other discourse in the play. Via the chastity of its chastest women, who are repeatedly compared to their Homeric and Virgilian forebears, *The Widow's Tears* reads the inheritance and standing of Jacobean society. That relationship to a heroic past is simultaneously constructed and deconstructed, for Tharsalio identifies Eudora and Cynthia with the culture's prime symbols of chastity so that he may prove that chastity a sham—"Your way is not to win Penelope by suit, but by surprise" (1.1.144–45); "Dido hath betroth'd her love to me" (2.4.190). In this self-serving enterprise Tharsalio becomes, as Henry Weidner observes, the Ulysses of "the iron age," of an inverted, "falsely heroic world" in which the apparent moral order is a mere image of its former self (524–27). As the new Aeneas, the new Ulysses of a fallen Homeric world, Tharsalio inverts the meaning of all courtesy, all praise, and through the women he subverts, Homeric myth undergoes Ovidean metamorphosis.

Cynthia, a paragon by her husband's own account, becomes the prime test case. Because male status and identity are made to depend on the bodily purity of the spouse, the latter becomes the symbolic center of the arrogated superiority that Lysander and all his class presume. In the integrity of Cynthia's gentle body are planted the status and privileges of hierarchy, just as priority of place and the principle of degree finally rest on Cressida in the final scenes of *Troilus and Cressida*. So fraught with significance is Cynthia's sexual body that Lysander must compulsively ascertain its inviolability by feigning death so that he may personally "make trial of her" (2.1.30). But in judging her he will end with a judgment of himself and his world.

Lysander's often-cited speech attacking his upstart brother's profligate way of life is actually about Tharsalio's subversive beliefs. In this problem-play metonymy, subversion is made plausible only if Cynthia's body *means* something that Lysander, descendant of a family with a six-hundred year pedigree, cannot imagine:

> I know him [Tharsalio] for a wild, corrupted youth,
> Whom profane ruffians, squires to bawds and strumpets,
> Drunkards spew'd out of taverns into th' sinks
> Of taphouses and stews, revolts from manhood,
> Debauch'd perdus, have by their companies
> Turn'd devil like themselves, and stuff'd his soul
> With damn'd opinions and unhallowed thoughts
> Of womanhood, of all humanity,
> Nay, deity itself. (2.1.42–50)

The manifest anxieties of the speech—the frightened vision of a society destabilized from below—gradually release deeper ones. Reverberating in

ever-expanding circles, the concluding verses invoke the foundational veri-
ties of Elizabethan hierarchy—womanhood, humanity, deity (Tricomi, "Social Disorder" 355). Cynthia's body ironically becomes Lysander's self-
knowledge. All the beliefs that make up Lysander's class identity are
epitomized in that body. The undermining of that body as a pattern of
gentle womanhood undermines the existing social order and humanity
itself, which God is viewed as authorizing.

The issue can be seen from the reverse angle as well. If Tharsalio is right
and a philosophy propounded in the stews proves a fair-seeming civilization to be foul, in effect "ripe unto rottenness," then the entitlements of the
superior classes and an ancient order evaporate. Against such prospects
English high culture speaks in its sermons and its antimasques, as well as
its mocking but apprehensive representations of the "natural" order turned
upside down by the likes of Wat Tyler, John Ball, and Jack Cade. In *The
Widow's Tears* all these freighted possibilities are seriously countenanced,
but the issue is carried on the backs and in the bellies of its gentry women.

Compared to *The Widow's Tears*, the debate mode in *The Dutch Courtesan*
is more pronounced and closer to that in *Measure for Measure* because the
latter plays explicitly treat the problematic ordering of sexual behavior. But
whereas *Measure for Measure* works a relentless contrast between its abstinent, high-minded principals and its sexually irrepressible low-life characters, *The Dutch Courtesan* uses Malheureux and Freevill to launch radically
incompatible views on the management of sexual behavior. Unable to
agree on the major terms of their debate, Malheureux condemns the bawdy
house, arguing that "the strongest argument that speaks / Against the
soul's eternity is lust," whereas Freevill challengingly calls it "a house of
salvation" (1.1.81–82, 137). Predicting that attending a brothel will make
Malheureux "repent" (139), Freevill destabilizes the traditional notion of
virtue, suggesting that his friend's abstinence is a sin of which fully developed human beings must repent. From this central question of what kind
of signified the bawdy house is—a place of "salvation" or damnation—all
the issues that radiate from *The Dutch Courtesan* proceed.

Exhibiting a characteristic problem-play reflexiveness, *The Dutch Courtesan* turns back on itself to question its own categories. If in *Measure for
Measure* Escalus, hearing the malapropisms of Constable Elbow and Pompey
the bawd, reflects, "Which is the wiser here: Justice or Iniquity?" (2.1.172–
73), *The Dutch Courtesan* uses its debate mode to probe whether human
salvation proceeds from sexual liberty or abstinence. This larger inquiry is
founded on at least two pillars of thought. The most obvious and imposing

translates each individual's sexual conduct into a spiritual destiny. The play demands to know how extramarital sexual appetite is to be read ontologically, whether it is in some originary sense a natural good or, in orthodox Christian terms, simply a vice. The second pillar is erected on a humanistic discourse of individual "freedom" and autonomy. In Freevill's blithe formulation, freedom follows the disregard of sexual prohibitions. For Malheureux, freedom is achieved by subjugating bodily desire in the name of a higher self that monitors and redirects base impulses. In both discourses, the social arrangements that are to be made for managing sexual desire depend upon how freedom and salvation are to be constructed.

Not surprisingly, Marston's comedy develops the case with a shiftiness that makes final assessments problematic. *The Dutch Courtesan* uses Freevill to pose a casuistic, lawyerly defense of prostitutes when he argues that if women sell their bodies, better persons sell their souls and that "All things are made for man, and man for woman" (1.1.126). How seriously is this disquisition to be taken? The mock demand at speech's end, "Give me my fee!" (127), acknowledges the sophistical bravura of the position; yet Freevill *has* in part taken the position he jokes about. In this way Freevill's libertinism is staked out brashly but uneasily in an unsettling fantasy. The parallel rhetorical display in which Cocledemoy both rails at and defends Mary Faugh's profession as a "necessary damnation" (1.2.24–25) argues a third position between Freevill's and Malheureux's. It too reproduces the problematic tentativeness of the previous arguments.

Critics have observed that Marston's interest in questions of nature and custom derives, as Gustav Cross has shown, from his reading of Florio's Montaigne. But to me the more striking features of his theatrical deployment of Montaigne are that pre-marital sexual relations are the locus for the inquiry and that Malheureux, the person whose sexual appetite is at issue, must, like the problem-play principals, be placed under surveillance. Judgment is passed both upon him and the philosophy for which he stands. Malheureux becomes the object of Freevill's scrutiny because the comedy seeks out the destructive social implications of illicit sexual desire. Its project is thus to use surveillance to normalize sexual desire.

Taking up the heterodox belief that the uninhibited expression of sexuality makes one like "the free-born birds [who] / Carol their unaffected passions!" (2.1.64–65), the play works hard to explode this view. It begins by representing Malheureux's mad desire to possess Franceschina as so extreme that he must acknowledge "I cannot choose" (2.1.136) and is therefore anything but free. Under the pressure of irrational desire, the would-be autonomous subject is shown to lose his humanness. And beneath the manifest question, How is Malheureux to reclaim his humanity? an unacknowledged issue lurks: how is premarital sexual desire to be negotiated on terms that will permit males to maintain their social status and honor? That the problem is preeminently male is evident from the stews themselves, which are shown to serve men of fair position from many nationalities. As Mary Faugh says of her clientele, "I have made you [, Franceschina,] acquainted with the Spaniard, Don Skirtoll; with the Italian, Master Beieroane; with the Irish lord, Sir Patrick; with the Dutch merchant, Haunce Herkin Glukin Skellam Flapdragon; and specially with the greatest French, and now lastly with the English. . . , an honest gentleman. And am I now grown one of the accursed with you for my labor? Is this my reward? Am I call'd bawd?" (2.2.13–20). Lords, masters, and gentlemen all line up. The problem, in the wider context of the comedy, is how incontinent male desire is to be managed in respect to establishing stable, lasting marital relationships.

Idealized images of Sir Philip Sidney and other celebrated gentlemen who were said always to have controlled their passions are not invoked when the issue is how most gentlemen behave in fact. To the contrary, the new realism of Nashe and Robert Greene was founded on the risqué representation of the newly acknowledged truth of male sexual desire, and Marston's play belongs to this popular fare. For Marston the problem is establishing a realistic code of conduct. At first the problem seems to be approached with confidence. Freevill has all the answers. He loved Franceschina with his heart, he says, until "my soul showed me the imperfection of my body, and placed my affection on a lawful love"—Beatrice (1.2.90–91). The remedy for premarital male desire, it seems, is indulgence. Instead of repressing their sexuality as the unhappy Malheureux has done, men should avoid its maddening effects by gaining sexual experience ("practice," as it were) before settling their affections on a bride.

The formulaic patness to this solution has a long history in European culture. As Susan Baker observes, it conforms to the ideology of medieval chivalric romance, which reserves "emotional intimacy to same-sex friendships [Freevill-Malheureux], desire to an idealized lady [Beatrice], and physical intimacy to a wicked enchantress [Franceschina]" (220). Such a solution runs up against two major cultural contradictions that Marston's play at least partially acknowledges. Unlike *Measure for Measure,* in which the rigid code of virtue of the upper classes is sharply separated from the

irrepressible sexuality of those beneath, *The Dutch Courtesan* draws attention to the unequal power relations between privileged men and déclassé
women, thereby permitting the abusiveness of those relationships to be
represented—up to a point. Thus Franceschina's discovery that Freevill has
fobbed her off on Malheureux as if she were an unfeeling piece of goods
begets a ringing protest. Freevill can blithely claim that courtesans "sell but
only flesh, no jot affection" (2.1.137–38), but his shallow thought is met
with the reality of Franceschina's feelings of betrayal. Sexuality and affection are not so easily compartmentalized. "Do you take me to be a beast, a
creature that for sense only will entertain love," Franceschina complains
(2.2.126–27). "Lie with you [Malheureux]?" she explodes, "Oh no! You men
will out-lie any woman" (2.2.123). Her protest discloses an interior life that
belongs more to the Edwardian problem play than to Jacobean comedy—
"Sall I, or can I trust again? O fool, / How natural 'tis for us to be abus'd!"
(2.2.134–35).

The marginal social position of the whore reverberates from Elizabethan
and Victorian culture to our own time. Uncannily and despite the strangeness of Franceschina's accent, *The Dutch Courtesan* maps a social transaction that is still recognizable, and it poses the question, To what destructive
institutional uses are society's prostitutes put? This issue opens still wider
as the free-speaking Crispinella launches a feminist critique of marriage as
an institution in which power is exercised for men's comfort, not women's.
Her rousingly comical speech employs the metaphor of the erect penis to
depict female subjection: "A husband generally is a careless, domineering
thing that grows like coral, which as long as it is under water is soft and
tender, but as soon as it has got his branch above the waves is presently
hard, stiff, not be bowed but burst; so when your husband is a suitor under
your choice, Lord, how supple he is, how obsequious, how at your service,
sweet lady! Once married, got up his head above, a stiff, crooked, knobby,
inflexible, tyrannous creature he grows; then they turn like water, more
you would embrace, the less you hold" (3.1.70–77). There is more than
licentious humor here. With this characteristic problem-play imagery, *The
Dutch Courtesan* makes its turn toward a symbolic understanding of sexuality: the tumescent phallus is read as male dominance in the marital relationship. The comedy also reinterprets the romantic conventions of male
service in *amour courtois* as mere ritual because the courtesy disappears as
soon as the "beloved" is secured as a sexual object. So too, the deflating
mockery of the male's detumescent state emphasizes that the behavior of

the male is unpredictable and his dominance sustained by asymmetrical power relations in the marital relationship. The entire speech may be taken as a burlesque of the male body "lower stratum" and thus a Rabelaisian exercise in demystifying patriarchal authority by returning its symbolic authority to its grossly physical source (Bakhtin 73–96).

By these interrogations of the codes that govern the construction of gendered relationships, *The Dutch Courtesan* entertains reforming possibilities. At the least, Crispinella's critique of marriage formation establishes a substantial ground for separating Beatrice's conventional views from her own independent-minded practice, in which the individual voices of Crispinella and her fiancé may be clearly heard. The play also comes within sight of exposing Freevill's philosophy of self-realization as predicated on a system of repression. It problematizes the construction of the marital relationship and calls into question the double standard that supports it. Up to this point, *The Dutch Courtesan* is a problem play of the first order. But then it draws back from its own radical insights.

Bussy D'Ambois, by contrast, never draws back. The most philosophical problem play of the group, it is closest to *Troilus and Cressida* because its central issues are dramatized through a symbolic sexuality and because the action is made, self-consciously, to reflect back upon itself metatheatrically. When the express subjects of debate are value, worth, and honor as in *Troilus and Cressida* (2.2), these are all brought to a dramatic crux through the suffering, wayward body of Tamyra. Even the probings of law and custom in *Bussy D'Ambois* are finally concretized in the symbolism of nature as a female body, whose significance is read in terms of her sexuality.

Given its manifest concern with heroic self-assertion, *Bussy D'Ambois* may not appear to be predicated on the female sexual body, but it is. Years ago Moody Prior identified a puzzling problem when he asked how Bussy's pursuit of Tamyra is related to his heroic pursuit of native noblesse (111). For many, Bussy's affair with Tamyra is a distraction from the tragedy's central concern with evaluating Bussy's challenge to kingship and civil law. This view, coupled with the insight that Bussy's career is presented from indeterminate perspectives, fortifies the commonplace that *Bussy D'Ambois* is a great flawed tragedy (J. Smith 45–61; Ferguson 223–29; Schwartz 175–76; Ornstein 58–59). When the play is thus read as a political tragedy and traditional closure is posited as an unquestioned good, this denigrating evaluation is to be expected. But when Bussy's ungovernable valor and "arrogance" in pursuing Tamyra are read as interrogating the entire ethical system that authorizes moral judgments, the tragedy's problem-play mode begins to reveal itself.

Bussy's career is a claim to the entitlements of great place, all conventional marital and social boundaries notwithstanding. His refusal to cede his right to court the Duchess, his rebuke of the Guise for participating in the St. Bartholomew Massacre, and his leading the disdainful courtiers to a dueling dance of death are constitutive expressions of this claim. Despite the king's law against dueling,[8] Bussy insists that Henry "Let me be King myself (as man was made) / And do a justice that exceeds the law" so as to "make good what God and Nature / Have given me for my good" (2.1.193–99). This eloquent speech foregrounds the play's challenging ideology.

The problem, of course, is that the play challenges even its challenging ideology. Bussy's courting of the Duchess, his slaying of the courtiers, and his affair with Tamyra all appear to implicate him in the very deformities he opposes.[9] Yet he is hailed by the Nuntius as "Great D'Ambois," "the bravest man the French earth bears" (2.1.91.137).[10] The play is thus sustained by a dual set of indeterminate ethical perspectives. Bussy's career, which is presented as a floating signified, illustrates these points because it engenders a series of unresolved contemplations about the nature of law and individual freedoms in modern society. The most crucial of these is King Henry's mythic identification of Bussy as

> A man so good, that only would uphold
> Man in his native noblesse, from whose fall
> All our dissensions rise; that in himself
> (Without the outward patches of our frailty,
> Riches and honour) knows he comprehends
> Worth with the greatest: Kings had never borne
> Such boundless eminence over other men,
> Had all maintain'd the spirit and state of D'Ambois;
> Nor had the full impartial hand of Nature
> That all things gave in her original,
> Without these definite terms of Mine and Thine,
> Been turn'd unjustly to the hand of Fortune—
> Had all preserv'd her in her prime, like D'Ambois;
> No envy, no disjunction, had dissolv'd
> Or pluck'd out one stick of the golden faggot

In which the world of Saturn was compris'd,
Had all been held together with the nerves,
The genius and th'ingenuous soul of D'Ambois. (3.2.90–107)

Henry's appeal to an original nature is the passage's controlling topos; its conventional argument is that in the Golden Age private property—"these definite terms of Mine and Thine"—did not exist. Only upon the advent of kings did individuals lose the primary power they once held over their own lives. There followed unfair imposition of hereditary rights and titles and the appearance of envy. In this understanding, the sway of positive law, embodied in the monarch, is coterminous with the Fall of Man, and Bussy's petition that the king "do a Right, exceeding Law and Nature: / Who to himself is law, no law doth need, / Offends no King, and is a King indeed" (2.1.202–4) is an attempt to emancipate the autonomous individual from the law's enslavement.

Bussy's petition, like his career, thus reappropriates and radically internalizes this concept of monarchical power. The warrant for this reappropriation is genealogical. Both Bussy and Henry trace Bussy's pedigree to an originary Mother Nature from whose undefiled fecundity all entitlements come.[11] The nostalgic impulse—call it primitivist—is thus to return a complex society driven by constraining law and custom to an imagined previous condition in which human freedoms were sealed as natural and good. By this genealogy, Bussy's arrogance and impudence should be reread as an attempt to rewrite the logos on which the social order validates itself by claiming an inviolate, prior natural order as his mother.

Symbolically laden as they are, these identifications are not stable. As ontological essences, neither nature nor man (meaning men) nor woman proves to exhibit a fixed or determinate identity. The issue is made to turn on the sexual identity of Nature herself. If she is whorish or purposeless in her favors, then her issue becomes illegitimate and consequently Bussy himself is disinherited, disfranchised. In this spirit, Bussy becomes the vehicle for contemplating the nature of the Mother Nature that has begotten him.[12] When Monsieur and Guise contemplate the man whom their bravos are about to destroy, Monsieur takes the view that Nature lacks a *telos* because she is "stark blind herself" and will as soon confer "that which we call merit to a man" like Bussy as effect "his ruin" (5.3.4, 18–20). By contrast, the Guise adopts the extreme view that Nature is a whore because she will just as soon fashion someone with "all the wondrous fabric man should have" as leave it "headless for an absolute man" (5.3.32–33). However the tragedy is interpreted, the core problem is situated in the puzzled reading of Nature's sexual body.

At this metalevel the tragedy's troubling indeterminacy prompts Millar MacClure to conclude, "*Bussy* is not a demonstration but an experience. Chapman is not solving a problem, but finding one. What room is there for heroism in the world? The sibylline answer is: None, or some" (125). This insight gives us warrant to read the tragedy as fruitfully unresolved. Even so, MacClure's philosophic focus on the problem of the hero is narrow for a tragedy that interrogates the sexual codes on which the taboos of English culture are written. The tragedy also dramatizes an irrefragable ethical dilemma—how a just social order, which ought to ally itself with an ideal natural order, is be squared with the entitlements of patriarchal marriage and the ownership of Tamyra's wayward body.

(Ir)Resolutions

The Dutch Courtesan, Bussy D'Ambois, and *The Widow's Tears* not only exhibit the characteristic social-sexual issues belonging to the problem play but resolve those issues problematically. The two comedies exhibit a bed trick or a symbolic substitution of bodies that works toward the same witty but problematic ends that appear in *Measure for Measure* and *All's Well That Ends Well.*[13] So too, all these problem plays, including *Hamlet,* write the spiritual health of the social order problematically and apprehensively on the symbolic bodies of women.

Earlier critics of *The Widow's Tears* were fond of remarking that Tharsalio's misogyny becomes the play's misogyny.[14] Read as ugly satire, the play's patriarchal moralism appeared easy to discern. Nowadays, poststructuralist perspectives encourage the observation that the satire destroys itself on the very principles by which it builds. Are women truly the monstrous ones? Although Tharsalio would unproblematically have us believe so, his view is feelingly challenged by Lycus. The entire issue is treated reflexively by Tharsalio as theatrical performance, the theater of Cynthia's grief becoming an image of the world's deceptive playmaking (Niobe's tears, as in *Hamlet,* is the trope). When Tharsalio sneeringly inquires how Cynthia "performed" the news of her husband's slaughter, Lycus retorts: "Perform it, call you it? You may jest; men hunt hares to death for their sports, but the poor beasts die in earnest. You wager of her passions for your pleasure, but she takes little pleasure in those earnest passions. I never saw such an ecstacy of sorrow since I knew the name of sorrow. Her hands flew up to her head like Furies, hid all her beauties in her dishevel'd hair, and wept as she would turn fountain. . . . I was so transported with the spectacle that in despite of my discretion I was forc'd to turn woman and bear a part with her. Humanity broke loose from my heart, and stream'd through mine eyes" (4.1.33–45). Clearly, both Lycus and Tharsalio are overseers who make judgments about woman's nature. Nonetheless, their views are not consonant. In Lycus's understanding Cynthia's "tears are true" (4.1.141), and she is the victim of men's cruel sport. Although he accepts the shibboleth that "women's truths are weak" (4.1.141), the weakness Lycus perceives begets a strong measure of sympathy.[15] By contrast, Tharsalio's dislocating, metatheatrical rejoinder, "In prose, thou wept'st" (4.1.46), distances all sympathetic feeling and discounts Cynthia's subject position.

In a real sense the cult of chastity that Cynthia begets also produces her: she plays the idol she has been made. To apply a concept Judith Butler develops from Foucault in *Gender Trouble,* a woman whose behavior is regulated by the requirements of chastity is "by virtue of being subjected to them, formed, defined, and reproduced in accordance with the requirements of those structures" (2). Such cultural prescriptions define Tharsalio's own oversight. In his jaundiced view, if women's lust is genuine their love must not be. He cannot acknowledge the paradoxical concordance of the two; no Venus-Virgo for him (Strong, *Cult of Elizabeth* 47).

As the play proceeds, Tharsalio's satiric viewpoint comes under increasing scrutiny, as do his motives. Tharsalio's competition with his firstborn brother makes him wish Cynthia the worst. Having wagered four horses and a chariot on her fall, he is heavily invested in the outcome. How well can Tharsalio come out, searching out as he does the limits of female love and fidelity? At one point, he is even made to urge that Cynthia's trial go forward "till the vessel split again" (3.1.190). This disturbing imagery, which suggests a womb-splitting death for Cynthia, reappears when Lycus draws attention to Lysander's jealous testing, which is a form of espionage. In bewilderment Lycus asks Tharsalio, "Would any heart of adamant, for satisfaction of an ungrounded humor, rack a poor lady's innocency as you intend to do? It was a strange curiosity in that Emperor [Nero], that ripp'd his mother's womb to see the place he lay in" (3.1.1–4). Use of the rack, we know, was not a punishment in England but an instrument of torture to ascertain truth (Langbein 84). Its tropic invocation at this juncture points both to the zeal of Cynthia's interrogators and the cruelty of delivering such pain to a woman who has no guilty knowledge to communicate.

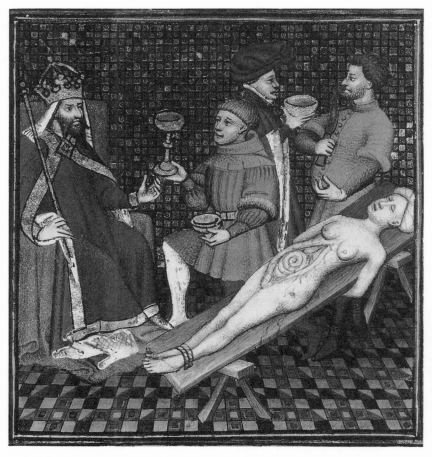

Fig. 4. "Nero's Autopsy of His Mother." From a French translation of Boccaccio, *The Fates of Illustrious Men*, fifteenth century. Courtesy of the Bibliothèque Nationale.

In the elaborated trope of the ripped-up womb, there is also a voyeuristic fascination with and abhorrence of the female sexual organ. The male's compulsive desire to search out the sexual truth it harbors is exhibited as objective, albeit ruthless, "scientific" examination. In fact, Nero's autopsy of his mother's body is part of the Renaissance tradition; a picture of the inquiry with the mother's organs exposed from the pudendum to the breastbone is recorded in a fifteenth-century translation of Boccaccio's *Fates of Illustrious Men* (fig. 4). Similar pictures appear in autopsies of women's bodies, including the reproductive organs, as in the frontispiece

Fig. 5. "Frontispiece" of Andrea Vesalius's *De humani corporis fabrica*, 1543. Courtesy of the Newberry Library.

of Vesalius's *De humani corporis fabrica* (1543) (fig. 5), where a horde of men, beholding at once the image of death and the origins of human life, look on. The point, of course, is that for all its supposed powers the probing knife cannot master the truth it seeks. Its truth is turned back upon the investigator. In our inquiry, the ripped-up womb is an especially significant cultural trope because it figures the problematic relationship between the surveillant and the surveilled. As the "truth" of that relationship is established through surveillance, so ironically are the identity and status of husband and wife.

Through this tropic sexual discourse more generalized anxieties about the character of English society are also embedded. In particular, Tharsalio's metatheatrical critique of Cynthia's grief is prompted by the apprehension that the cult of chastity makes Cynthia too powerful: "she look[s] to be deified, to have hymns made of her, nay to her; the tomb where she is, to be no more reputed the ancient monument of our family, the Lysandri, but the new-erected altar of Cynthia, to which all the Paphian widows shall after their husbands' funerals offer their wet muckinders for monuments of the danger they have pass'd" (4.1.114–19). Against nature, Tharsalio implies, this cult threatens to replace the reverence felt for ancestral patrilineal families, here the Lysandri. The locus of these concerns has a foundation in the concrete reality of the making of monuments under the cult of Elizabeth as Cynthia/Diana. Only by recognizing them for the threatening innovations they were seen to be (Strong, *Cult of Elizabeth* 16, 125–26) can we properly historicize Tharsalio's mockery. Throughout the period monuments to chastity were fashionably constructed in great country estates, including the gardens at Kenilworth and Theobalds and the Temple and Grove of Diana at Nonsuch, the last of which actually featured a statue of the goddess bathing while Acteon, with antlers growing from his head, looks on (Strong, *Renaissance Garden* 45–50, 66–68). So when Lycus avows Cynthia's "virtues may justly challenge a deity to enshrine them" (4.1.124–25), his cultural paean to female power ought to reverberate—and so should Tharsalio's hard-headed critique of it: "My sister may turn Niobe for love; but till Niobe be turn'd to a marble, I'll not despair but she may prove a woman" (4.1.130–32).

The cultural apprehensions attendant upon this fetishizing of female chastity are ostentatiously staged in the closing acts. Jealous to the point of insanity, the "dead" Lysander cannot wait for Tharsalio to summon him; he must return on his own as a sentinel to inspect firsthand his wife's chastity and then under the most contrived of conditions test a fidelity he

Fig. 6. "Acteon Watching Diana and Her Nymphs Bathing." Joachim Anthoniesz Wtewael, 1612. Abbott Lawrence Fund, courtesy of the Museum of Fine Arts, Boston.

has never had reason to doubt his entire married life. In these circumstances Lysander, like the monument at Nonsuch, enacts the role of a modern-day Acteon (1.2.22; see fig. 6), salaciously spying upon his own chaste wife and destroying himself by seducing her. In him the figure of Acteon is savagely restaged as a satiric, tragic, farcical tale of the voyeur intelligencer-husband who is made to discover himself in a mixed, compromising madness. The turn by which Cynthia, after hearing her soldier explain how the crucified body he was guarding has disappeared, offers to replace the lost body with her husband's own is, if narrowly viewed, another demonstration of the play's misogyny. From a wider perspective, it discloses Lysander's masochistic enactment of the compulsions of his culture as he helplessly pursues his own annihilation—surveillance as self-destruction. Discovering what he has secretly desired to witness all the time, Lysander is emotionally disemboweled by the dogs of his own prurient curiosity, and he cuckolds himself in the bargain.

In this way the satire ironically discloses Lysander's surveillance as an act of subjectification, not mastery. His espionage produces both his wife's identity and his own. Cynthia herself expounds the meaning of the crucial event. Alerted by Tharsalio's timely information that her sentinel lover is her "dead" husband, and contemptuous of Lysander's deception, she prepares an imposture of her own. At the very moment when her enraged husband-lover-sentinel begins to choke her, she turns the tables and forces him to face his self-cuckolding moment of beastly transformation, his "uncrowning," as Bakhtin would say. "Ill-destin'd wife of a transform'd monster, / Who to assure himself of what he knew, / Hath lost the shape of man!" she exclaims, continuing, "Go, satyr, run affrighted with the noise / Of that harsh-sounding horn thyself hast blown. / Farewell; I leave thee there my husband's corpse; / Make much of that" (5.1.479–87). Ovidian metamorphosis has overtaken the high and mighty male testers as well as the female paragons, and we are left to ponder the deformity of a society where compulsive entrapment produces its own problematic truths.

Not content, however, to rest on a satiric note of social disintegration, *The Widow's Tears* works its way back to a "happy" resolution through the bed trick. Coaxed to believe Cynthia knew his identity the whole time, a chastened Lysander becomes reconciled to his matchless wife. But the resolution undercuts itself in its very making. From one point of view, the play is a "dark and 'mirthless' comedy" (Preussner 263) whose self-negation and nihilism are produced by its own compulsive surveillance and possessiveness; from another, its deconstruction of the fallen idol of chastity calls into question the legitimacy of the Jacobean social order; from yet another it scrutinizes and ridicules a patriarchal order obsessed by an idealized and finally inhuman construction of female chastity.

The disordering implications of these insights are shown to circulate through the society. The final scene presents the pseudo-solutions of the new upstart Governor, who has "come in person to discharge justice" and who "In matters of justice" proclaims himself to be "blind" (5.1.563, 598–99). Emblematic of this anarchic order, the Governor's "new discipline" promises, all at once, to place asses and braggarts at the head, hunt lechery and jealousy out of the kingdom, extirpate cuckolds, and spay young women for marrying again. Radical and contradictory, this emblematic chaos is predicated, once again, on a new sexual order, everything turned "topsy turvy" (5.1.619). This manner of invoking a pervasive sexual symbolism to represent an endemic social disorder is one that cultural anthropologists such as Victor Turner find significant because it illustrates how "overt symbolisms of sexuality and hostility between the sexes" can be "channeled toward master symbols representative of structural order, and values and virtues on which that order depends" (93).

In *The Widow's Tears* this consummating scene has its tumultuous moment of discovery when Cynthia and her sentinel are observed "drawing on" (5.1.26). The situation is reminiscent of that in which Troilus, caught in his own obsession, observes Cressida making love with Diomede and thereby experiences the destruction of his own worldview. Both are examples, once again, of surveillance as the voyeurism that produces the hidden, portentous truth of one's own identity (Foucault, *History of Sexuality* 1:69) and the deflating truth about one's own society as well—that its transcendent principle of order is subject to mutability. But whereas Troilus metaphysically asserts the shattered truth of his transcendent ideal against all the evidence of the senses—"This she? no, this is Diomed's Cressida. / If beauty have a soul, this is not she" (5.2.137–38)—*The Widow's Tears* makes Lysander and Cynthia into a metaphysical conundrum. Lysander is and is not cuckolded; Cynthia is and is not constant to him. What we have, then, is an act of prestidigitation in which one self substitutes for the same self, simultaneously providing perfect knowledge and perfect ignorance. Such disclosures bring about problematic closures. Making the bed trick a metaphor for the constructedness of our knowledge, *The Widow's Tears* rejoices in the undecipherability of Lysander and Cynthia's conjugal act, that impenetrable act of darkness that attracts to it all discoverings.

If *The Widow's Tears, Measure for Measure,* and *All's Well That Ends Well* all offer a bed trick to escape the consequences of the dark view they present, *The Dutch Courtesan* offers, circuslike, a ring trick. The crucial problem-play issue is framed by the choice that confronts Malheureux. Before Franceschina will sleep with him, Malheureux must slay Freevill and present her with the ring intended for Beatrice. Unlike the problem issue of *Measure for Measure,* which weighs the supreme values of human life and chastity against one another, Marston's play establishes its problem proposition by weighing an absolute evil (murder of a male friend) against the power of heterosexual desire. The latter is posed as a test, not so much of Malheureux's character, the local concern, as of the compulsivity of male sexuality, ominously rendered as unreason. On the outcome rests the play's evaluation of the moderating forces of culture as they work to fortify the power of rational judgment. The fully cognizant decision Malheureux makes to murder Freevill ("To kill my friend! Oh, 'tis to kill myself!" [2.2.198]) vividly stages the intractability of such desire, even in a hitherto virtuous gentleman. In this way the play broaches the radical consequences such desire has for the ordering of society.

But just as Vincentio avoids these consequences by presenting Ragozine's head in place of Claudio's, Freevill lends his ring to Malheureux so that the latter can fake his friend's death. As a metonymic trick—the ring for the body—the device resembles Helena's triumphant presentation to Bertram of the marriage ring he believed she would never come to wear (ring and body trickily and symbolically reunited). By these means neither Bertram nor Malheureux has to face the forbidding consequences of his intemperate desire—and neither does the audience.

A similar analogical reliance upon conventional tropes takes over as *The Dutch Courtesan* resolves the problems of custom and desire by falling back on a conventional discourse of the "natural," deceptively recommended as self-evident. Ironically, the iconoclastic Crispinella becomes the bearer of this wisdom. She who fearlessly speaks of pricks in public comes to reify "virtue" as an essence rooted in nature. Echoing Montaigne, she declares, "I consider nature without apparel; without disguising of custom or compliment. . . . She whose honest freeness makes it her virtue to speak what she thinks will make it her necessity to think what is good. I love no prohibited things, and yet I would have nothing prohibited by policy but by virtue" (3.1.35–41).

Though the speech seems to challenge the audience's received beliefs— a hallmark of the problem play—it actually works to deny the play of custom in the "virtuous" ordering of sexual conduct. Baker's historical construction of the sexual issues in the play shows its relationship to a contemporary debate on sexual intercourse in companionate marriages (218–32). Whereas Montaigne and others stressed moderation in sexual activity, a second, challenging view, which may be called Puritan, encouraged sexual activity (as against celibacy) and held that spouses owe their bodies to each other, and it for this latter view that Crispinella speaks. The "virtue" to which Crispinella appeals, however, is guaranteed under the name of the "natural" and endowed with a transcendent essence that finally places it beyond investigation. When Crispinella rejects Beatrice's asseveration that "severe modesty is women's virtue," arguing that "Virtue is a free, pleasant, buxom quality" (3.1.46–48), she challenges conventional notions of virtue by examining their necessity in the light of nature. Yet Crispinella's endorsement of an unconfined (especially female) sexuality ultimately functions as a domesticating device to promote the institution of marriage because that is where this "freedom" is to be expressed. In the same normalizing manner, Cocledemoy's irrepressible daring, represented as outside of custom, brings the hypocritical city father and familist Mulligrub to the bar of satiric judgment as if his punishment were "natural" as well as poetic. In both plots, this "natural" wisdom is enlisted in the name of reformation, but it is really another form of cultural appropriation because the play fails to probe these problematic inscriptions.

For these reasons, the darkness enveloping *The Dutch Courtesan* will not lift, despite its tragicomic form. Freevill's refusal to come forward until Malheureux is sentenced to be executed for murdering his friend is usually read as a Calvinistic demonstration of the lustful depravity that must be wrung out through terror. This is fine, but it misses the central point that Freevill as overseer actively works to shape Malheureux's sexual conduct in "productive" ways (Foucault's characteristic emphasis) to reclaim him for gentle society. The critical fact that he allows Malheureux to be brought before the bar of justice before being "freed" from the law's grip and from his concupiscent desire brilliantly illustrates how juridical and cultural surveillance work hand in glove to achieve their reforming ends.

An even darker exhibition of cultural domestication is revealed in the final treatment of Franceschina's unrestrained appetites. Just as Angelo, despite having "slept" with Isabella, refuses to stay Claudio's execution, Franceschina not only refuses to fulfill her vow to sleep with Malheureux after he purportedly slays Freevill, but she exposes him to the charge of murder. She even humiliates Beatrice by telling her, "dis your ring he gave me" (4.4.57). By these acts the Franceschina who had been represented with some understanding of her social circumstances is epiphanically unveiled as a witch. Her villainy becomes an essence. As a consequence, a social critique of her marginalization is no longer necessary. In the end she is simply a "comely damnation!" a "fair devil / In shape of woman" (5.3.44–48). The spectacular message is clear: "We are in no way responsible for what happens to Franceschina, for she is from the devil." Despite the antiquated language of Freevill's imprecations, the shape of this scapegoating echoes uncannily across several centuries.

Yet the wheels of Marston's plot, trampling over Franceschina's body, jangle on toward a happy ending, leaving behind graven marks of cultural contradiction. Only by displacing the problem of the unrestrained male passions onto this demonized female (as if to say, "the devil's dam has aroused these dark passions in me") can the comedy roll on toward its self-congratulatory conclusion. This air of self-congratulation, which the comedy shares with *Measure for Measure,* proceeds from the secure knowledge that those who walk in light have been permanently separated from those consigned to thrash about in darkness. At this level the comedy dissolves the contradictions in Elizabethan sexual practices that have threatened to break the play apart. But at another level it only crystallizes them. In a kind of Derridean supplementarity, the more demonic Franceschina is made to behave (to destroy our human concern for her and, ironically, to "reclaim" Malheureux for the god-fearing), the greater do the wrongs against her appear. The more completely the play demonizes her, the more does it call attention to her victimization. This problematic crux may be put generically. As Carol Pollard explains, "Since the criteria for judging a work of art are created in large part by the work itself, conflicting backgrounds provide conflicting criteria, upsetting the harmony of the romantic/comic conclusions and creating disruptive but constructive tension" (54).

Further irreconcilable tension appears in Franceschina's lament after being taken into custody—"me ha' lost my will" (5.3.58). This last complaint could have provided opportunity for a tragic dramatization of Franceschina's victimization, but in Marston's rendering it merely illustrates her psychopathology. To invert the emphasis, at the point at which Franceschina speaks her own demonization—"O Divila, life o' mine art! Ich sall be reveng'd! Do ten tousand hell damn me, ich sall have the rogue troat cut" (2.2.40–42)—she has become a ventriloquist's puppet. Franceschina's heavy Dutch accent along with her whore's name function as prejudicial linguistic markers—or shall we call them stigmas? The tongue that speaks Franceschina utters a strange, untethered language of aggression made to signify an alien class, an alien nation, an alien spirit. Name, dialect, national origin, class, and gender are the outward marks of an unalterable otherness constructed as spiritual damnation, and each signified circulates almost interchangeably in a "gentle" economy that buys bodies for lust and then (ex)changes the used-up product for an unused one.

This is the opposite of a symbolic sexuality circulating to define the entire culture; this is a sexually specific symbolism that defines the culture by what it is not. The dramatic act that portrays the temptress as devil works to deflect every social problem onto a reified scapegoat so that neither is brought into perspective. An ending in which Franceschina's natural beauty has been prejudicially redefined as spiritual blight does a great deal more than reverse the trend of the opening acts; it burkes the original questions so sharply defined. Crispinella's critique of the institution of marriage is lost in the unrelieved final assault upon Franceschina. The problem of the domineering phallus as a metonym for the day-to-day social oppression women suffer in marriage has indeed been raised but is then buttoned up and put away.

And there are other unresolved issues as well. Through Crispinella the comedy challengingly presents the view that marriage is an institution in which women must endure the onslaught of male desire even when that desire is not mutual and when women must still serve as homemakers and nurses to their husbands. Marriage itself, the play shows, is made into a stable institution by an arrangement in which gentlemen may freely make premarital sexual liaisons with a class of servant females for whom respectable marriage is not open. These women, whose marginal position deprives them of a social voice, are to be consumed as part of the economy of marriage formation.[16] The idea goes back at least as far as Musonius Rufus, whom Foucault cites for his "classical" view that "'The man who has relations with a courtesan or a woman who has no husband wrongs no one for he does not destroy anyone's hope of children'" (*History of Sexuality* 3:169). The Franceschinas of Marston's society are to perform the services gentlemen require so that a class of respectable women can be safeguarded for the purposes of marriage and child rearing.

But here a crux presents itself. If England's Franceschinas are to be avoided, how are young gentlemen to preserve their honor in the face of their socially dangerous and, as the play represents it, compulsive premarital sexual desire? By what means are the Malheureuxes of this society to eschew a cloistered virtue and realize their full humanity? Indeed, how are society's libertarian Freevills to conduct themselves in the future, having come to know that the brothel offers only a devilish illusion of salvation? A conclusion that permits Malheureux to be spared the noose and Freevill to have his conventional wedding with Beatrice smothers these questions. In this way the unresolved social-sexual issues so acutely identified in the opening acts remain to disturb the moral intellect.

So does the cultural power of theater. *The Dutch Courtesan* exhibits the repressive logic underlying family formation in gentry culture and yet validates it—a clear example of containment. One class of woman is brought up for respectable marriage; a vilified underclass is fit only to serve illicit male desire. But the very service this class of women performs (for money) permanently devalues their status and bars them from respectability. Their beauty is therefore culturally revalued as alluring deception, the proof of their appetitive, serpentine nature and the warrant for their marginalization.

The respective symbolic names Beatrice and Franceschina bear, the language they speak, the plots in which they are cast, all demonstrate the power of theater to promote, promulgate, and validate a dichotomous English society. And if this is true for Jacobean society, one observes how effectively the filmmaking industry in Hollywood can work to validate the same normalizing "family values" when, for example, it plots to represent in stereotypical terror the "other woman" as a Glenn Close *Fatal Attraction*, and then, once she has worked her terror upon the errant husband can (by audience demand) be killed off so that normal marital life may resume. With similar panache, Hollywood can work to allay contemporary qualms about class fissures as when in *Pretty Woman* the attractive underclass prostitute can, fairy-tale-like, turn her venal tryst with a rich gentlemen into a romantic, mutually beneficial marriage. By thus transcending the issues of class and gender inequality, the film allows them, happily, to disappear.

By contrast, the ending of *Bussy D'Ambois* frankly exhibits its gaping wounds, social and metaphysical. Despite its strangely conflicted rather than condemnatory exhibition of spousal torture, the play speaks to values about which we continue to care. The tragedy has, furthermore, the substantial virtue that it interrogates the central terms by which it constructs the world. If nature is a central trope, the nature of that nature is constantly being interrogated. Bussy's pedigree as "Man in his native noblesse" is made to depend, we have seen, upon an original Mother Nature whose purity is ironically the source of her fecundity. In the name of this original Nature, Bussy pursues Tamyra. Thomas Randolph follows this line of thought in "Upon Love Fondly Refused for Conscience' Sake" and makes it explicit, when he writes, "It was not love, but love transform'd to vice, / Ravish'd by envious avarice, / Made women first impropriate: all were free: / Enclosures mans Inventions be. / I' th' golden age no action could be found / For trespass on my neighbours ground" (2: 631, ll. 11–16). But in *Bussy D'Ambois* a signal irony surfaces from such premises. The sexual body of Tamyra is the opposite of Nature's. By virtue of her having been joined in marriage to Montsurry, it has been redefined and bound by the laws of the modern state. Strategically, Tamyra is caught in the middle between two paradigms that read her sexuality in completely different ways. Because that body is literally the focus of the problem-play issues the tragedy raises, its final disposition discloses something crucial about the way the tragedy negotiates the cultural conflicts invested in her person.

The crucial text is, once again, Henry's speech asserting that the "terms of Mine and Thine" did not obtain in the original state of nature—in short, that private property and individual ownership did not exist until the advent of the modern, fallen state. From this proposition it follows that the institution of marriage is a contractual relationship authorized by the modern state and church. It is also a relationship organized for regulating the sexual activity of the partners, especially the aristocratic wife, upon whose body the legitimacy of the family and the honor of the husband depend (Neely, "Female Sexuality" 212–13; cf. Tennenhouse, *Power on Display* 113–14). This idea of marriage as ownership, as private property, helps to frame Bussy's challenge to the court. His wooing of the Duchess, discounting her social superiority and marital status, recognizes no such boundaries. Similarly, Bussy's affair with Tamyra is undertaken without the least recognition that the laws of marriage have assigned her to another. This is not to say that Bussy's affair is innocent of political or social aspiration but that he does not recognize as legitimate the usual normalizing constraints upon his right to pursue Tamyra's perfections, as he calls them.

The tragic consequences of this double reading of Tamyra's person are written on her bleeding body. Protective of her as he is, Bussy cannot prevent Montsurry's discovery that Tamyra has taken a lover. The unparalleled direction that opens the fifth act, "*Enter* MONTSURRY *bare, unbraced, pulling* TAMYRA *in by the hair,*" begins to stage the spectacle of Tamyra's body. As the revised B-text underscores, Montsurry also initiates a bizarre dialogue filled with physical and psychological violence aimed to show that his coercive will is somehow her will as well:

Tamy: O Help me Father.
Frier: Impious Earle forbeare.
  Take violent hand from her, or by mine order
  The King shall force thee.
Monts: Tis not violent; come you not willingly?
Tamy: Yes good my Lord. (5.1.1a–d)

As the debased revenger of his violated prerogatives, Montsurry judges that Tamyra's "arms have lost / Their privilege in lust" and then "*Stabs her*" (5.1.122–25). Nine lines later, he "*Stabs her again.*" A third stage direction orders servants to "*place* TAMYRA *on the rack*" (136.1). Readers may view these directions simply as atrocities, but the logic of this madness is compelling. The piercing retribution of Montsurry's knife works impotently to reassert his husbandly prerogative while the rack subdues, immobilizes, and displays Tamyra as on a bed, her body open to him. Tamyra's sexual body is thus staged as a spectacle of ownership. But the theatrical emblem it is made to signify, "Tamyra belongs to Montsurry," is at once as an impotent wish fulfillment or charade and an indisputable reality.

Another dimension to Montsurry's vengeance is his use of the rack, which had an express but limited place in the Tudor-Stuart judicial system.[17] Part of a calibrated regimen of "truth-seeking" deployed to reshape the minds even more than the bodies of the accused through coerced confessions, the rack may be viewed as the ultimate, concrete trope of surveillance, as it marks the body with its desire to know. Because the rack was employed as an instrument of interrogation to obtain concealed informations of import to the state (Langbein 84; Peters 72), Montsurry's use of it richly suggests that he has assumed the role of offended justice even as he delivers unmeasured, outraged revenge. Indeed, his actions bring home the intimate relationship between cultural oversight of the sexual body and juridical surveillance, with its explicit system of punishments.

The racking of Tamyra shows grand ideas of state justice being appropriated for domestic purposes. The entire episode corroborates an important generalization framed by John Archer—that the "invasion of women's secrets corresponds to the Renaissance tendency to conceive of power as the surveillance and subjection of the female body" (105). Montsurry's lordly vengeance unlocks the workings of the constitutive discourses of fidelity and justice in unexpected ways. Far from being treated as normative, his claim over Tamyra's body in the name of an offended justice is revealed as so laden with contradiction, so beyond measure, that it becomes its own critique. The ritual element in Montsurry's recourse to the rack dramatizes a "wild justice" that in its violence and iconography is actually a rape. Ironically, the law, with its sanctioned view of possession, of "mine and thine," has given rise to a madness; it has produced its own confutation in tortuous caricature.

The problem of the social construction of the marital relationship is reenacted and, at the same time, called into question when Tamyra cries out, "O who is turn'd into my Lord and husband? / Husband? My Lord? None but my lord and husband, / . . . / O help me husband" (5.1.144–46). At this moment, Comolet suddenly falls dead. Strategically uncalled for because Comolet must later return (as his own ghost), the friar's death is enacted for the sole purpose of underscoring the "rape of honour and

religion" and the "wrack of nature" (read "rack"; 5.1.147–48) he has witnessed. At this point, Tamyra's maimed body is more than a picture of
patriarchal tyranny; it is framed as an image of a defiled society and of a
nature wracked by Tamyra's racking. These correspondences make clear
that the torturing interrogation of Tamyra, the wayward noble wife, signifies a radically disjointed society that must be knit together in some new
way. But the ineradicable fact that the play cannot resolve is that Tamyra's
ungovernable sexual passion and Bussy's ungovernable valor are two aspects of the same problematic challenge. As A. R. Braunmuller helpfully
puts it, in the play's action and metaphysics, "they are complementary, and
they contradict the most deeply held patriarchal convictions of early modern England" (45).

For this same reason, Montsurry too is ensnared by the authoritarian
social structure that makes him all at once an executor and a helpless
subject. The notion that nature is a rack that torments everybody is ratcheted
into prominence when Montsurry complains that an unnatural wrong has
been done to *him:* "methinks the frame / And shaken joints of the whole
world should crack / To see her parts so disproportionate; / . . . / . . . O
what a lightning / Is man's delight in women! what a bubble, / He builds
his state, fame, life on, when he marries!" (5.1.170–80). Tamyra's abused
body is in some way the outward image of Montsurry's own anguish, even
though he authors her punishment and, like Lysander, literally frames his
anguish on his wife's body. The racking of Tamyra is thus more than a
horrific emblem of revenge; it critiques the issues of marriage formation
and sexual conduct central to the problem play, and it corroborates Turner's
insight that "overt symbolisms of sexuality and hostility between the sexes
are channeled toward master symbols representative of structural order"
(93).

These issues of structural order finally ensnare Bussy as well. The man
who would set aside the tyranny of society's order is shot from behind.
Enraptured by his mission, Bussy at first contemplates his greatness—until
Tamyra reveals her blood-stained breasts. Then the posturing ceases. Bussy's
fervent reaction, "O, my heart is broken" (5.3.178), brings him to the sear-
ing recognition of his project's failure. His despair may be seen as the end
of the archetypal myth of the hero whose mask is torn away to reveal the
despair underlying the quest, a despair that springs from the anxiety that
heroism is not enough, is never enough.[18] Bussy's ambition to "bring up a
new fashion / And rise in Court with virtue" (1.1.125–26) ends by bringing

endless pain and misery to the person he most sought to protect. Further-more, his heroism has effectively displaced neither the tyranny of marital possession nor the system of property underlying it.

Both fundamental problems remain to torment Tamyra, for she is prob-lematically and theatrically placed between lover and husband. Her place-ment on the stage illuminates the tragedy's insoluble dilemma. Caught between two sets of social practices, two systems of organizing relation-ships, Tamyra exhibits the fractured thought in which the tragedy itself is ensnared. Enamored as she is of Bussy and the wild valor of his native noblesse, Tamyra remains a creature whose values and social position belong to a postlapsarian world:

> . . . if I right my friend
> I wrong my husband: if his wrong I shun,
> The duty of my friend I leave undone;
> Ill plays on both sides; here and there, it riseth;
> No place, no good so good, but ill compriseth;
> . . . .
> O husband? dear friend? O my conscience! (5.3.212–30)

The prostrate, broken body of Tamyra is again symbolic. So are her torn allegiances. They betoken fractures in the tragedy itself, which remain unhealed even at play's end. With her husband there can be no reconcilia-tion, although Montsurry wishes for it on his knees. If merely for his honor's sake, his wife, a fallen woman in the mundane way of seeing, must leave his home. Such a conclusion is an ending but not a resolution. Far from disclosing a flawed tragedy, however, this ending impressively con-veys the utter inadequacy of the institution of marriage and of propertied arrangements of persons. A reconstituted society seems to be the only answer, but the pathways seem blocked at every turn.

In all the problem plays that concern us, the spectacle of the errant female body or else the spectacular turns that preserve its sexual integrity underline the cultural importance of social and sexual boundaries. The concern with sexual conduct in these plays is, however, only a by-product of more deeply inscribed cultural tropes. As I have emphasized through-out, this is because the sexual female body bears such symbolic signifi-cance: the reading of it circulates as a metonym for the fundamental values of English high culture generally. And unlike the monologic sermon or conduct book, which provided prescriptive responses to the same ideologi-

cal issues, the plays we label problem plays, with their symbolic representations of sexuality and distinctive debate mode, offer a critique of culture
that is turned outward and public by the process of playwrighting and
production. Strange as these plays may appear to us with their obsessive
oversight, regulation, and punishments of illicit sexual desire, the issues
they depict continue to speak to us. Through the regulation, surveillance,
and representation of sexual desire our culture makes and remakes itself,
even as it makes and remakes the self-consciousness of its people, male and
female.

Affectivity and New Historicism

The Mothering Body Surveilled
in *The Duchess of Malfi* and *The Duchess of Suffolk*

Our concern with the symbolic sexuality of women provides the opportunity to extend the subject to the sexual mothering body in familial settings. Again my focus is on representation in the theater, where the mothering body is both reproduced and constituted and the rigorous oversight of that body is rejected as unnatural. A distinctive feature of the plays I will examine is their powerful affectivity. Insofar as that affectivity was exhibited to popular audiences as a form of persuasive politics, my aim is to trace its cultural significance, both for early modern audiences and for us today who seek ways to engage its meaning.

When Renaissance new-historicist criticism treats the subject of the family, an undeniable problem bubbles up. That problem is part of a troubling tension between new-historicist and feminist modes of criticism. Walter Cohen has described the situation succinctly, observing that although new historicism's "recurrent concern with gender aligns it with feminism, its subordination of gender to power leads it away from characteristically feminist concerns."[1] This orientation has provoked strictures. Lynda Boose has complained with justice that new historicists have declined "an alliance with feminism," allowing instead something that "is more like a progressive eradication of even the subject of women, accomplished by means of several (though, I would emphasize, not necessarily conscious) critical displacements . . .—usually race or class—. . . [by which] women are silently eradicated from the text, leaving only one gender for consideration."[2] If new historicism is to treat feminist concerns effectively, it must find ways, as Foucault did in his later, more flexible formulations, of treating power within power, "exercised from innumerable points, in the interplay of nonegalitarian and mobile relations."[3] Any adequate historicism must explore such paradigms if it is to treat the multivocalism that is part of the ceaseless play of culture and if the concerns of students of women's history are to be written into a cultural historicist practice.[4]

To apply this notion to Renaissance family life, it may be observed that assessments of family relations as no more than a replication of the power relations of the state are being increasingly challenged as critics seek out the incipient and manifest contradictions within power.[5] Patriarchy is not a single transhistorical reality but a dynamic set of power relations that must be examined in their historical particularity.[6] The fact, moreover, that contemporary arguments were developed by Robert Filmer and others seeking to bring family and state into ideological conformity indicates that the two institutions were not equivalent. For this latter reason alone, I would say that the relationship between the early modern family, conceived as a fundamental social unit, and the state was complex, changing, and potentially adversarial. The theoretical and historical warrant for adopting this view I would formally characterize in the following way:

First, if Foucault's influence on new-historicist practice in Renaissance studies is acknowledged, then a problem in appropriating his thought to this period must also be acknowledged. The primary site for Foucault's archaeological studies was French history and culture in the late seventeenth and eighteenth centuries—the high period of French absolutism. But the historical conditions that obtained in this period cannot be appropriated to those of early seventeenth-century England as Goldberg does in *James I* without substantial revision to account for the more dispersed power relations that existed between the English king (not monarch) and other English institutions (including family, church, and Parliament), not to mention the less visible kinds of power encoded in England's cultural inheritance. Alternatively stated, the techniques, disciplines, and strategies that Foucault speaks about in characterizing the eighteenth-century project of coordinating the operation of disparate institutions were not nearly so well developed in early modern England as they were in Enlightenment France. Although it may be appropriate to invoke the pervasiveness of power—in the Foucaultian sense of being dispersed everywhere—the ap-

plication of this notion to a monarch-centered conception of power becomes reductive not only of Foucault's thought but of the historical conditions of English society.[7]

Second, numerous seventeenth-century social contract theorists conceived of the family not only as a quasi-independent social and economic
unit and not only as possessing a history different from that of the state but
as being antecedent to it.[8] Patriarchal theorists Robert Filmer and Thomas
Hobbes developed their concepts of political obligation, Gordon Schochet
emphasizes, by appealing to the belief that the family preceded the state
and was endowed with "natural rights" (136–58, 225–43). Further distinguishing between their views, Collins characterizes Hobbes's thought as
ridding the state and civil order of "eschatological purpose" while emphasizing Filmer's denial that the state existed separately from social nature, a
social nature sustained by familial relations and ordered by patriarchal
authority (149–52). Just as God had endowed Adam with absolute powers
to dispense life and death over all family members without appeal, Filmer's
argument went, so the kings enjoyed those same powers once the paternal
heads of families ceded these original rights (*patraie potestas*) to form a
country. James I followed this same line of reasoning in claiming his divine
right powers by virtue of his position as *"Parens patriae"* ("Speech of 1609"
307). The king, he argued, "becomes a naturall Father to all his Lieges at his
Coronation: And as the father of his fatherly duty is bound to care for the
nourishing, education, and vertuous gouernment of his children; euen so is
the king bound to care for all his subiects" (*The Trew Law of Free Monarchies*
55). The repeated use of these arguments illustrates that the family was
recognized not only as distinct from but prior to the state, and this priority
is what compelled theorists of governmental authority to *derive* the state's
powers from it.

Third, although there is a pronounced analogic relationship in the mutual obligations that bind subjects to rulers and those that bind wives to
husbands, the institutions of state and family were nonetheless constituted
quite differently. For example, although James and Elizabeth frequently
protested their love for their subjects, the relationship of English princes to
subjects was primarily a legal one involving obligations to dispense justice
and to uphold the laws of the realm. The relationship between family
members was also legally constituted through the institution of marriage—
"wedlock"—but the nature of that bond (in contrast to that of the state),
especially in the ranks beneath the aristocracy, was also intensely personal,
involving the arousal of sexual desire, sexual intercourse, childbirth, and

the raising of children. Also, such closeness was promoted very often by the need to maintain the viability of the household as a common economic enterprise in which moral and religious values were also transmitted. An uncompromising materialist analysis may dissolve the affectivity of these relationships in the material reality of power; it may further deconstruct these familial relationships to highlight their inequality or repressiveness, but such strategies do not for all that establish the adequacy of a theoretical model solely based on a homogenizing concept of power.

In treating this subject, I find myself coming to a view of family life very different from that provided by Lawrence Stone in *The Family, Sex and Marriage in England, 1500–1800*. Stone's much-cited view is that the emotional bonds between family members were weak by modern standards. After pointing to the high infant mortality rates as proof that it was "folly to invest too much emotional capital in such ephemeral beings" and calling attention to the customs in propertied families of sending their children to wet-nurses and, later, of entering them as servants in other households, Stone concludes that the relationship between parents and children was "normally extremely formal" and "usually fairly remote" in these families (105, 112, 105). Similarly, Stone concludes that there was little affectivity between well-to-do husbands and wives who, not unexpectedly, found their "emotional outlet[s]" elsewhere (102). Obviously, Stone's account of familial relations in gentry households can be used to support the notion that family relationships resembled business or state relations much more closely than we might think.

This issue is of considerable importance, for where the emotional bonds among family members are strong, attempts by governmental authorities to loosen or transpose them may meet with something less than compliance. Stone's arguments may eventually fall to contrary evidence (Hey 213–14; MacFarlane 105–10) and direct challenges by other social historians (Wrightson 71, 101–3). But whatever the outcome of this social-historical debate, my own cultural evidence on the dissenting side proceeds from a different source—"imaginative" representations of royal and aristocratic family life in the early modern theater. The plays we shall examine not only represent aristocratic (or royal) mothers with their spouses and children; they represent them by means of a powerful affectivity which, as we shall see, works to new cultural and political ends.

Turning to the Elizabethan-Jacobean drama, we are immediately confronted with an irony. Accustomed though we have become to look toward

Shakespeare's drama on every issue, his plays are by no means the most appropriate place to examine the deployment of the affective nuclear family. It is even difficult to find examples in Shakespeare of a fully functioning family with mother, father, and growing children.[9]

The point bears elaborating. Shakespearean comedy is full of witty, resourceful heroines with restricting fathers, but the issue in these romances is marriage, not the conjugal life following. *Romeo and Juliet,* it is true, gives us in the Capulets a father, mother, nurse, and nubile child, but the dramatic emphasis falls only obliquely on child rearing and the domestic life. Instead it treats that transitional event in family history when a young woman prepares to leave her household of origin. The history plays treat with epic amplitude the rigors of rule and dynastic conflict so that young children, when they do appear (e.g., Rutland in *3 Henry VI* or the Yorkist child princes of *Richard III*), are introduced only to be slaughtered and thereby to underline the ruthlessness of political intrigue. Among Shakespeare's mature tragedies, a peculiar barrenness appears. The marriage of Calpurnia and Caesar is childless as are those of Portia and Brutus, Othello and Desdemona. The marriage of Claudius and Gertrude is astonishing in that not one scene depicts them alone together. Their marriage generally speaks in public, and always it is the son-stepson who in tormented, lurid visions imagines what that private relationship is really like. *Lear* too gives us grown children (all cast by the folkloric extremities of preternatural good and evil), no mother, and a grandfatherly father at the verge of death. In the imagination of the ancient king, upon which the play intently fixes, woman's sexual body is regarded not intimately or warmly but anxiously and symbolically as a psychosexual nightmare: "Down from the waist they are Centaurs, / Though women all above; / But to the girdle to the gods inherit, / Beneath is all the fiends': there's hell, there's darkness, / There is the sulphurous pit, burning, scalding, / Stench, consumption" (4.6.124–29).

Macbeth does indeed introduce the intimacies of married life, but even before Lady Macbeth greets her husband, she has renounced, once again preternaturally, witchlike, her womanly sexuality, to satisfy an overleaping political ambition through self-induced demonic possession. Indeed, the experience of motherhood is introduced solely to be abjured. And whereas in *Lear* the female body (because ambitious) is imagined as fiendish, in *Macbeth* that fiendishness is made to originate in the mother herself, whose breasts will release gall, not milk, and whose tender recollections of the smiling babe sucking at her breast are invoked solely to be dashed with her baby's brains.[10]

Hardly ever does Shakespeare depict sustained, positively affective marital relationships or growing children in familial settings. Even in the late romances, where we might expect to find them, these relationships are largely absent. The forgotten wife/mother of Prospero and Miranda is a pattern that recurs in *Pericles* in the absent wife Thaisa. Even in *The Winter's Tale,* where Leontas's and Hermione's marital relationship is celebrated, that celebration is rendered in a single scene as an edenic dream (1.2) from which we are summarily banished to entertain Leontes's paranoia, his remanding his pregnant wife to prison, separating her from her young son, denying Hermione the nursing of her newborn daughter, and, finally, exposing her babe to the elements on a foreign shore.

From such representations as these, it is hard to resist the observation that the privy mark of Shakespeare's dramaturgy is that the shared marital life is an absence, to be recaptured if at all in dream and penance. Were Shakespeare to remain the sole measure of Renaissance practice, his manner of representing families (or even married women) might continue to stand as a normative expression. But there is no warrant for such privileging. It would be more salutary to examine plays in which families and family formation are a central dramatic concern. Two such plays featuring aristocratic *and* affective nuclear families are Webster's *Duchess of Malfi* (1614) and Thomas Drue's *Duchess of Suffolk* (1624). Along with Lope de Vega's *El mayordomo de la duquesa de Amalfi* (ca. 1605), which I will briefly treat, they show the bonds created over several years following the remarriage of each duchess to a man of lower rank and the birth of children whose safety is threatened by an intruding despotic state. As in *Macbeth,* these duchess plays depict a couple caught at the intersection between their domestic cares and the exigencies of the state, but in them the nuclear family becomes an alternative to the coercive demands of the open-lineage, patriarchal family described by Stone (4–7), which is at one and the same time the tyrannical authority of the state.

As the more powerful ideological representation, I will treat Webster's tragedy first and then in conjunction with Lope's *El mayordomo* use *The Duchess of Suffolk* to urge the political significance of a theatrical representation of the conjugal mothering body—a representation whose very power inheres in its being proffered as apolitical.

Through Duke Ferdinand's implacable resolve to use his hired intelligencer Bosola to bring his sister's personal life under his control, an autocratic but hardly depersonalized patriarchy pruriently and menacingly pries into the domestic spaces where the Duchess of Malfi would dwell in privacy. This premise has prompted a series of recent essays treating the Duchess's tragedy in terms of the placement and displacement of female sovereignty (Jankowski 163–79), the installation of women as "subjects" (Belsey, *Subject* 200–207),[11] the sociopolitical significance of marrying beneath oneself (Selzer 71–80), and as a conflict between emergent and residual modes of conduct (Rose 157–63). The same concerns can also lead to a liberal interpretation that yokes the tragedy to Jonson's *Sejanus* or Samuel Daniel's *Philotus,* where the theme is that individuals ought in their own homes to be spared the surveillance of an Argus-eyed state. Frank Whigham's new-historicist analysis takes a different course, interpreting Ferdinand's need to shut up his sister as an aristocratic resistance to the upward mobility represented by the Duchess's marriage to her steward, a conflict he describes anthropologically in terms of exogamous and endogamous impulses.

Whigham's reading of the codes underlying the tragedy isolates one set of social concerns, while feminist and liberal readings attend to others. Be this as it may, these analyses leave unaddressed a concern to explore the source of the powerful affective messages the tragedy delivers. *The Duchess of Malfi* works more personally, intimately, than most plays because it seeks to tap the deep concerns human beings have for being taken care of unconditionally. This it achieves by first making the Duchess an all-giving, nurturing mother and wife and then unleashing the anxiety of showing that caregiver being taken away, abused, and put to death. Ironically, the discursive mode by which the tragedy works upon its audience forsakes simile by locating the values of marital love (both sexual and affective), motherly care, love, and selfhood *in the body* of the Duchess.

No other tragedy in the Elizabethan-Jacobean drama displays such care in encouraging its audience to feel the corporeality of its central character. Webster's Duchess may embody an abstract idea—of "integrity of life" or the freedom of nature or political sovereignty—but those ideas are conveyed concretely: her procreant body is made to express nature's life-nourishing possibilities. More than this, even the Duchess's spirituality, her manner of approaching Christ, is achieved through her humanity, which becomes synonymous with her physicality. This is why Ferdinand's assault upon it is felt to be horrific, why his psychopathology, in accordance with the Doctor's Paracelsian diagnosis, is shown to be a madness that leads to lycanthropia.[12] The brother hunts down and tortures the woman who proves to sustain even him. Identified though she is with birds of nature—the robin redbreast, the wren, the lark—and with deeply rooted forests and meads, and even with the soul's imprisonment in the body, the Duchess is never a disembodied symbol. Although limited by her subject positions as widow and prince, she is also represented in the humanist manner as affectionate as well as directive, possessing genuine agency and rights (Belsey, *Subject* 199–200)—all of which are realized dramatically in the Duchess's sexual body.

But it is more than this. The Duchess's spirituality is indistinguishable from her humanity, which, ironically, is realized *through the body.* The palpability of the Duchess's body in its stereotypical vulnerability to illness and emotional distress is everywhere. Having engendered a marriage to her liking with Antonio, the Duchess risks a precarious freedom, living a clandestine domestic life that hides her husband and then the changes in her pregnant body from her voyeuristic brother and his spy. But the body tells its own story. As Bosola disdainfully observes, the Duchess "Is sick a-days, she pukes, her stomach seethes, / The fins of her eyelids look most teeming blue, / She wanes i'the' cheek, and waxes fat i'th' flank" and "Wears a loose-bodied gown" (2.1.67–71).[13] For the Duchess herself pregnancy brings the unsettling experience of otherness, of life happening to her; yet her safety lies in the ability to control the messages her would-be irreproachable aristocratic body conveys. "Your arm Antonio, do I not grow fat? / I am exceeding short-winded" (2.1.111–12). After ravenously consuming the apricots Bosola has proffered, she breaks into "an extreme cold sweat" that presages labor, feels her belly "swell," and confides to Antonio, "I fear I am undone" (2.1.159, 161–63). So too, at the moment of birth, Bosola reports hearing "a woman shriek" (2.3.1) and, after hearing it again, reports the sound came from the Duchess's lodgings. In this way, the Duchess's body becomes the center of dramatic intrigue: for her to reveal that body as a pregnant one, possessed of a growing life inside, is to be betrayed, and all because she will not surrender that body up to serve the theatrical requirements of a patriarchal despotism that would put it on display as an insignia of family pride and status.

The occasion of the Duchess's betrayal strengthens this sense of illicit encroachment, personal violation, and trespass by suggesting the prying open of a private space of family. Represented as apolitical, "natural," and conjoining—as in the Duchess's marriage ceremony itself—body and spirit, the family counterpoints the patriarchal state, which is depicted as idea-driven, unresponsive to human need, and ultimately depraved. Ferdinand's surreptitious entry into the Duchess's quarters literalizes this intrusion into a sacrosanct domain. Through his tool, Bosola, this relentless surveillance is then used to bring about the tragic peripety. In a thoroughly ironic scene Bosola successfully elicits the identity of the Duchess's husband by praising (true praise as it turns out) the steward the Duchess has pretended to dismiss. Pleased and comforted by this appraisal of the loyal spouse she has not dared appear with in society, she confides, "This good one that you speak of, is my husband"; "I have had three children by him" (3.2.275, 279). Pride in her husband and pride in the children she has borne him—in short, her wifely and maternal love—ends by exposing all of them to retribution and death.

The Duchess's children are extensions of her. For this reason, they do not have speaking parts; rather, they have a corporeal presence. At Loretto they appear with their parents in the dumb show and in the episode preceding the Duchess's capture they are divided for safety's sake, Antonio fleeing with the eldest, the Duchess with the younger buntings. Much more than a harbinger of the deaths to come, the scene dramatizes their parting as a spiritual and physical tearing apart, a de-parting of the family body, the joined flesh of marriage.[14] Feeling his separation from the Duchess as a loss of a part of himself, Antonio laments, "Best of my life, farewell," and bids farewell to the Duchess's serving woman Cariola "And thy sweet armful" (3.5.59, 81). The Duchess, in her turn, cannot decide "which is best, / To see you dead, or part with you" (63–64). Antonio compares the physical separation of their family to "some curious artist" (ironically adumbrating Vincentio Lauriola's artistry) taking "in sunder / A clock, or watch," which he vainly hopes will be put back in a better order (61–63). In these lines the family is figured as a harmonious working unit, the clock, whose innards are being eviscerated. Antonio's vain hopes expresses an irony, that time will put it back in better order.

Because the Duchess has disposed her body in ways Ferdinand does not approve, he makes war both upon her and the family body she has brought forth. This he brings about first by putting her under surveillance and then by controlling the body itself, by imprisoning the Duchess. This incarceration, often read psychoanalytically as Ferdinand's attempt to possess his sister, is also a poetically symbolic "confinement" for the Duchess's impermissible pregnancies, the "bastard-making" that affronts the royal dignity. The confinement Ferdinand creates is total. In her prison the Duchess becomes an object of study, her mind and body to be examined from afar.

Under these conditions, her dress, her words, her every reaction are open to Ferdinand's manipulation.

This incarceration effectively makes the Duchess a solitary inmate in what Erving Goffman would describe as a "total institution," by which he means an institution in which the "territories of the self are violated; the boundary that the individual places between his being and the environment is invaded and the embodiments of self profaned" (*Asylums* 4, 23). This homology between the Duchess's situation in a totalizing institution and that of inmate in an asylum is made explicit in the scene where Ferdinand looses upon the Duchess the madmen from "the common hospital" (4.1.125). As a totalizing institution "the common hospital" reproduces the madness it contains; the Duchess, deprived of the external supports that give her identity, is driven toward the same end. She acknowledges as much when she says, "I'll tell thee a miracle, / I am not mad yet" (4.2.24–25).

Imprisonment is nothing if not the subjugation of the body. Consistent with this idea, the imagery of menace in *The Duchess of Malfi* is insistently corporeal. In this manner, the Duchess, in a premonitory metaphor that suggests her brother's hostility toward her procreative functions, complains, "men preserve alive / Pheasants and quails, when they are not [yet] fat enough / To be eaten" (3.5.109–11). Similarly, the imprisonment itself is literalized as a psychosexual assault upon the Duchess's hitherto privileged body—privileged in its birthing functions and its aristocratic status: "Damn her! that body of hers" (4.1.119). Wishing to obliterate the body that produces the family, its cohesiveness, its interpersonal connectedness, Ferdinand shapes in wax the fantasy of its dismemberment. He is himself obsessed with dismemberment, and his lycanthropia, we recall, takes the form of dismembering the buried dead and stealing their parts. By inducing the Duchess to view as real the artificial, murdered figures of her husband and her children, Ferdinand brings her to experience the dismembering of her domestic world, the amputation of the family members that constitute her relatedness to life. This is the source of the strange hold the scene exerts over its audiences. The Duchess experiences this sight as a killing act performed directly upon herself. It "wastes me more," she moans, "Than were't my picture, fashion'd out of wax" and stabbed in an act of witchcraft by a "magical needle" (4.1.62–64). That is, the effect of witnessing the bodies of her husband and children is more immediate in its death-producing effect on her than the voodooist's slaying of his enemy by stabbing the totem. This identification of self with family, as if the killing of the one sympathetically kills the other, is the source of the scene's dreadful emotional power. In Ferdinand's sadistic play of death, the Duchess's empathetic identification with her husband and children parallels that of the audience (as much abused by the sight as she) in its empathetic witness of the Duchess as its own defeated mother and protector. The spectacle on the great stage releases a core anxiety—that the inexplicable enmity of the world, the all-powerful Other, will destroy every member of our family unit, leaving us bereft, without support, love, or safety.

The scene brings the audience to behold a site (sight) "at which art is no longer *only* language" and is perhaps beyond language—the spectacle of family death and our own "sensory engagement" with its meaning.[15] So too, the tragedy's literalization of metaphor brings the audience to experience in concrete imaginative forms the spectacular dismemberment of the affective family body as an integral unit. The literalization appears with uncanny wittiness in Ferdinand's letter saying that he wants Antonio's head in a business and horrifically in the image-in-action of the severed hand Ferdinand proffers to the Duchess. Ironically, the unremarkable gesture by which she kisses it suggests the warmth of her affection for Antonio. Her concern that Antonio's cold flesh means he has not fared well after his travel expresses an intimate solicitude; it is a devotion of herself to the mundane experiences of another, which have no social value other than that the someone she cares about has had them. The Duchess's subsequent recognition that the hand is detached from the body also releases an anxiety of an extreme sort, for the message is that to love without permission is to bring upon oneself ceaseless punishment and terror. This hand, which also bears the Duchess's wedding ring, is the tragedy's most straightforward representation of Ferdinand's attempt to sever, physically, the marital bond; it is also part of his war upon the family and its self-presuming autonomy.

Although the Duchess could easily be positioned to play the martyr, she repeatedly renounces the role, wishing instead that "Heaven, a little while, [should] cease crowning martyrs / To punish them" and asking in a more political vein why she must "Account it praise to suffer tyranny" (4.1.106–7, 3.5.74). These values disclose the emergence of a worldview that refuses to accept self-abnegation as a Christian ideal. It is through her involuntary rather than self-inflicted suffering that her spirit reaches to God and for this reason that she marks her patriarchal big brothers as tyrants. With similar emphasis, the Duchess declines to become a repressed model of female celibacy: "Why should only I / Of all the other princes of the world / Be cas'd up, like a holy relic? I have youth, / And a little beauty" (3.2.137–40). This is not the language of social or sexual renunciation. In fact, the Duchess's relationship to Antonio is remarkable for its gentle sexual humor, a humor that frames their sexuality as comfortable and familiar without ever becoming smutty, as when the Duchess teasingly responds to Antonio's request to sleep with her by urging the fashion that noblemen kneel to "purchase a night's lodging of their wives" and by the teasing query, "Alas, what pleasure can two lovers find in sleep?" (3.2.6, 10).

These values are writ small as well as large. They appear in seemingly inessential details, in the Duchess's observations that her hair is graying and tangled and in Cariola's wry, indecorous description of her as "the sprawling'st bedfellow" (3.2.13). They appear in her instruction that her boy take syrup for his cold and her daughter be reminded to say her prayers. They also appear in the Duchess's low-key, "small" conversations in the domestic scenes and during her imprisonment, as when she asks Cariola, "Dost thou think we shall know one another / In th' other world?" (4.2.18–19). The theme throughout is relatedness, and is expressed in the Duchess's certain belief that in the next life people will continue to be connected to one another, to be in touch, as it were, by sight. This conviction expresses a doctrinal as well as a social faith, for belief in the Redemption was closely tied to concerns about the resurrection of the whole body and the survival of the full personality.[16] The patience, calm, constancy, and courtesy the Duchess exhibits throughout the tragedy are Webster's distinctive contributions to the story, and they work to reinforce the conviction that merely by being herself she lives the pattern of Christ's human love. For this same reason, the Duchess's loss of control upon seeing the effigies of her children and husband is felt to be terrifying. Ferdinand's "unnatural" assault threatens to destroy the family as a social, sanctified unit.

The unstudied palpability of these details is most unusual in the drama and bears comparison with that other female prince, Shakespeare's Cleopatra, whose body is a bravura presentation made into a performance as calculated and public as the impersonation in which "Egypt" packages herself as Venus on a barge on the river Cyndus. Webster's Duchess operates on a much smaller scale; her princely ambition is to secure her entitlement to a room of her own with husband and children, where she may be the self she longs to be.

Unlike *Macbeth*, where the maternal body is made to unwish itself for political dominion, *The Duchess of Malfi* makes the nurturant female body and its extension, the affective domestic nuclear family, alternative sites of allegiance to the extended patriarchal family through whom the authority of state devolves. The latter, we see, has been constituted as an intrusion, a tyrannical busybody encroaching on the private family, which is now deployed as *the* originary social unit, natural and beyond politics. Without doubt, the attempt to sustain a center of value outside the patriarchal Renaissance state can bring a terrifying retribution. Antonio's dying words, "And let my son fly the courts of princes" (5.4.71), acknowledges as much.

Nonetheless, to conclude from such an issue of events, as one new-historicist reading does, that the Duchess's tragedy is yet another endorsement of the monarch's power is to deprive this tragedy of its *resistant* powers of display. So too, to conflate the tragedy of the Duchess with that of Desdemona, Cleopatra, and Tamyra, making the fundamental insight that they all function as admonitory exhibitions of the punishment that must come to aristocratic women who "obscure within themselves the boundary differentiating what belongs to the body politic from what must be kept outside" (Tennenhouse, *Power on Display* 120), is to collapse the abstraction of the "body politic" into what the tragedy presents as the unassimilated, unrecuperated mothering body of the Duchess.

Such a reading also forgets that Jacobean tragedy increasingly depends for its profound effect not upon hortatory demonstration but sympathetic identification. Though *The Duchess* itself obviously appeals to the ethical notion of *"integrity of life"* (5.5.119), it conveys this message at a much deeper level through the mothering body of the Duchess, which makes its audience aware of the "unspeakably common," the need for the "fusion of human bodies through the group, the precisely nonverbal and nonanalytical supportive stratum of our lives" (Wilshire 23). For a play that has been described as a tragedy of spiritual transcendence and a political tragedy of state, it is well to remember the substantial claims of the female body and of Caroline Bynum's judgment that women, following a pattern established in the Middle Ages, "reached God not by reversing what they were but by sinking more fully into it" (172).

The very meaning of the body—even the body of a female prince—is thus revealed to be recursive. Its meaning is partially produced by internal processes of self-reflection, and that meaning is itself negotiated as part of a complex social process that exceeds objective attempts to fashion it definitively or univocally. The Duchess herself assigns it a distinctive signifi-

Fig. 7. The Pelican Emblem. "Quod in te est, prome" ("Bring forth what is in you"). From Whitney, *A Choice of Emblemes*, 1586. Courtesy of the University of Illinois.

cance. "Dispose my breath how please you," she says, "but my body / Bestow upon my women, will you?" (4.2.223–24). In the reckoning of the tragedy, whatever there is in life that's worth having proceeds from her. She is the pelican mother who, Christ-like, with her life's blood nurses those who cannot live without her (fig. 6). Her caregiving body provides the play's only health; she suckles everyone, even her enemies:

In my last will I have not much to give;
A many hungry guests have fed upon me,
Thine will be a poor reversion[, Cariola].
. . . .
Go tell my brothers, when I am laid out,
They then may feed in quiet." (4.2.197–99, 232–33)

This culminating moment of tragedy creates not so much tears but, as Bert States observes in his phenomenological study of theater, "an empathetic experience wherein we are dissolved in what could be called a magnificent loneliness, felt most deeply in the absolute stillness of the auditorium when tragic characters say such things as 'Thou shalt come no more'" (171).

As a discourse of power, *The Duchess of Malfi* is formidable because it represents the nurturant, royal, female body as belonging both to a fully individuated self and to a transcendental order of nature. This discourse too stands in an explicit relationship of tension to a patriarchal discourse of authority based on political obligation and civic honors. Furthermore, by drawing the relations within the Duchess's immediate family as private, consensual, and thus extrapolitical, the tragedy situates patriarchal authority *outside* this private space. Paternal authority is not made invisible by this sensory engagement with the maternal; rather, it is singled out in its prohibitive, public, and repressive functions as the object of obloquy. And by being juxtaposed to the maternal principle, paternal authority is experienced all the more effectively as unnatural and life-denying.[17]

The reading I have just presented presses the claim that *The Duchess of Malfi* is a distinctive, culturally significant text. The larger question, however, is whether the tragedy ought to be viewed as extraordinary or whether it is part of a persisting discourse of the aristocratic mothering body within the domain of theatrical representation. In responding, I can call attention to Lope de Vega's reworking of Matteo Bandello's 1554 *Novelle, The Duchess of Amalfi's Steward* (*El mayordomo de la duquesa de Amalfi*) (ca. 1605) and to Drue's *Duchess of Suffolk.* These show clearly that such an affective discourse was widely available to playwrights. They used it to affirm a form of authority distinct from and—at particular points in these plays—in opposition to a civic authoritarianism nominally located in a patriarchal head, whose powers were not yet firmly bounded by a concept of private and public space.

Lope's verse tragedy is notable in its own right as a product of popular, outdoor, Spanish theater and has recently been translated into English, in no small measure because Lope's tragedy is also a retelling of the story of the Duchess of Amalfi.[18] But from the perspective I have just described, the most significant feature of Lope's tragedy is its care in eliciting the emotions brought on by parenthood and in using these emotions to constitute the enclosed nuclear family as a refuge from patriarchal authority. A central example of his mode of dramaturgy is revealed following the Duchess's delivery of a daughter, when her husband, Antonio, delivers a long soliloquy on the event. An alloy of joy mixed with pathos (because the child must be sequestered from the Duchess's powerful brother Julio de Aragon), its central section reads,

> She gave me a son, who is raised
> in such absolute secrecy
> that a mountain is made the fortress
> for this body, who is my hope.
> And now her illness is feigned
> for the birth of a daughter, so beautiful[,]
> . . . .
> one the sun, the other the moon.
> O what children, blessed heaven!
> O what glory! O what gifts!
> Come night, obscure the earth.
> If I call her my little moon,
> you must keep her veiled for me.
> Moon of night my girl must be
> when I bear her light away.
> Come, Night. Be not afraid.
> She cannot blaze out your shadows,
> for I must wrap her up,
> and cover her with my cloak
> to hide her spendour. Come. (2.177–202)

This likening of the boy to Antonio's sun and the daughter to his moon has the effect, gender-defined though it surely is, of magnifying Antonio's experience of parenthood, recording it as a cosmic event in the small universe of the affective nuclear family. Such purple passages not only continue to build identification with Antonio and Camilla (the Duchess) as conjugal lovers and hounded parents; they also work to constitute the vengeance that flows from Julio's authoritarianism and its values of lineage, kinship, patronage, and local community as inhuman.[19]

Like Webster's tragedy, Lope's represents the joys of conjugal love as natural, and it goes considerably further by mystifying the "maternal instinct." Because not only the Duchess's lying-in but the children's rearing must be furtive, Antonio farms each babe out to a peasant wet-nurse, the spunky, affectionate Bartola, whose own child has just died and who takes immediately to the newborn, exulting "Yes, baby sweetheart, my life. / My little duchess. / . . . This is the baby I bore. / It is living; I'm comforted" (2.598–619). Bartola's humorously displaced husband, Doristo, universalizes these maternal ejaculations, explaining, "Even the soberest woman / goes ga-ga at baby prattle. / If the baby so much as coughs / her mama swears she said, 'Daddy'" (2.605–8). Years later, when the Duchess's two children, ages six and eight, are again presented to her in their peasant dress, all unaware of their blood ties, they experience a kind of inner recognition, each child testifying to being overcome by a sudden unexplained surge of love for the Duchess—"my heart is moved inside me" (3.100). The verse embellishes what is already present in the spectacle of the reunited family. Represented as a spiritualized recognition scene, the reunion presumes an empathetic audience and shamelessly seeks to tap what Bruce Wilshire describes as "deeper sympathies about which it [the audience] has never learned to speak in words" (23).

This experience of motherhood and paternity and of the family body reunited is clothed in a precious ordinariness. The love for children is shown to cut across class divisions (including those separating Bartola from the Duchess; Julio from Antonio) and, following a logic of adorational mystification, yearns to make the whole world one. Of course, in the end it does not. Instead, the powerful emotions marshaled in valorizing the nuclear family are pitted against the tyranny of the patriarchal, open-lineage family. In the latter, the artificialities of degree and patrimony are prized over the "natural" affections. On this point the denouement depends. Believing that the Aragonians' naked sword "will be sheathed by pity" when Julio and his brother see their niece and nephew, their "two small angels" (3.38–40), Antonio determines to present his little children to Julio. But as Aragonian patriarch and head of state, the Duke feels only the scandalous crime committed against his house by a mean marriage that has debased and dishonored his family. In consequence, he has his sister poisoned but ensures that she live long enough to see a table he has had decorated with the heads of Antonio and her two children. To mark the loathsomeness of this vengeance, Lope has the young Duke of Amalfi, the Duchess's son by her first, approved marriage, vow vengeance—only to be sneeringly slighted by Julio, who calls him a mere boy. Such an unmodulated conclusion stimulates raw emotions, and by highlighting the absence of "natural" affection in Julio, the tragedy treats his patriarchal fury as the product of an unnatural, if unanswerable, despotism. At a deeper, personal level the spectacle of the dismembered family body, its members detached from one another and the integrity of the individual members cut away and detached, evokes horror by showing us the violation of bodily identity, which is constitutive of our identity as persons and of our corporeal connectedness to those closest to us. To behold this spectacle and—if the audience is able—to believe in its killing power is to experience from another direction the "magnificent loneliness" that tragedy strives to elicit.

Also performed before a popular audience, the Palsgrave's Men at the Fortune, *The Duchess of Suffolk* presses the values of family sentiment to shape attitudes toward the political nation. This it does through the spectacular opposition established between the aristocratic but vulnerable mothering body of the Duchess of Suffolk and a cadre of government informers and pursuivants who dog her every move. Set in the reign of Queen Mary, when Bishop Bonner was persecuting England's Protestants, *The Duchess of Suffolk* theatricalizes the plight of the celebrated Catherine Willoughby (1520–80), the Puritan widow who was forced to flee England to continue practicing her faith.[20] Like *The Duchess of Malfi,* Drue's tragicomedy emphasizes the widowed Duchess's independence in choosing to marry her steward Bertie out of motives of affection and regard. Careful not to challenge the principles of degree, Bertie is the spiritual successor—even if not the equal in blood—of the Duke of Suffolk, whom the steward praises as having "suckt his Nutriment of life" in "honor's wombe" (Act 1).[21] These images of lactation and gestation carry the values of the play and are used as counterpoint to the imagery of surveillance and the savage hunt that define the Marian regime. When, for example, the Duchess and Bertie are forced to one of their several separations, Bertie, amid kisses and tears, complains that the "watching eyes of inquisition / Steales covertly vpon our purposes," so that he and the Duchess fear even to "peepe out" their thoughts (Act 2). The operant term *peepe* suggests the oppression they endure and their reduction to a childlike condition of fear.

This imagistic matrix is reinforced by the melodramatic plot. In melodramatic contrast to the historical Duchess, who escaped to the Continent with her entire entourage (Heineman 207), Drue's Duchess carries her daughter on foot, accompanied by a single wet-nurse whose presence highlights the Duchess's life-giving powers and vulnerability.[22] Everywhere, the play measures the Duchess's nurturant, motherly productivity against the savage predatoriness of Bonner's popish inquisitors. Courageous and resourceful as she is, even defending her husband against marauders, the Duchess's vulnerability as a parturient mother exposed, moreover, to assault are matters for pathos and apprehension. In these scenes the source of the play's hold upon its audience rests on the alienation between the innocent Duchess as mother and the unfeeling world. For the very reason that the audience is not living the Duchess's life but can witness her plight at a contemplative remove, it can experience through her, without resistance, its deepest needs and vulnerabilities.

Such vulnerability, which the audience experiences only in its role as sympathetic spectator, is made vivid by the Duchess's sentimental attempt to kiss away the hungry cries of her nursling, her "treasure," because the infant's innocent wailing threatens to betray her place of refuge in the forest (Act 2). The babe's miraculous silence hard upon its mother's kissing inscribes the child's love for its mother as percipient and mystical. In a wondrous reversal of role, the prescient babe answers its mother's urgent need. Later, amid thunder, snow, and rain, the Duchess finds herself on a cold, stone church porch beside a graveyard giving precarious birth to a male heir. The need of the hotly pursued Duchess to lie in and regain her strength jeopardizes her escape, drawing sympathy to her even as it underlines the sanctity of her life-giving aristocratic body. So too, after eluding her enemies in a hearse with her baby, literally taking new life from death's shape, the Duchess must preserve (what has become) her hallowed body against the sexual assault of robbers. During each of these harrowing experiences, the values of conjugal love and familial affectivity are reaffirmed in the face of "the other," Queen Mary's papist bloodhounds. As the Duchess says after being reunited with Bertie, at the moment before the birth of her son, "Having my Husband, Child, and this my servant, / I am the richest Princes on the earth" (Act 3).

The political uses of the "apolitical" mothering body and its affective family become explicit in the closing action. This sets the Duchess's traumatic exile against the Protestant martyrdoms of Ridley, Latimer, and Cranmer, each of whom is actually brought on stage before their burning. In this nationalistic spirit, the play makes the Duchess's return from her Marian exile coterminous with Elizabeth I's enfranchisement from "her prison, to a royall Throne" (Act 5). This conjunction identifies the Duchess's trials with those of Elizabeth and by metonymic transposition represents England's Protestant heritage as maternal, heroic, and productive. By contrast, Mary's popish state, the abhorred "other," is identified with despotic incarceration and surveillance. Underscoring these significances, the Duchess is delivered from her enemies by the Palsgrave, a hero whose namesake, Frederick of Bohemia, became Protestantism's great hope in the Thirty Years' War then raging.[23]

The play's final identification of the Duchess's trials with those of Elizabeth shows that there is no intrinsic opposition between the discourses of the mothering body and of the nation-state. The former could be elicited in opposition, but both could also be realigned—and were—with the power of state.[24] In *The Duchess of Malfi, The Duchess of Amalfi's Steward,* and *The Duchess of Suffolk* the conjugal mothering body is represented on the margins of power; however, the fact that these bodies are marked as "aristocratic" or "royal" lends to them a special authority. In them the authority signified by blood is joined with the concept of "great creating nature" to reify a natural order to which the current political order ought to conform.

Throughout this chapter, I have urged that an effective cultural historicism must take account of the affectivity of texts, which is one of the distinctive attributes of plays and poems. Affectivity is one of the principal means by which plays exert their authority. Affectivity, moreover, is part of history, part of the lived experience of the past. Playmakers, by their recourse to it, persuasively addressed issues of their time and through it solicit our attention today. Inescapably, the production of affectivity is a constitutive part of the powerful production of valuing. By treating that affectivity responsively and critically, we enlarge the range of understanding by which our cultural-historicist and feminist concerns with representation may be represented to ourselves. Simply put, the affectivity of the past is part of our cultural identity; denial of it is a debilitating blindness.

Considered together, the plays we have examined show that representing aristocratic or royal women as mothers and lovers was a theatrical practice and that the ideology attendant upon their representation contended with the developing but more entrenched discourse of patriarchal authority. The noble women in these plays are powerful not because they are in power but because their lives are represented as coterminous with life-giving possibility itself. Valorizing as they do conjugality, nurturance, privacy, selfhood, and spiritual wholeness, these plays nevertheless move well beyond a discourse of domesticity. They articulate a cultural politics, as is evident from the fact that they are constituted as *histories.*

Whereas the Jacobean problem plays use their sexual matter to interrogate notions of justice, Webster's and Lope's tragedies on the Duchess of Malfi and Drue's tragicomedy on the Duchess of Suffolk disclose an ideology of the nuclear family that cordons off as sacrosanct a space where government officials are no longer to intrude. In marked contrast to the *Utopia* of Thomas More discussed in chapter 2, which presents for serious commendation a society whose vision of the common good is achieved through a comprehensive system of surveillance, the Duchess plays positively resist such surveillance, portraying it as the prurient and/or tyrannical encroachment of public officials, an offense to great creating nature.

In each of these chapters, I have approached this subject of surveillance from discrete but converging perspectives, and although I have eschewed any attempt to come to definitive conclusions or even closure, my account does not suggest that the postmodern condition signifies an end to history. Rather, it signifies another beginning from which other beginnings become possible. Building on many of the insights of new-historicist studies, I have urged that a viable cultural historicism must, through the inclusion of canonical and noncanonical literary and theatrical texts, iconographic representations, and recursive cultural practices, continue to develop procedures for reading texts symbolically, processually, and diachronically from multiple perspectives. In literary studies, in particular, modernist criticism must find ways of breaking out of its cerebral, inveterately suspicious manner of reading, as if all texts spoke a repressive language from the center. That is why I have stressed the importance of treating the affectivity of the textual past. Our affective responses, constructed and historicized as they are, are part of the meaning that the past holds for us. By continuing to revise and reform current critical practices in ways such as this, we work toward ensuring that studies in cultural historicism remain adaptable and pertinent. By "pertinent" I mean something simple and important—the development of a historical consciousness that models our perspectives on the present and so provides the basis, as I said in chapter 2, from which a plausible future may be imagined and subsequently shaped.

Notes

Throughout this book, all references to Shakespeare's plays and poems are to The Riverside Shakespeare. Unless otherwise stated, dates to plays are from Silvia Wagonheim's revised third edition of Harbage and Schoenbaum's Annals of English Drama. References to the Oxford English Dictionary and The Dictionary of National Biography are cited as OED and DNB, respectively.

Chapter One

1. Most notably, Michaels and Knapp, "Against Theory" (723–42), and Greenblatt, "Shakespeare and the Exorcists" (163–65). See also De Man's influential arguments in *Resistance to Theory*.

2. Howard, "The New Historicism" (13–14); White, *Tropics of Discourse* (89). Unless otherwise noted, all citations of Howard in this chapter refer to this essay.

3. The beating up on E. M. W. Tillyard for his compendious *Elizabethan World Picture* (although very little for his other books) is characteristic of this use of a single work to represent a diverse tradition. Also, history as a problematic, ideational, nonpositivist enterprise was expounded by Collingwood (205–81) years before the new historicism appeared.

4. The term originates in Greenblatt's *Renaissance Self-Fashioning* (4–5), appears as the title in "Towards a Poetics of Culture," and is redefined in *Shakespearean Negotiations* as "study of the collective making of distinct cultural practices and inquiry into the relations among these practices" (5).

5. On the transcendental assumptions that underlie historical understanding, especially as applied to Foucault, see D'Amico (chap. 5, esp. pp. 90–91).

6. On Rorty and Peirce as belonging to the correspondence theorists, Lovejoy and Dewey, see Rorty's "Academic Freedom" (62n.8) and "Putnam and the Relavist Menace." Rorty's position renouncing correspondence is set forth in *Objectivity*.

7. See Almeder (153–54, 184–85). For an explanation of Peirce's concept of the sign, see especially Greenlee (23–49). I speak throughout the paragraph about the redactors or reinterpreters of Peirce's triadic because Peirce himself, in more than one essay, supports the belief that "the method of science is the only objective method for the determination of the truth" (Almeder 109). But

this view is by no means a necessary consequence of Pierce's triadic epistemology.

8. Throughout this paragraph I am thinking of Freud's essay "The Uncanny," with its attention to unconscious memory in which the world appears at once strange and familiar. Freud's perspective can be adapted, I believe, to explain historical consciousness, particularly in respect to the disorienting features of the past and its powerful, affective hold over us.

9. See also Porter's "History and Literature: 'After the New Historicism.'"

10. Montrose acknowledges the point in "New Historicisms" (400–401). Besides Greenblatt, other notable practitioners employing this technique include Mullaney, Helgerson, and Fumerton.

11. On new historicism's use of functional anthropology see M. Jardine (290–91); Collins, "Where's the History?" (231); cf. Montrose, "New Historicisms" (398–401). Unless otherwise noted, citations to Collins throughout this study refer to this essay just cited.

12. For another critique of unproblematic appeals to "patriarchy" as a totalizing manner of argumentation, see Fox-Genovese (217).

13. The attack has been joined by others whom I have little space to treat, but see Himmelfarb and Lerner and also Jehlen's contribution to the essay by Walkowitz and Chevigny (24, 31–37).

14. See Hayden White's theory that the grounds for the new-historicist method of reading texts in problematized, nonempirical ways is warrant enough for speaking of "history as a text" ("New Historicism" 297). It may also be observed that the concept of "cause" came into the English language from France in the thirteenth century (*OED*, s.v.), a fact that underlines the point that human beings have had other modes of explanation. By the same token, the discernment of causes in the modern, philosophical sense is itself a way of seeing, of making sense of the world.

15. This is one further reason for Montrose's plural title, "New Historicisms," a point underlined by Cox and Reynolds's account of the "versions" of new historicism. Montrose has dissociated himself from certain now notable features of what others have characterized as "the new historicism." Greenblatt's revised version of "Invisible Bullets," evidently produced to mute the criticisms of method brought on by the original, is another indication that a period of reassessment is under way.

16. Foucault's centrality to new historicism is manifest in the title of Lentriccia's essay "Foucault's Legacy—A New Historicism?" On Foucault's importance to a new historicism see Simpson. Foucault is also my starting point because his method, despite his theory of the discontinuous eruption of epistemes, is able to acknowledge the pastness of the past.

17. Goldberg's account of the history of the word *sodomite* as "anyone performing a sexual act not aimed at procreation within the bonds of marriage" (*Sodometries* 9) underlines the generic character of "sodomitic" activity, the terms of which survive today. The criminalization of sexual acts under twentieth-century sodomy laws includes both homo-and heterosexual behaviors (un-

less otherwise stipulated) and may include oral sex, anal sex, sex with animals, and masturbation (8–11).

18. See Howard's list of nine critics who object that the focus on monarchical power and on the theater as recuperation too often "precludes examining the possibility of . . . social change and contestation" (*Stage and Social Struggle* 11–12).

19. *Criticism* (11). See also Pechter's account of "the detachment of new-historicist criticism," which includes a review of the work of numerous critics, including Belsey and Lentriccia (299–300).

20. There is also a fallacy in the polar judgment that texts must be viewed either "scientifically," that is, with detachment and "suspicion," or "appreciatively." The affectivity of texts may be registered intellectually as well as viscerally. A criticism that engages and then wrestles with one's emotional responsiveness to the text, which is what Kathleen McLuskie does when she *refuses* the affective power of *King Lear* (98–100), is a fuller and more useful criticism, I would contend, than one that is not.

Chapter Two

1. Titles such as Erickson's "Rewriting the Renaissance, Rewriting Ourselves" attest to new historicism's interest in mutually constitutive activities, but the relationship between the way the historical past is constituted and the way we situate ourselves in the present remains largely untheorized. Even the chiastic formulations that Montrose has made famous in the dictum that we must concern ourselves with "'the history of texts'" and "'the textuality of history'" ("Renaissance" 8, "Professing" 20) leads more quickly to a critical practice than to an understanding of the relationship between method and ideology.

2. *Discipline and Punish* (293–308). Otherwise unidentified citations to Foucault in this essay are to this primary text.

3. For an astute, qualified endorsement of the first impulse, see R. W. Chambers (125–32); on the second, Kautsky. For a general survey with assessments, see Elliott.

4. On Foucault's epistemes, see *Discipline*, Part I, "The body of the condemned" and "The spectacle of the scaffold" (3–69); cf. Part II, "Generalized punishment" and "The gentle way in punishment" (73–131). On the notion of the subject I follow Paul Smith's distinction between the "human agent," the site where resistance may be produced or played out, and the "subject," with its connotation of being subjected (xxv).

5. All citations from More's *Utopia* in my text are to the Adams edition.

6. Such a critique of humanism may be aligned with Foucault's response to Sartre's own latter-day humanism, existentialism, in which the self is forever burdened with personal responsibility for every act taken: Foucault responded to this injunction by calling it "terrorism." See Miller's biographical account of Foucault's relationship to Sartre's modern brand of humanism (38).

7. Among prerevolutionary philosophes, a surprising number composed

treatises whose scientific and/or mathematical interests inform utopian proposals. Examples are Fénelon's "Salentum: Frugal and Noble Simplicity" from *Les Aventures de Télémaque* (1699); the Abbé de Saint-Pierre's *Projet pour rendre la paix perpétuelle en Europe* (1713); and Rousseau's chapter "The People of the Ideal Commonwealth and the Expression of their General Will" in *Le Contrat Social* (1762). All appear in Manuel and Manuel's *French Utopias*.

8. See Wallerstein, chaps. 1 and 2, treating, respectively, "Capitalist Agriculture" and "Mercantilism."

9. Unless otherwise noted, citations from Bacon's works are to the Spedding edition.

10. See John Archer, who develops this argument by invoking Lacan's concept of the gaze—"'I see only from one point, but in my existence I am looked at from all sides'"—and then applies it in a manner similar to Greenblatt's in *Renaissance Self-Fashioning* to courtiers and Renaissance courtly observers (10).

11. Framing this concept as an absolute, Liu remarks of post-structuralist and new historicist discourses, "The hidden telos of any analysis of ideological struggle, after all, is that at the end of struggle lies new, free, or true Man (in a relativistic idiom: the salient class or type of man at the time)" (732).

12. Helgerson's concept of negation elucidates the contrast I am drawing. He argues that Golden Age fantasies "negate so fundamental an element of human society that without it society ceases to exist. Negating artifice as they do, is like negating mortality" ("Inventing Noplace" 108).

13. "Two Lectures," *Power/Knowledge* (81–85). On the need for local knowledge, as against integrative and synthesizing projects, see Flax's exegesis (42–43, 222–36).

14. For the demand that new historicists acknowledge that critics can occupy an undefiled space outside of power, see M. D. Jardine. For a critique of this demand, see Maslan (98–103).

Chapter Three

1. See Giddens's account of change within structural reproduction (*Central Problems* 103–20); also Collins's "Where's the History?" (231–33). Elton's tendentious rejection of poststructuralist methods is set forth in *Return to Essentials* (3–26).

2. I have stopped short of describing Elton's approach as "positivistic," a term commonly abused among cultural critics to mean the writing of history "as it really was" (*wie es eigentlich gewesen*) in Otto Ranke's famous phrase. Although Elton's interest in the history—or progress—of English democratic government is clear (e.g., *The Tudor Constitution*; "Reform by Statute"; *Reform and Renewal*), other aspects of his work, evidenced in "A High Road to Civil War?" reject the grand Whiggish narrative that the progress of democratic liberties in England resulted in an "inevitable" civil war.

3. For an analysis of the principles of what we would now call traditional historiography, see Heller (Part II, "Historiography as episteme"). Elton summarizes his views in *Practice of History*.

4. Ingram argues that these practices were employed strictly for *"legally purposeful"* ends (245), but Quaife's data are more voluminous and varied (50–53). On skimmingtons and charivari, see Underdown (110–11), Quaife (200), and Newman (131–45).

5. Following the influential theoretical accounts of the cultural formation of identity by Althusser, Foucault, Kristeva, and Lacan, recent studies in women's history have documented the informal control of subjects. Over the last decade Belsey (*Subject of Tragedy* 192–200, 220–21), Butler (16–25), and Flax (passim) have presented incisive critiques of female identity formation. In the early modern period, the construction of women's character through the imposition of the values of silence, deference, chastity, and obedience has also been corroborated through visual culture. See the woodcut in Ozment showing the Chaste Woman as a model for emulation with a lock on her mouth and a serpent guarding her nether parts (66–67).

6. Citations from *The Revenger's Tragedy* are to Gibbons' edition.

7. My account of metaphor and metonymy absorbs features of White's definitions in *Tropics of Discourse* (5–6, 72–74). White contends that historical discourse, like literature, is fundamentally figurative (94). At this metalevel all discourses are unavoidably united (197–217). Historical tropes, however, unlike those in imaginative literature, are bound by the additional constraint that they purport to "refer" (to past events). In White's view the explanatory mechanisms that weave such events together are unavoidably tropological.

8. This is a very different defense of literary function from that steadfastly articulated by Greenblatt. Resisting the implications of the new-historicist precept that "literary and non-literary 'texts' circulate inseparably" (Veeser xi), he holds that the language of "literary art" is "the single greatest cultural creation that may be appropriated without payment [i.e., 'the quid pro quo of economic exchange']" and describes Shakespeare's plays as "easily the most powerful, successful, and enduring artistic expressions in the English language" (*Shakespearean Negotiations* 9, 13). See also *Renaissance Self-Fashioning* (6) and *Learning to Curse* (170–71). Greenblatt has concerned himself much less with the cultural implications of metaphoric form, but see *Shakespeare Negotiations* under "Symbolic Acquisition" (10–12).

9. I concur with Holstun's argument that new historicists need to take up noncanonical texts much more than they do and avoid using them as mere prologues to discussions of canonical texts (192–93). An underlying thematic in chapters 5–7 of this book is the deformities consequent to a bard-obsessed criticism.

10. Throughout this study, citations from Jonson's *Poems* are to vol. 8 of Herford and Simpson; citations from *Sejanus* and *Poetaster* are to vol. 4.

11. For extended treatments of the functional relationship between literature and historical knowledge, see White, *Tropics of Discourse* (esp. 81–100), and La Capra's critique of White's book (72–83) along with La Capra's chapter "Who Rules Metaphor" (118–44), an analysis of Paul Ricoeur's *Rule of Metaphor*.

12. In other sonnets the narrator's feelings of self-worth are couched in the legalistic terminology of "charters," "bonds," "patents," "judgments," and the

like. These tropes show, obviously, that the experience of "eternal" love is constituted within a historicized juridical discourse. Brook Thomas's essay in *College English* makes the point (516–17).

13. I need not repeat Spivack's arguments in *The Allegory of Evil* except to remark that the psychomachia of the medieval morality plays and of *Dr. Faustus,* in which the good and bad angel contend for the soul of the protagonist, survives in sublimated forms in Prince Hal's "two fathers" (see Spivack, "Falstaff and the Psychomachia") and in Iago's satanic seduction of Othello's mind.

14. J. Archer 103. In his essay on *Sejanus,* Archer goes on to argue that Jonson's Roman plays "embody an ambiguous attitude toward surveillance at court and the sort of knowledge it produces" (96). Insofar as these plays express anxiety over sovereignty, they represent, he reasons, "the movement away from the representation of sovereign power by a single individual and toward the idea of the abstract state" (96).

15. The government records Nicoll cites reveal an extraordinary world of intelligencing and counterintelligencing in London, in which poets and scholars played significant roles ("The Intelligence Connection" 91–165). On Ben Jonson as a double agent, see John Archer (119–20).

16. See also Laclau and Mouffe (142). On the necessity of positing some form of "self" in cultural studies, see Flax (231).

17. Elton's notion of change is restricted because it concerns itself very little with the effect of cultural formations and is built upon sociological-political concepts of causation. I emphasize this point because the categorical concept of change is one that new-historicist practitioners ought to treat much more than they have.

Chapter Four

1. On Elizabeth's symbolic person see Jankowski (61–72) and Strong's *Gloriana* (esp. 62–69, 95–107).

2. On these matters, see Geertz's works, especially "History and Anthropology."

3. Holdsworth (4:355). For an example of a modern use of law enforcement procedures to raise revenues, see "Officers Write" (p. Al).

4. Holdsworth (4:357); Elton, "Informing" (149–50); cf. Beresford (231–32). In Elizabeth's reign the penalty was often half the imposed fine. See *Tudor Proclamations* ([listed by number] 521, 784). On the varying percentages of rewards, ranging from a third to half, see Russell (54) and Holdsworth (4:356, 9:240).

5. See *Tudor Proclamations* ([listed by number] 428, 521, 542, 565, 573, 577, 612, 655, 672, 699, 721, 784, 807, 810).

6. Stephens (235–36 [2d numerical ser.]). Composition payments to common informers, Davies estimates, ranged widely from one pound up to ten (50–58).

7. Superscripts to *The Wasp* are normalized, abbreviations expanded. Knights of the post were themselves subjects of contemporary satire of the legal system. See Milligan.

8. The first citation is from the Star Chamber's censure of Sir John Stafford

for turning informer, reported by Davies (63n); the second from *Stuart Proclamations* (1:No. 217).

9. Sometimes the tension between governmental policy and societal norms was made explicit. Allowing for a change of venue to Rome, that tension is registered in Jonson's *Sejanus* (1603) as well as Massinger's *Roman Actor* (1626), where "Caesar's spy" and consul Aretinus (1.1.35) plants himself among theatergoers to report any speech that might be construed as seditious. The players' grievance is that because they "galld [Aretinus] in our last Comedie," "He would silence us for ever" (1.1.37–38). Paris and his acting company complain that it is almost impossible to "Speake our thoughts freely of the Prince, and State, / And not fear the informer" (1.1.68–69). Such historically situated representations of informers are predicated on analogic habits of reading and playwrighting (Patterson, *Censorship* 49–58; Tricomi, *Anticourt Drama* 72–75, 158–59; Tricomi, "Earl of Pembroke").

10. On this point see Lentriccia's criticism of Foucault and the new historicism ("Foucault's Legacy") for failing to specify the conditions for meaningful rebellion—although Lentriccia neglects Foucault's statements on this matter (see *Language* 205). See also Leinwand's thoughtful attempt to mediate the bipolar terms of this debate through "a negotiation-based model of social relations that can account for change or for resistance to change" (480).

Chapter Five

1. I adapt Giddens's model of social change from *Central Problems in Social Theory* to the theater as an institution that presents an image of society's face to itself. The form of that self-presentation may be compared to Goffman's account of individuals presenting themselves metatheatrically to the world by means of the social roles they enact.

2. From *Shakspere and His Predecessors*. Unless otherwise noted, all page citations to Boas are to this work.

3. Howard critiques Frye's transhistorical reading of Shakespeare as an expression of "the mythic realm of man's timeless and collective existence," endorsing instead the historicist view that literature is "inextricably bound up with the contradictions and discontinuities of the Elizabethan cultural matrix, sometimes mediating or harmonizing conflicts and sometimes merely reflecting them" ("Difficulties of Closure" 114). See also Price's critique of six major generic approaches to *All's Well That Ends Well* (133–36).

4. Foucault's concept of genealogy, which owes something to Nietzsche, is cultural and replaces the older term archaeology (*The Order of Things*). I follow him in distinguishing between the development of a problem-play discourse in the late Victorian period and a more limited, traditional search for the "origins" of the term in a single author or text. On the method, see Foucault's "Nietzsche" in *Language* (139–64) along with Harootunian (110–37), Shiner (382–87), and Hunt (7–9).

5. Dates of plays from the Victorian and Edwardian periods are from Rowell's "Play-List, 1792–1914" (*Victorian Theatre* 151–57). Dates of Chapman's plays are from my own study.

6. Taylor 15–18, 81–91. The Victorian-Edwardian problem play is the primary subject in Balmforth, Carlson, and Simon. On the new drama, see Weales, Introduction (vii–xviii), and Rowell, *Victorian Theatre* (31–74, 103–40).

7. Cited by Trewin (49).

8. The distinction between eternal theater and, in Shaw's view, the more important social drama of modern times is elaborated in "The Problem Play," from which I have quoted (444, 446).

9. This notion is ambiguous. It may refer either to the literal irresolution detected in *Troilus and Cressida* or to a thematic irresolution, a failure to discern coherence or unity of meaning at higher levels of interpretation (Jameson's "allegorical" level [31]) as in *All's Well* and *Measure for Measure*.

10. Lawrence (22). See also Rossiter, who identified the dramatic techniques governing the problem-play mood as "an art of inversion, deflation and paradox" (117). His account of the problem play's features refines that of his predecessors (116–17).

11. Schanzer made the probing of "the complicated interrelations of character and action, in a situation admitting of different ethical interpretations" (3) central to his definition. The result of this latitudinarian approach, which ignores the centrality of sexuality, is that it radically revises the historical meaning of the Shakespearean problem-play concept. Consequently, an almost entirely new group appears. In Schanzer's pantheon the group becomes *Julius Caesar, Antony and Cleopatra*, and *Measure for Measure*, with many others partially qualifying.

12. Compared with Shakespearean drama, the treatment of sexual issues in Victorian-Edwardian drama tends to be literal rather than symbolic. Nevertheless, as Weales' sharply observes, the social themes of "position in society, the family, sex and marriage" tend to be explicit in Edwardian theater and the "serious political and economic concerns are implicit" (xiii–xiv).

13. See *The Arraignment of Ferneseede* (352). The same symbolic coding also appears in the homilies "An Exhortacion to Obedience," "Against Whoredom, and Adultery," and "Against Disobedience and Wylfull Rebellion," where challenges to authority and sexual transgressions were viewed as inviting providential retribution against the commonwealth (*Certain Sermons*, esp. 162, 174, 214). Similarly, public humiliation for sexual misconduct, ritualistically enacted in the churches and the marketplace, where the offense was read and forgiveness implored, functioned to appease God, create docile subjects, and perpetuate communitarian values.

14. On the reconstituted ideology of the sixteenth-century household as a "freeing" social institution for women, see Ozment (1–49); on the Tudor appropriation of patriarchal symbolism see Schochet (57–58). The displacement of the priestly class elevated families, especially the husband, whom William Gouge depicted as "the highest in the family. . . . [He hath] authoritie ouer all . . . committed to his charge: he is as a king in his owne house" (258). Gouge also counsels mutual assistance: "The husband by his helpe aiding his wife, addith much authoritie vnto her, and so causeth that she is not despised, nor lightly esteemed" (259).

15. In the first part of the sentence I paraphrase Bynum (202). For an account of the spiritual significance of the body for the human community from the early Middle Ages, see Brown (428–47).

16. For a splendid analysis of representations in medieval and Renaissance art of the Virgin Mary, who becomes "our prescription for motherhood generally," see Mullins (152–75).

17. The relationship between the restraint of female sexuality and the maintenance of social order has become a subject of anthropological examination. See, for example, Hirschon (66–88).

18. Quaife (51), citing from *Session Rolls* 95 (July 8, 1657).

19. Quaife (64, 68), citing from *Session Roles* 90 (October 21, 1654) and 91 (December 6, 1655).

20. A methodological point: if the method is purely sociological, the issue can readily become the extent to which women were in fact viewed misogynistically as empty "vanities," "shrews," and "seductresses" (Henderson and McManus 47–63). Wrightson contrasts the evaluations of roles appropriate to women as reported in conduct books with the quite disparate practices revealed in diaries and other personal statements (89–104). Obviously, such approaches are useful, but the method risks taking manifest expressions of conflict between the sexes—e.g., the pamphlet wars about women—as the fundamental category of understanding while neglecting or perhaps only nodding at the powerful symbolic discourse operating underneath. Elizabethan-Jacobean theater, placed at the intersection between discursive and symbolic modes of discourse, affords the study of both.

21. Even before Boas's book appeared, Dowden aired the notion in a proto-psychoanalytic work (1885) that pointed to an aberrational mood of disillusionment in three Shakespeare "comedies" that spoiled the bard for comedy. These were the same that Boas came to designate as problem plays. Although Dowden's explanation enjoys few adherents today, its way of constructing the critical problem, along with Boas's study, has had a lasting effect.

22. I employ the term *Jacobean* as F. P. Wilson did, to denote the tonality of plays that first appeared a few years before the death of Elizabeth I in 1603 and continued beyond the first decade of the seventeenth century. The term *Jacobean problem play* is thus a convenience.

Chapter Six

1. Tennenhouse develops this relational concept in terms of statecraft and the body politic in "Representing Power" and *Power on Display* (103–15). Other important discussions of the idea appear in essays on *Measure for Measure* by Jaffa and Baines.

2. The public debate on issues of gender might be understood in a fashion analogous to the Freudian concept of the manifest content of dreams. Beneath that lies the symbolic system that provides the mechanism for understanding the clues or, in modern terms, the codes that give rise to the symptomatic issues of public debate.

3. Citations from *The Widow's Tears* are to the Smeak edition.

4. Citations from *The Dutch Courtesan* are to Wine's edition. Comparisons of *The Dutch Courtesan* to *Measure for Measure* are not unusual. See Wine (xxiii).

5. The clash of modes of representation, usually the satiric with the romantic (or the comic) and the tragic, clearly contributes to the problem-play mode itself. See Gross (260–61). On the tensions produced by making the conventions of comedy clash with realistic or satiric treatments, see Kastan (585–86) and Price (133–36).

6. Citations from *Bussy D'Ambois* are to Brooke's edition.

7. Brooke's terminology. By identifying Bussy's opponents with "the stench of corruption" and "nausea and perverse appetite" (xl), he conveys the problem-play atmosphere Chapman creates. Boose's account of the prurience of so much Elizabethan fiction as couched in "a language not of lascivious delight but of sexual scatology—of slime, poison, garbage, vomit, clyster pipes, dung, and animality" ("1599 Bishops' Ban" 193) applies just as well to each of Bussy's enemies, but not, clearly, to Bussy in his relationship to Tamyra.

8. The play anachronistically reenacts James's own prohibitions "Against Private Challenges," February 4, 1614 (*STC* 8497) and "A Publication . . . Against Private Combats," 1613 (*STC* 8498).

9. This view is taken by numerous critics, including Ribner (31–34), Bement (187–98), J. Smith (50–52), and Ornstein, the last of whom holds that we become lost in a "muddled . . . high design" (58).

10. Waith interprets Bussy's career in the light of a pattern of imagery that links him to Hercules, the great flawed exemplar of human endeavor (88–111). Waddington pieces out the mythological ironies that accrue from Bussy's dual associations with Prometheus and Hercules, and so the play's moral ambiguities.

11. See Goldberg's Foucaultian interpretation of Bussy's monarchical identity (*James I* 159) and Tricomi (*Anticourt Drama* 82–83) on the parliamentary arguments for the entitlements accruing from ancient freedoms and immemorial rights.

12. By opening the question of ontology to reflection, the tragedy interrogates those categories that define property as "natural" and, as Jordan shows, normally write woman as an inferior ontological category whose "privileges of rank [rest] on the sufferance of her husband" (92).

13. Like Shakespeare's two dark comedies, *The Insatiate Countess* exhibits a bed trick, but it outdoes the others by showing a *double* bed trick in its subplot, which permits a comic conclusion in dramatic counterpoint to the tragic main plot. In particular, the subplot treats the sexual failures of two gentlemen, thereby counterpointing and commenting upon the focus subject of the main plot, the doings of an insatiate noble lady. On these matters, see Melchiori's introduction to Marston's *Insatiate Countess* (26–30).

14. Among the many examples, see the views of Ward (2:440–41), Parrott (2:803), and Kreider (86). The view is also widespread among late mid-century critics, Schoenbaum (334–35) and Herring (158) chief among them.

15. For an attempt to save even Tharsalio from the charge of misogyny, thereby adding another element of perturbation to the play's interpretation, see Juneja's essay.

16. The relationship of *The Dutch Courtesan* to the commercialization of sex and "the economic pressures at work in Jacobean society as a whole" (257) has been effectively explored by Horwich.

17. Langbein adduces evidence showing only eighty-one cases authorizing by official warrant the use of torture between 1540 and 1640 (82). The rack was normally used for suspected high crimes such as treason, sedition, murder, and occasionally to produce evidence in respect to robberies and religious offenses (94–123).

18. On the archetypal hero as "puer"—adolescent narcissist whose archetypal mask covers the depression beneath—see Goodrich-Dunn's interview with Morris Berman, who critiques the work of Joseph Campbell (16–17).

Chapter Seven

1. Cohen (33). Goldberg's "Shakespearean Inscriptions," an attack on Linda Bamber's *Comic Women, Tragic Men: A Study of Gender and Genre in Shakespeare*, makes these tensions explicit. Tennenhouse's *Power on Display* treats the "politics of misogyny" and is an example of the new-historicist orientation because it explicitly aims "to dissolve the sexual theme" into the primary components of Jacobean drama: "kingship versus kinship; natural versus metaphysical bodies of power; the signs and symbols of state versus the exercise of state power" (102, 123).

2. "The Family in Shakespeare Studies" (729). See also Neely, "Constructing the Subject." Earlier feminist critics were also given to totalizing procedures by overwriting the coverall term *power* with the subsuming term *patriarchy*. For example, McLuskie counsels renunciation of the pleasures of Shakespeare's plays because his work is irretrievably patriarchal. In a chapter called "The Patriarchal Bard," she writes, "When a feminist accepts the . . . intellectual pleasures of this text she does so in male terms" (98). See also Weedon's analysis of the bourgeois family as a site of capitalist patriarchy and the locus of women's oppression (17–19).

3. *History of Sexuality* (1:92). Even in one of the early interviews recorded in *Power/Knowledge*, "Power and Strategies" (1977), Foucault argued "that there are no relations of power without resistances" and that "resistance [like power] is multiple and can be integrated into global strategies" (142).

4. See Paul Smith's supple critiques of Althusserian theory and Foucault's totalizing practice (14–21, 89, 168n) and his account of an ideologically framed subject who is nevertheless capable of resistance and limited agency (56–69, 152–60).

5. Catherine Belsey has stressed that the early seventeenth-century family began to manifest a complex identity as a private as well as a public or dynastic institution (*Alternative Shakespeares* 169–73). See Margaret Ezell on the household authority of "the patriarch's wife" (33–35, 61). See Susan Wells for a sophisticated discussion of the historical emergence of the idea of family as applied to *The Duchess of Malfi* (69).

6. In addition to the critics cited in note 5, see Sarah Hanley's essay on collaborative female resistance to the "Family-State Compact" established in seventeenth-century France.

7. Stone's nicely phrased point that "authoritarian monarchy and domestic patriarchy form a congruent and mutually supportive complex of ideas and social systems" (152) is good, so long as it is remembered that such ideas were actively challenged, as Collins's discussion of Selden's antiauthoritarianism shows (*Divine Cosmos* 153–54), and so long as no one loses sight of the findings of Schochet (120) and Keith Thomas (42–62), showing that rejection of patriarchal authority was not uncommon.

8. For example, Michael Hunton's *Treatise of Monarchie* (1643), discussed by Collins in *Divine Cosmos* (157–58).

9. Max James emphasizes Shakespeare's recurring representation of fragmented families (ix). His summary description of the range of family conflict in Shakespeare includes no examples of growing children or their mothers. More characteristic types of family conflict occur between brothers or marriageable females and their disapproving fathers (191–92). See also Erickson's *Patriarchal Structures,* which treats the gendered constructs underlying wide-ranging images of the family in Shakespeare's work.

10. See Adelman's psychoanalytic reading of *Macbeth,* which develops the view that Shakespeare empties out the possibility of a productive representation of the female principal. Female feeling, which symbolizes a welcome androgyny, is celebrated in Shakespeare's heroic men, not his women.

11. In contrast to Belsey's view, Lisa Jardine stresses that the Duchess is defined by the polar stereotypes of the chaste woman and whore and that the tragedy's concerns with legitimacy, hereditary rights, and the transmission of property illustrate the Duchess's helplessness in enforcing her own claims to authority (91).

12. A Foucaultian perspective reveals that the very presence of the Doctor (as in *Macbeth*) works to distinguish the category of the "abnormal" from the "normal." The Doctor's medical discourse traces the progress of the play itself, showing that Ferdinand's behavior, not the Duchess's, wanders beyond the bounds of the human, while all that is "human" and spiritually regenerative is lodged in or proceeds from the life-bearing Duchess.

13. Citations from *The Duchess of Malfi* are to the Brennan edition.

14. The *OED* records one of the earlier meanings of "depart" as "To sever or separate a thing *from* another" as "To departe us from Godde's love" (s.v., sixteenth century). The earlier marriage service employs the words: "Till death do us depart."

15. The notion of "sensory engagement" as immediate and distinct from language is developed in the phenomenological theatrical criticism of States, from whom the citation is also taken (7).

16. The Redemption, the Resurrection of the body, and the Incarnation are all interconnected. See Bynum (149–50, 239–97).

17. Throughout this paragraph, I adapt the categories Butler employs in her critique of Kristeva's notion of "maternal drives" as a precultural essence in its relation to the "Law of the Father" (79–91). Kristeva and Butler both theorize the female body in explicit relation to the "paternal law" and, in Butler's terminology, to "Subversive bodily Acts."

18. In the Cynthia Rodriguez-Badendyck edition, from which citations to the play are taken.

19. Stone sets forth features, describing them as comprising the Open Lineage Family, which he says began ca. 1530 and predominated from 1580 to 1640 (7).

20. For a biographical account of the Duchess of Suffolk, see Hogrefe (82–103).

21. Citations by act number are from *The Duchess of Suffolk* are the unlineated, irregularly paginated, Huntington Library copy of *The Life of the Duches of Suffolke* (STC 7242).

22. The evidence Paster adduces showing that upper-class mothers who suckled their own children were viewed as performing a special act of love and sacrifice (199) does not appear to apply to Suffolk's play. The wet-nurse and mother together appear to sustain the ideals of maternal love and care.

23. Frederick William, Count Frederick V, Elector Palatine of the Rhine, was simply called "the Palsgrave" by the English (Akrigg 142). After marrying James's daughter Elizabeth in 1613, he quickly became a popular hero. The troupe that performed *The Duchess of Suffolk* bore the ensign "the Palsgrave's Company" (Herbert 18, 27). By bringing the Palsgrave on the stage, Drue capitalized doubly on his company's identity.

24. Stone might well identify this final emphasis with the "Restricted Patriarchal Nuclear Family," with its "more universalistic loyalties to the nation state and its head, and to a particular sect or Church" (7).

Bibliography

Adelman, Janet. "Bed Tricks: On Marriage as the End of Comedy in *All's Well That Ends Well* and *Measure for Measure*." *Shakespeare's Personality*. Ed. Norman N. Holland, Sidney Homan, and Bernard J. Paris. Berkeley: U of California P, 1989. 151–74.

———. "'Born of Woman': Fantasies of Maternal Power in *Macbeth*." *Cannibals, Witches, and Divorce: Estranging the Renaissance. Selected Papers from the English Institute, 1985*. Ed. Marjorie Garber. Baltimore: Johns Hopkins UP, 1986. 90–121.

Akrigg, J. P. V. *Jacobean Pageant, or the Court of King James I*. New York: Atheneum, 1974.

Almeder, Robert. *The Philosophy of Charles S. Peirce: A Critical Introduction*. Oxford: Blackwell, 1980.

Althusser, Louis. "Ideology and Ideological State Apparatuses." *Lenin and Philosophy and Other Essays*. Trans. Ben Brewster. New York: Monthly Review P, 1971. 127–86.

Anon. *Histoire du grand ét admirable royaume d'Antangil*. (History of the great, admirable realm of Antangil). Leiden, 1616. Rpt. in *French Utopias: An Anthology of Ideal Societies*. Trans. and ed. Frank E. Manuel and Fritzie P. Manuel. New York: Free P, 1966. 35–42.

Archer, John M. *Sovereignty and Intelligence: Spying and Court Culture in the English Renaissance*. Stanford: Stanford UP, 1993.

Archer, William. *The Old Drama and the New: An Essay in Re-valuation*. Boston: Small, Maynard, 1923.

The Arraignment and Burning of Margaret Farneseede. London, 1608. Rpt. in *Half Humankind: Contexts and Texts of the Controversy about Women in England,*

1540–1640. Ed. Katherine Usher Henderson and Barbara F. McManus. Urbana: University of Illinois Press, 1985. 351–59.

Bacon, Francis. *The Works of Francis Bacon.* Ed. James Spedding, R. C. Ellis, and D. D. Heath. 15 vols. London: Longman, Green, 1857–74.

Baines, Barbara J. "Assaying the Power of Chastity in *Measure for Measure.*" *Studies in English Literature* 30 (1990): 283–301.

Baker, Susan. "Sex and Marriage in *The Dutch Courtesan.*" *Another Country: Feminist Perspectives on Renaissance Drama.* Ed. Dorothea Kehler and Susan Baker. Metuchen, N.J.: Scarecrow Press, 1991. 218–32.

Bakhtin, Mikhail. *Rabelais and His World.* Trans. Helene Iswolsky. Cambridge, Mass.: MIT Press, 1968.

Balmforth, Ramsden. *From Richardson to Pinero.* London: John Murray, 1936.

———. *The Problem-Play in British Drama, 1890–1914.* New York: Henry Holt, 1928.

Barker, Francis. *The Tremulous Private Body: Essays on Subjection.* London: Methuen, 1984.

Beaumont, Francis. *Poems. The Works of the English Poets, from Chaucer to Cowper.* Ed. Alexander Chalmers. Vol. 6. 1810. New York: Johnson Reprint Corporation, 1970. 173–221.

———. *The Woman Hater. The Dramatic Works in the Beaumont and Fletcher Canon.* Vol. 1. Ed. Fredson Bowers. Cambridge: Cambridge UP, 1979.

Belsey, Catherine. *Alternative Shakespeares.* Ed. John Drakakis. London: Methuen, 1985.

———. *Critical Practice.* London: Methuen, 1980.

———. *The Subject of Tragedy: Identity and Difference in Renaissance Drama.* London: Methuen, 1985.

Bement, Peter. "The Imagery of Darkness and of Light in Chapman's *Bussy D'Ambois.*" *Studies in Philology* 64 (1967): 187–98.

Benveniste, Emile. *Problems in General Linguistics.* 1965. Trans. Mary Elizabeth Meek. Miami: University of Miami Press, 1971.

Beresford, M. W. "The Common Informer, the Penal Statutes and Economic Regulation." *Economic Historical Review,* 2nd ser. 10 (1957): 221–38.

Boas, Frederick S. *From Richardson to Pinero: Some Innovators and Idealists.* London: J. Murray, 1936.

———. *Shakspere and his Predecessors.* 1896. New York: Greenwood Press, 1969.

Bond, Ronald B. "'Dark Deeds Darkly Answered': Thomas Becon's Homily against Whoredom and Adultery, and Its Affiliation with Three Shakespearean Plays." *Sixteenth Century Journal* 16 (1985): 191–205.

Boose, Lynda E. "The Family in Shakespeare Studies; or—Studies in the Family of Shakespeareans, or—The Politics of Politics." *Renaissance Quarterly* 40 (1988): 707–42.

———. "The 1599 Bishops' Ban, Elizabethan Pornography, and the Sexualization of the Jacobean Stage." *Enclosure Acts: Sexuality, Property, and Culture in Early*

Modern England. Ed. Richard Burt and John Michael Archer. Ithaca: Cornell UP, 1994. 185–203.

Bourne, Edward. *A Looking-Glass Discovering to All People What Image They [Informers] Bear.* London, 1671.

Bradshaw, Graham. *Misrepresentations: Shakespeare and the Materialists.* Ithaca: Cornell UP, 1993.

Braunmuller, A. R. *Natural Fictions: George Chapman's Major Tragedies.* Newark: University of Delaware Press, 1992.

Bray, Alan. *Homosexuality in Renaissance England.* London: Gay Men's Press, 1982.

Brindley, Marianne. *The Symbolic Role of Women in Trobriand Gardening.* Pretoria: U of South Africa P, 1984.

Brown, Peter. *The Body and Society: Men, Women and Sexual Renunciation in Early Christianity.* New York: Columbia UP, 1988.

de Bruyn, Lucy. *Woman and the Devil in Sixteenth-Century Literature.* Tisbury, Wiltshire: Compton Press, 1979.

Burke, Edmund. *Reflections on the Revolution in France.* 1790. Ed. J. G. A. Pocock. Indianapolis: Hackett, 1987.

Burt, Richard. *Licensed by Authority: Ben Jonson and the Discourses of Censorship.* Ithaca: Cornell UP, 1993.

Butler, Judith. *Gender Trouble: Feminism and the Subversion of Identity.* New York: Routledge, 1990.

Bynum, Caroline Walker. *Fragmentation and Redemption: Essays on Gender and the Human Body in Medieval Religion.* New York: Zone Books, 1991.

Calendar of State Papers, Domestic Series, Edward VI, Elizabeth, James I: 1547–1625. 12 vols. Ed. Robert Lemon et al. 1865. Nendeln, Liechtenstein: Kraus Reprints, 1967.

Campanella, Tommaso. *The City of the Sun.* From *Civitas Solis, dea reipublicae Platonicae.* 1623. *Famous Utopias of the Renaissance.* Ed. Frederic R. White. Trans. T. W. Halliday. [1946]. New York: Hendrick's House, 1955. 153–204.

Carlson, Susan L. "Two Genres and Their Women: The Problem Play and the Comedy of Manners in the Edwardian Theatre." *Midwest Quarterly* 26 (1985): 413–24.

Castel, Charles I. (Abbé de Saint-Pierre). "A Proposal for Everlasting Peace." From *Projet pour rendre la paix perpétuelle en Europe.* 1713. Trans. as *A Project for an Everlasting Peace in Europe, First Proposed by Henry IV of France, and approved of by Queen Elizabeth. . . .* 1714. *French Utopias, An Anthology of Ideal Societies.* Ed. Frank E. Manuel and Fritzie P Manuel. New York: Free P, 1966. 81–90.

Certain Sermons or Homilies (1547) and A Homily against Disobedience and Willful Rebellion (1570). Ed. Ronald B. Bond. Toronto: University of Toronto Press, 1987.

Chambers, E. K. "Shakespeare." *Encyclopedia Britannica.* 11th ed. 1910.

————. *Shakespeare: A Survey.* London: Macmillan, 1925.

Chambers, R. W. *Thomas More.* London: Jonathan Cape, 1953.

Chapman, George. *Bussy D'Ambois.* Ed. Nicholas Brooke. London: Methuen, 1964.

————. *The Revenge of Bussy D'Ambois.* Ed. Robert J. Lordi. Salzburg: Institut für Englische Sprache und Literatur, Universitat Salzburg, 1977.

————. *The Widow's Tears.* Ed. Ethel M. Smeak. Lincoln: U of Nebraska P, 1966.

Chartier, Roger. *Cultural History: Between Practices and Representations.* Trans. Lydia G. Cochrane. Ithaca: Cornell UP, 1988.

Cohen, Walter. "Political Criticism in Shakespeare." *Shakespeare Reproduced: The Text in History and Ideology.* Ed. Jean E. Howard and Marion F. O'Connor. New York: Methuen, 1987. 18–46.

Coke, Sir Edward. *The Third Part of the Institutes of the Laws of England.* London, 1644.

Collingwood, R. G. *The Idea of History.* New York: Galaxy, 1956.

Collins's Peerage of England. 9 vols. Ed. Egerton Bridges. London, 1812.

Collins, Stephen L. *From Divine Cosmos to Sovereign State: An Intellectual History of Consciousness and the Idea of Order in Renaissance England.* New York: Oxford UP, 1989.

————. "Where's the History in the New Historicism? The Case of the English Renaissance." *Annals of Scholarship* 6 (1989): 231–47.

Compact Edition of the *Oxford English Dictionary.* Oxford: Oxford UP, 1971.

Cox, Jeffrey N., and Larry J. Reynolds. "The Historicist Enterprise." *New Historical Literary Study: Essays on Reproducing Texts, Representing History.* Ed. Jeffrey N. Cox and Larry J. Reynolds. Princeton: Princeton UP, 1993.

Cross, Gustav. "Marston, Montaigne, and Morality: *The Dutch Courtesan* Reconsidered." *English Literary History* 27 (1960): 30–43.

Daly, Peter M., Leslie T. Duer, and Anthony Raspa, eds. *The English Emblematic Tradition.* Toronto: University of Toronto Press, 1988.

D'Amico, Robert. *Historicism and Knowledge.* New York: Routledge, 1989.

Davies, John. *The Poems of Sir John Davies.* Ed. Robert Krueger. Oxford: Clarendon P, 1975.

Davies, Margaret G. *The Enforcement of English Apprenticeship, 1563–1642: A Study in Applied Mercantilism.* Cambridge, Mass.: Harvard UP, 1956.

De Man, Paul. *Resistance to Theory.* Minneapolis: University of Minnesota Press, 1986.

The Dictionary of National Biography. Oxford: Oxford UP, 1906.

Dolan, John P. Introduction. *Utopian and Other Essential Writings of Sir Thomas More.* Ed. and trans. James J. Greene and John P. Dolan. New York: New American Library, 1984. 26–28.

Dollimore, Jonathan. *Radical Tragedy: Religion, Ideology and Power in the Drama of Shakespeare and His Contemporaries.* Chicago: U of Chicago P, 1980.

————. "Transgression and Surveillance in *Measure for Measure.*" *Political Shakespeare: New Essays in Cultural Materialism.* Ed. Jonathan Dollimore and Alan Sinfield. Ithaca: Cornell UP, 1985. 72–87.

Dowden, Edward. *Shakespere: A Critical Study of His Mind and Art.* New York, 1881.

Drue, Thomas. *The Life of the Dutches of Suffolke.* London, 1631. [*STC* 7242].

Eagleton, Terry. *William Shakespeare.* Oxford: Blackwell, 1986.

Eccles, Mark. "Jonson and the Spies." *Review of English Studies* 13 (1937): 385–97.

Elliott, Robert C. "The Shape of Utopia." *English Literary History* 30 (1963): 317–34.

Elton, G. R. "A High Road to Civil War?" *From the Renaissance to the Counter-Reformation: Essays in Honor of Garrett Mattingly.* Ed. Charles H. Carter. Charlottesville: UP of Virginia, 1969. 325–47.

————. "Informing for Profit: A Sidelight on Tudor Methods of Law-Enforcement." *Cambridge Historical Journal* 11 (1954): 149–67.

————. *Policy and Police: The Enforcement of the Reformation in the Age of Thomas Cromwell.* Cambridge: Cambridge UP, 1972.

————. *Political History: Principles and Practice.* New York: Basic, 1970.

————. *The Practice of History.* Sydney: Sydney UP, 1967.

————. *Reform and Renewal: Thomas Cromwell and the Common Weal.* Cambridge: Cambridge UP, 1973.

————. "Reform by Statute: Thomas Starkey's *Dialogue* and Thomas Cromwell's 'Policy.'" *Proceedings of the British Academy* 54 (1968): 165–88.

————. *Return to Essentials: Some Reflections on the Present State of Historiographical Study.* Cambridge: Cambridge UP, 1991.

————. *The Tudor Constitution: Documents and Commentary.* 1960. 2nd ed. Cambridge: Cambridge UP, 1982.

————. *The Tudor Revolution in Government: Administrative Changes in the Reign of Henry VIII.* Cambridge: Cambridge UP, 1953.

Emmison, F. G. *Elizabethan Life: Morals and the Church Courts.* Chelmsford: Essex County Council, 1973.

Erickson, Peter. *Patriarchal Structures in Shakespeare's Drama.* Berkeley: U of California P, 1985.

————. "Rewriting the Renaissance, Rewriting Ourselves." *Shakespeare Quarterly* 38 (1987): 327–37.

Ezell, Margaret J. M. *The Patriarch's Wife: Literary Evidence and the History of the Family.* Chapel Hill: U of North Carolina P, 1987.

Fabricant, Carole. "Binding and Dressing Nature's Loose Tresses: The Ideology of Augustan Landscape Design." *Studies in Eighteenth-Century Culture* 8 (1979): 109–35.

Ferguson, A. S. "The Plays of George Chapman." *Modern Language Review* 14 (1920): 223–29.

Filmer, Robert. *Patriarcha and Other Political Works*. Ed. Peter Laslett. Oxford: Blackwell, 1949.

Fineman, Joel. "The History of the Anecdote: Fiction and Fact." *The New Historicism*. Ed. H. Aram Veeser. New York: Routledge, 1989. 49–76.

Flax, Jane. *Thinking Fragments: Psychoanalysis, Feminism, and Postmodernism in the Contemporary West*. Berkeley: U of California P, 1990.

Foucault, Michel. *The Archaeology of Knowledge and the Discourse on Language*. Trans. A. M. Sheridan Smith. New York: Pantheon, 1972.

————. *The Birth of the Clinic: An Archaeology of Medical Perception*. Trans. A. M. Sheridan Smith. London: Tavistock, 1973.

————. *Discipline and Punish: The Birth of the Prison*. 1977. Trans. Alan Sheridan. New York: Vintage, 1979.

————. *The History of Sexuality*. Vol. 1. Trans. Robert Hurley. New York: Random House, 1978.

————. *Language, Counter-Memory, Practice: Selected Essays and Interviews by Michel Foucault*. Ed. Donald F. Bouchard. Trans. Donald F. Bouchard and Sherry Simon. Ithaca: Cornell UP, 1977.

————. *Madness and Civilization: A History of Insanity in the Age of Reason*. Trans. Richard Howard. New York: Pantheon, 1965.

————. *The Order of Things, an Archaeology of the Human Sciences*. New York: Random House, 1970.

————. *Power/Knowledge: Selected Interviews and Other Writings, 1972–77: Michel Foucault*. Ed. Colin Gordon. Trans. Colin Gordon et al. New York: Random House, 1980.

Fox-Genovese, Elizabeth. "Literary Criticism and the Politics of the New Historicism." *The New Historicism*. Ed. H. Aram Veeser. New York: Routledge, 1989. 213–24.

Fraser, Nancy. "Foucault's Body-Language: A Post-Humanist Political Rhetoric." *Salmagundi* 61 (1983): 55–70.

Freeman, Goodlove. *A Dialogue between Hodge and Heraclitus, or, A Character of an Informer*. London, 1682.

Freud, Sigmund. "The Uncanny." 1919. *On Creativity and the Unconscious: Papers on the Psychology of Art, Literature, Love, Religion*. Ed. Benjamin Nelson. New York: Harper & Row, 1958. 122–61.

Frye, Northrop. *The Myth of Deliverance: Reflections on Shakespeare's Problem Comedies*. Brighton: Harvester P, 1983.

Fumerton, Patricia. *Cultural Aesthetics: Renaissance Literature and the Practice of Social Ornament*. Chicago: U of Chicago P, 1991.

Geertz, Clifford. "Deep Play: Notes on the Balinese Cockfight." *Daedalus* 101 (1972): 1–37.

———. "History and Anthropology." *New Literary History* 21 (1990): 321–35.

———. *The Interpretation of Cultures.* New York: Basic, 1973.

———. *Local Knowledge: Further Essays in Interpretive Anthropology.* New York: Basic, 1983.

Gibbons, Brian, Ed. *The Revenger's Tragedy.* London: Ernest Benn, 1967.

Giddens, Anthony. *Central Problems in Social Theory: Action, Structure and Contradiction in Social Analysis.* London: Macmillan, 1979.

———. *The Constitution of Society: Outline of the Theory of Structuration.* Cambridge: Polity P, 1984.

Gies, Frances, and Joseph Gies. *Marriage and the Family in the Middle Ages.* New York: Harper & Row, 1987.

Goffman, Erving. *Asylums: Essays on the Social Situations of Mental Patients and Other Inmates.* Garden City, N.Y.: Anchor, 1961.

———. *The Presentation of the Self in Everyday Life.* Garden City, N.Y.: Doubleday, 1959.

Goldberg, Jonathan. *James I and the Politics of Literature: Jonson, Shakespeare, Donne, and Their Contemporaries.* Baltimore: Johns Hopkins UP, 1983.

———. "Shakespearean Inscriptions: The Voicing of Power." *Shakespeare and the Question of Theory.* Ed. Patricia Parker and Geoffrey Hartman. New York: Methuen, 1985. 116–37.

———. *Sodometries: Renaissance Texts, Modern Sexualities.* Stanford: Stanford UP, 1992.

Goodrich-Dunn, Barbara. "Walking the Critical Path." *Common Boundary* July-August 1991: 12–21.

Gouge, William. *Of Domesticall Duties.* London, 1622.

Graff, Gerald. "Co-optation." *The New Historicism.* Ed. H. Aram Veeser. New York: Routledge, 1989. 168–81.

Greenblatt, Stephen. "Invisible Bullets: Renaissance Authority and Its Subversion. *Glyph* 8 (1981): 40–61. Cited from rev. version in *Shakespearean Negotiations: The Circulation of Social Energy in Renaissance England.* Berkeley: U of California P, 1988. 21–65.

———. *Learning to Curse: Essays in Early Modern Culture.* New York: Routledge, 1990.

———. *Renaissance Self-Fashioning: More to Shakespeare.* Chicago: U of Chicago P, 1980.

———. "Shakespeare and the Exorcists." *Shakespeare and the Question of Theory.* Ed. Patricia Parker and Geoffrey Hartman. New York: Methuen, 1985. 163–87.

———. *Shakespearean Negotiations: The Circulation of Social Energy in Renaissance England.* Berkeley: U of California P, 1988.

————. "Towards a Poetics of Culture." *The New Historicism.* Ed. H. Aram Veeser. New York: Routledge, 1989. 1–14.

————, ed. *Representing the English Renaissance.* Berkeley: U of California P, 1988.

Greenlee, Douglas. *Peirce's Concept of Sign.* The Hague: Mouton, 1973.

Gross, Gerard J. "The Conclusion to *All's Well That Ends Well.*" *Studies in English Literature* 23 (1983): 257–76.

Hanley, Sarah. "Engendering the State: Family Formation and State Building in Early Modern France." *French Historical Studies* 16 (1989): 4–27.

Harbage, Alfred, rev. by S. Schoenbaum. *Annals of English Drama 975–1700.* Rev. 3d ed. Sylvia S. Wagonheim. London: Routledge, 1989.

Harootunian, H. D. "Foucault, Genealogy, History." *After Foucault, Humanistic Knowledge, Postmodern Challenges.* Ed. Jonathan Arac. New Brunswick: Rutgers UP, 1988. 110–37.

Harrison, William. *The Description of England.* [1587] Ed. Georges Edelen. Ithaca: Cornell UP for the Folger Shakespeare Library, 1968.

Heineman, Margot. *Puritanism and Theatre: Thomas Middleton and Opposition Drama under the Early Stuarts.* Cambridge: Cambridge UP, 1980.

Helgerson, Richard. *Forms of Nationhood: The Elizabethan Writing of England.* Chicago: U of Chicago P, 1992.

————. "Inventing Noplace, or the Power of Negative Thinking." *The Forms of Power and the Power of Forms in the Renaissance.* Ed. Stephen Greenblatt. Norman: U of Oklahoma P, 1982. 101–21.

Heller, Agnes. *A Theory of History.* London: Routledge & Kegan Paul, 1982.

Henderson, Katherine Usher, and Barbara F. McManus, eds. *Half Humankind: Contexts and Texts of the Controversy about Women in England, 1540–1640.* Urbana: U of Illinois P, 1985.

Herbert, Sir Henry. *The Dramatic Records.* Ed. Joseph Quincy Adams. New York: Benjamin Blom, 1917.

Herring, Thelma. "Chapman and an Aspect of Modern Criticism." *Renaissance Drama* 8 (1965): 153–79.

Hexter, J. H. *Doing History.* Bloomington: Indiana UP, 1971.

Hey, D. G. *An English Rural Community: Myddle under the Tudors and Stuarts.* Leicester: U of Leicester P, 1974.

Himmelfarb, Gertrude. "Some Reflections on the New History." *American Historical Review* 94 (1989): 661–70.

Hirschon, Renée. "Open Body/Closed Space: The Transformation of Female Sexuality." *Defining Females: The Nature of Women in Society.* Ed. Shirley Ardener. London: Croom Helm, 1978. 66–88.

Hirst, Derek. "The Privy Council and Problems of Enforcement in the 1620s." *Journal of British Studies* 18 (1978): 46–66.

Hobbes, Thomas. *Leviathan, or the Matter, Forme and Power of a Commonwealth Ecclesiasticall and Civill.* 1651. Ed. Michael Oakeshott. Oxford: Blackwell, 1946.

Hogrefe, Pearl. *Women in Action in Tudor England*. Ames: Iowa State UP, 1977.

Holdsworth, William S. *A History of English Law*. 16 vols. London: Methuen, 1903–66.

Holland, Norman N., Sidney Homan, and Bernard J. Paris, eds. *Shakespeare's Personality*. Berkeley: U of California P, 1989.

Holstun, James. "Ranting at the New Historicism." *English Literary Renaissance* 19 (1989): 189–225.

Hoopes, James. "Review Article: Objectivity *and* Relativism Affirmed, Historical Knowledge and the Philosophy of Charles S. Peirce." *American Historical Review* 98 (1993): 1545–55.

Horwich, Richard. "Wives, Courtesans, and the Economics of Love in Jacobean City Comedy." *Drama in the Renaissance: Comparative and Critical Essays*. Ed. Clifford Davidson, C. J. Gianakaris, and John H. Stroupe. New York: AMS P, 1986. 255–73.

Howard, Jean E. "The Difficulties of Closure: An Approach to the Problematic in Shakespearean Comedy." *Comedy from Shakespeare to Sheridan: Change and Continuity in the English and European Dramatic Tradition*. Ed. A. R. Braunmuller and J. C. Bulman. Cranbury, N.J.: Associated U Presses, 1986. 113–30.

———. "The New Historicism in Renaissance Studies." *Renaissance Historicism*. Ed. Dan S. Collins and Arthur F. Kinney. Amherst: U of Massachusetts P, 1987. 3–31.

———. *The Stage and Social Struggle in Early Modern England*. London: Routledge, 1994.

Howell, Martha C. "A Feminist Historian Looks at the New Historicism: What's So Historical about It?" *Women's Studies* 19 (1991): 139–47.

Hunt, Lynn. Introduction. *The New Cultural History*. Ed. Lynn Hunt. Berkeley: U of California P, 1989. 1–22.

The Informers Looking-Glass. London, 1682.

Ingram, Martin. *Church Courts, Sex and Marriage in England, 1570–1640*. Cambridge: Cambridge UP, 1987.

Jaffa, Harry V. "Chastity as a Political Principle: An Interpretation of Shakespeare's *Measure for Measure*." *Shakespeare as Political Thinker*. Ed. John Alvis and Thomas G. West. Durham, N.C.: Carolina Academic P, 1981. 181–213.

James I. *Political Works of James I*. 1616. Ed. Charles H. McIlwain. New York: Russell and Russell, 1965.

James, Max H. *"Our House is Hell": Shakespeare's Troubled Families*. Westport, Conn.: Greenwood P, 1989.

Jameson, Fredric. *The Political Unconscious: Narrative as a Socially Symbolic Act*. Ithaca: Cornell UP, 1981.

Jankowski, Theodora. *Women in Power in the Early Modern Drama*. Urbana: U of Illinois P, 1991.

Jardine, Lisa. *Still Harping on Daughters: Women and Drama in the Age of Shakespeare*. Sussex: Harvester P, 1983.

Jardine, M. D. "New Historicism for Old: New Conservatism for Old?: The Politics of Patronage in the Renaissance." *Yearbook of English Studies* 21 (1991): 286–304.

Jonson, Ben. *The Complete Works.* 11 vols. Ed. C. H. Herford and Percy Simpson and Evelyn Simpson. Oxford: Clarendon P, 1925–52.

Jordan, Constance. "Renaissance Women and the Question of Class." *Sexuality and Gender in Early Modern Europe: Institutions, Texts, Images.* Ed. James G. Turner. Cambridge: Cambridge UP, 1993. 90–106.

Josselin, Ralph. *The Diary of Ralph Josselin, 1616–1683.* Ed. Alan Macfarlane. London: For the British Academy by Oxford UP, 1976.

Journals of the House of Commons. Vol. 1. (1547/1628). London, 1803.

Juneja, Renu. "Widowhood and Sexuality in Chapman's *The Widow's Tears.*" *Philological Quarterly* 67 (1988): 157–75.

Kastan, David Scott. "*All's Well That Ends Well* and the Limits of Comedy." *English Literary History* 52 (1985): 575–89.

Kautsky, Karl. *Thomas More and His Utopia.* 1890. New York: Russell and Russell, 1959.

Kenyon, Timothy. *Utopian Communism and Political Thought in Early Modern England.* London: Pinter, 1989.

Kolodny, Annette. *The Lay of the Land: Metaphor as Experience and History in American Life and Letters.* Chapel Hill: U of North Carolina P, 1975.

Kotker, Norman, Ed. *The Horizon Book of the Elizabethan World.* New York: American Heritage, 1967.

Kreider, Paul. *Elizabethan Comic Character Conventions as Revealed in the Plays of George Chapman.* Ann Arbor: U of Michigan P, 1935.

Kristeva, Julia. *Desire in Language: A Semiotic Approach to Literature and Art.* Ed. Leon S. Roudiez. New York: Columbia UP, 1980.

La Capra, Dominick. *Rethinking Intellectual History: Texts, Contexts, Language.* Ithaca: Cornell UP, 1983.

Laclau, Ernesto, and Chantal Mouffe. *Hegemony and Socialist Strategy: Towards a Radical Democratic Politics.* Trans. Winston Moore and Paul Cammack. Thetford: Thetford P, 1985.

Langbein, John H. *Torture and the Law of Proof: Europe and England in the Ancien Regime.* Chicago: U of Chicago P, 1977.

Lawrence, W. W. *Shakespeare's Problem Comedies.* 1931. Rev. ed. Penguin: Harmondsworth, 1960.

Leinwand, Theodore B. "Negotiation and New Historicism." *Papers of the Modern Language Association* 105 (1990): 477–89.

Lentriccia, Frank. *Criticism and Social Change.* Chicago: U of Chicago P, 1983.

———. "Foucault's Legacy—A New Historicism?" *The New Historicism.* Ed. H. Aram Veeser. New York: Routledge, 1989. 231–42.

Lerner, Laurence. "Against Historicism." *New Literary History* 24 (1993): 273–92.

Litvak, Joseph. "Back to the Future: A Review-Article on the New Historicism,

Deconstruction, and Nineteenth-Century Fiction." *Texas Studies in Language and Literature* 30 (1988): 120–49.

Liu, Alan. "The Power of Formalism: The New Historicism." *English Literary History* 56 (1989): 721–71.

Lope de Vega. *The Duchess of Amalfi's Steward. (El mayordomo de la duquesa de Amalfi)*. Ed. and trans. Cynthia Rodriquez-Badendyck. Ottawa: Dovehouse Editions Canada, 1985.

Lyotard, Jean-François. *The Postmodern Condition: A Report on Knowledge*. Trans. Geoff Bennington and Brian Massumi. Foreword Fredric Jameson. Minneapolis: U of Minnesota P, 1984.

MacClure, Millar. *George Chapman: A Critical Study*. Toronto: U of Toronto P, 1966.

MacFarlane, Alan. *The Family Life of Ralph Josselin: An Essay in Historical Anthropology*. Cambridge: Cambridge UP, 1970.

McLuskie, Kathleen. "The Patriarchal Bard: Feminist Criticism and Shakespeare, *King Lear* and *Measure for Measure*." *Political Shakespeare: New Essays in Cultural Criticism*. Ed. Jonathan Dollimore and Alan Sinfield. Ithaca: Cornell UP, 1985. 88–108.

Manuel, Frank E. "Toward a Psychological History of Utopias." *Utopias and Utopian Thought*. Ed. Frank E. Manuel. Boston: Beacon P, 1966. 69–98.

Manuel, Frank E., and Fritzie P. Manuel. *French Utopias: An Anthology of Ideal Societies*. New York: Macmillan, 1966.

———. *Utopian Thought in the Western World*. Cambridge, Mass.: Harvard UP, 1979.

Marston, John. *The Dutch Courtesan*. Ed. M. L. Wine. Lincoln: U of Nebraska P, 1965.

———. *The Malcontent*. Ed. M. L. Wine. Lincoln: U. of Nebraska P, 1964.

——— et al. *The Insatiate Countess*. Ed. Giorgio Melchiori. Manchester: Manchester UP, 1984.

Maslan, Mark. "Foucault and Pragmatism." *Raritan* 7 (1988): 94–114.

Massinger, Philip. *The Roman Actor*. Vol. 3. *The Plays and Poems of Philip Massinger*. 5 vols. Ed. Philip Edwards and Colin Gibson. Oxford: Clarendon P, 1976.

Michaels, Walter Ben, and Stephen Knapp. "Against Theory." *Critical Inquiry* 8 (1982): 723–42.

Middleton, Thomas. *A Chaste Maid in Cheapside*. Ed. R. B. Parker. London: Methuen, 1969.

Miller, James. *The Passion of Michel Foucault*. New York: Simon and Schuster, 1993.

Milligan, Burton A. "A Note on Knights of the Post." *Modern Language Notes* 61 (1946): 147–51.

Mink, Louis O. "Change and Causality in the History of Ideas." *Eighteenth-Century Studies* 2 (1968–69): 7–25.

Montrose, Louis. "The Elizabethan Subject and the Spenserian Text." *Literary*

Theory/Renaissance Texts. Ed. Patricia Parker and David Quint. Baltimore: Johns Hopkins UP, 1986. 303–40.

———. "New Historicisms." *Redrawing the Boundaries: The Transformation of English and American Literary Studies.* Ed. Stephen Greenblatt and Giles Gunn. New York: Modern Language Association of America, 1992. 392–418.

———. "Professing the Renaissance: The Poetics and Politics of Culture." *The New Historicism.* Ed. H. Aram Veeser. New York: Routledge, 1989. 15–36.

———. "Renaissance Literary Studies and the Subject of History." *English Literary Renaissance* 16 (1986): 5–12.

———. "'Shaping Fantasies': Figurations of Gender and Power in Elizabethan Culture. *Representations* 2 (1983): 61–94.

More, Sir Thomas. *Utopia.* Ed. and trans. Robert M. Adams. New York: Norton, 1975.

Moretti, Franco. "'A Huge Eclipse': Tragic Formation and the Deconsecration of Sovereignty." *Genre* 15 (1982): 7–40.

Mullaney, Steven. *The Place of the Stage: License, Play, and Power in Renaissance England.* Chicago: U of Chicago P, 1988.

———. "Strange Things, Gross Terms, Curious Customs: The Rehearsal of Cultures in the Late Renaissance." *Representations* 3 (1983): 40–67.

Mullins, Edwin. *The Painted Witch: Female Body—Male Art, How Western Artists Have Viewed the Sexuality of Women.* London: Secker and Warburg, 1985.

Mumford, Lewis. "Utopia, the City and the Machine." *Utopias and Utopian Thought.* Ed. Frank E. Manuel. Boston: Beacon P, 1965. 3–24.

Murfin, Ross C. "What Is the New Historicism?" *Hamlet.* Ed. Susanne L. Wofford. Boston: St. Martin's P, 1994. 368–76.

Nashe, Thomas. *To Saffron-Walden.* Vol. 3. *The Works of Thomas Nashe.* 5 vols. Ed. Ronald B. Mc Kerrow. 1910. Rpt. with corrections by F. P. Wilson. Oxford: Blackwell, 1958.

Neely, Carol Thomas. "Constructing Female Sexuality in the Renaissance: Stratford, London, Windsor, Vienna." *Feminism and Psychoanalysis.* Ed. Richard Feldstein and Judith Roof. Ithaca: Cornell UP, 1989. 209–29.

———. "Constructing the Subject: Feminist Practice and the New Renaissance Discourses." *English Literary Renaissance* 18 (1988): 5–18.

Newman, Karen. "Renaissance Family Politics and Shakespeare's *The Taming of the Shrew.*" *Renaissance Historicism: Selections from "English Literary Renaissance."* Ed. Arthur F. Kinney and Dan S. Collins. Amherst: U of Massachusetts P, 1987. 131–45.

Nicoll, Charles. *The Reckoning: The Murder of Christopher Marlowe.* London: Jonathan Cape, 1992.

Nietzsche, Friedrich. *Complete Works.* 18 vols. 1909–11. New York: Russell and Russell, 1964.

"Officers Write 54% Fewer Tickets to Protest New York Pact Impasse." *New York Times* 11 April 1991: A1.

Orgel, Stephen. *The Illusion of Power: Political Theater in the English Renaissance.* Berkeley: U of California P, 1975.

―――. "The Royal Theatre and the Role of King." *Patronage in the Renaissance.* Ed. Guy Fitch Lytle and Stephen Orgel. Princeton: Princeton UP, 1981. 262–73.

Ornstein, Robert. *The Moral Vision of Jacobean Tragedy.* Madison: U of Wisconsin P, 1960.

Ozment, Stephen E. *When Fathers Ruled: Family Life in Reformation Europe.* Cambridge, Mass.: Harvard UP, 1982.

Painter, William. *The Palace of Pleasure.* 3 vols. Ed. Joseph Jacobs. London, 1890.

Parrott, Thomas Marc. *The Plays of George Chapman: The Comedies.* 2 vols. 1914. New York: Russell and Russell, 1961.

Parry, Graham. *The Golden Age Restor'd: The Culture of the Stuart Court, 1603–42.* London: Manchester UP, 1981.

Paster, Gail Kern. *The Body Embarrassed: Drama and the Disciplines of Shame in Early Modern England.* Ithaca: Cornell UP, 1993.

Patterson, Annabel. *Censorship and Interpretation: The Conditions of Writing and Reading in Early Modern England.* Madison: U of Wisconsin P, 1984.

―――. *Shakespeare and the Popular Voice.* Oxford: Blackwell, 1989.

Patterson, Lee. *Negotiating the Past: The Historical Understanding of Medieval Literature.* Madison: U of Wisconsin P, 1987.

Peacham, Henry. *Minerva Brittana.* 1612. Leeds: Scolar P, 1966.

Pearse, Edward. *The Conformists Fourth Plea.* London, 1683.

Pechter, Edward. "The New Historicism and Its Discontents: Politicizing Renaissance Drama." *Papers of the Modern Language Association* 102 (1987): 292–303.

Peirce, Charles S. *Essays in the Philosophy of Science.* Ed. Vincent Tomas. Indianapolis: Bobbs-Merrill, 1957.

Peters, Edward. *Torture.* New York: Blackwell, 1985.

Petter, C. G., Ed. *Eastward Ho!* London: Ernest Benn, 1973.

Plato. *The Republic.* Trans. Richard W. Sterling and William C. Scott. New York: Norton, 1985.

Pollard, Carol W. "Immoral Morality: Combinations of Morality Types in *All's Well That Ends Well* and *The Dutch Courtesan.*" *Cahiers Elizabéthains* 25 (1984): 53–59.

Porter, Carolyn. "Are We Being Historical Yet?" *South Atlantic Quarterly* 87 (1988): 743–86.

―――. "History and Literature: 'After the New Historicism.' "*New Literary History* 21 (1990): 253–72.

Post, Robert C. "The Social Foundations of Defamation Law: Reputation and the Constitution." *California Law Review* 74 (1986): 691–742.

———. "The Social Foundations of Privacy: Community and Self in the Common Law Tort." *California Law Review* 77 (1989): 957–1010.

Preussner, Arnold W. "Chapman's Anti-Festive Comedy: Generic Subversion and Classical Allusion in *The Widow's Tears.*" *Iowa State Journal of Research* 59 (1985): 263–72.

Price, Joseph G. *The Unfortunate Comedy: A Study of "All's Well That Ends Well" and Its Critics.* Toronto: U of Toronto P, 1968.

Prior, Moody E. *The Language of Tragedy.* New York: Columbia UP, 1947.

Quaife, G. R. *Wanton Wenches and Wayward Wives: Peasants and Illicit Sex in Early Seventeenth Century England.* New Brunswick: Rutgers UP, 1979.

Rabelais, François. *Gargantua and Pantagruel.* Trans. Burton Raffel. New York: Norton, 1990.

Raeff, Marc. "The Well-Ordered Police State and the Development of Modernity in Seventeenth-and Eighteenth-Century Europe: An Attempt at a Comparative Approach." *American Historical Review* 80 (1975): 1221–43.

Raleigh, Walter (Sir). *History of the World.* London, 1614.

Raleigh, Walter. *Shakespeare.* New York: Macmillan, 1907.

Randolph, Thomas. *The Poetical and Dramatic Works of Thomas Randolph.* 2 vols. Ed. W. Carew Hazlitt. 1875. New York: Benjamin Blom, 1968.

Ribner, Irving. *Jacobean Tragedy: The Quest for Moral Order.* London: Methuen, 1962.

Riddell, Edwin, Ed. *Lives of the Stuart Age, 1603–1714.* New York: Barnes and Noble, 1976.

Rorty, Richard. "Does Academic Freedom Have Philosophical Presuppositions?" *Academe* 80 (1994): 52–63.

———. *Objectivity, Relativism and Truth.* Cambridge: Cambridge UP, 1991.

———. "Putnam and the Relativist Menace." *Journal of Philosophy* 90 (1993): 443–61.

Rose, Mary Beth. *The Expense of Spirit: Love and Sexuality in English Renaissance Drama.* Ithaca: Cornell UP, 1988.

Rossiter, A. P. *Angel with Horns and Other Shakespeare Lectures.* 4th Ed. London: Longman, 1970.

Rousseau, Jean-Jacques. *The Social Contract.* Trans. Maurice Cranston. Harmondsworth: Penguin, 1968.

Rowell, George. *Victorian Dramatic Criticism.* London: Methuen, 1971.

———. *The Victorian Theatre, a Survey.* Oxford: Clarendon P, 1956.

Russell, Conrad. *The Crisis of Parliaments: English History, 1509–1660.* Oxford: Oxford UP, 1971.

Salignac, François de (Fénelon). "Salentum: Frugal and Noble Simplicity." From *Les Aventures de Télémaque.* 1699. Trans. as *The Adventures of Telemachus.*

French Utopias: An Anthology of Ideal Societies. Ed. Frank E. Manuel and Fritzie P. Manuel. New York: Free P, 1966. 69–80.

Schanzer, Ernest. *The Problem Plays of Shakespeare: A Study of "Julius Caesar," "Measure of Measure," "Antony and Cleopatra."* New York: Schocken, 1965.

Schochet, Gordon. *Patriarchalism in Political Thought: The Authoritarian Family and Political Speculation and Attitudes Especially in Seventeenth-Century England.* New York: Basic, 1975.

Schoenbaum, Samuel. "*The Widow's Tears* and the Other Chapman." *Huntington Library Quarterly* 23 (1960): 321–38.

Schwartz, Elias. "Seneca, Homer, and Chapman's *Bussy D'Ambois.*" *Journal of English and Germanic Philology* 56 (1957): 163–76.

Select Cases before the King's Council in the Star Chamber, 1477–1544. 2 vols. Ed. I. S. Leadam. London: Selden Society. Vol. 16 (1902); Vol. 25 (1910).

Selzer, John L. "Merit and Degree in Webster's *The Duchess of Malfi.*" *English Literary Renaissance* 11 (1981): 70–80.

Shakespeare, William. *The Riverside Shakespeare.* Ed. G. B. Evans. Boston: Houghton Mifflin, 1974.

Shaw, George B. *Plays: Pleasant and Unpleasant.* London, 1898.

———. "The Problem Play" (1895). *European Theories of the Drama.* Ed. Barrett H. Clark. New York: Crown, Inc. Rev. ed. 1965. 443–47. Rpt. of "Should Social Problems Be Freely Dealt with in the Drama?" *Humanitarian* 6 (May 1895).

Sheridan, Alan. *Michel Foucault: The Will to Truth.* London: Tavistock, 1980.

Shiner, Larry. "Reading Foucault: Anti-Method and the Genealogy of Power-Knowledge." *History and Theory* 21 (1982): 382–98.

A Short-Title Catalogue of Books Printed in England, Scotland and Ireland. [*STC*]. Ed. A. W. Pollard, and G. R. Redgrave. London: Bibliographical Society, 1926. Rev. Ed. 1969.

Shuger, Debora Kuller. *Habits of Thought in the English Renaissance: Religion, Politics, and the Dominant Culture.* Berkeley: U of California P, 1990.

Simon, Elliott M. *The Problem Play in British Drama, 1890–1914.* Salzburg: Institut für Englische Sprache und Literature, 1978.

Simpson, David. "Literary Criticism and the Return to 'History.'" *Critical Inquiry* 14 (1988): 721–47.

Smith, Bruce R. *Homosexual Desire in Shakespeare's England: A Cultural Poetics.* Chicago: U of Chicago P, 1991.

Smith, James. "Revaluations: George Chapman." *Scrutiny* 4 (1935): 45–61.

Smith, Paul. *Discerning the Subject.* Minneapolis: U of Minnesota P, 1988.

"A Spie, Sent out of the Tower-Chamber in the Fleet." London, 1648.

Spivack, Bernardo. "Falstaff and the Psychomachia." *Shakespeare Quarterly* 8 (1957): 449–59.

———. *Shakespeare and the Allegory of Evil.* New York: Columbia UP, 1958.

States, Bert O. *Great Reckonings in Little Rooms: On the Phenomenology of Theater.* Berkeley: U of California P, 1985.

Stephens, John. *Essays and Characters, Ironicall and Instructive.* London, 1615.

Stern, Fritz, Ed. *The Varieties of History, from Voltaire to the Present.* 1956. Rev. ed. New York: Vintage, 1972.

Stone, Lawrence. *The Family, Sex and Marriage in England, 1500–1800.* London: Weidenfeld & Nicolson, 1977.

Strong, Roy. *The Cult of Elizabeth: Elizabethan Portraiture and Pageantry.* London: Thames & Hudson, 1977.

———. *Gloriana: The Portraits of Queen Elizabeth I.* Wollop, Hampshire: Thames & Hudson, 1987.

———. *The Renaissance Garden in England.* London: Thames & Hudson, 1979.

Stuart Royal Proclamations. 2 vols. Ed. James F. Larkin and Paul L. Hughes. Oxford: Clarendon UP, 1973–83.

Taylor, John Russell. *The Rise and Fall of the Well-Made Play.* New York: Hill and Wang, 1967.

Tennenhouse, Leonard. *Power on Display: The Politics of Shakespeare's Genres.* London: Methuen, 1986.

———. "Representing Power: *Measure for Measure* in Its Time." *The Power of Forms in the English Renaissance.* Ed. Stephen Greenblatt. Norman, Okla.: Pilgrim Books, 1982. 139–56.

Thomas, Brook. "The Historical Necessity for—and Difficulties with—New Historical Analysis in Introductory Literature Courses." *College English* 49 (1987): 509–22.

———. *The New Historicism and Other Old-Fashioned Topics.* Princeton: Princeton UP, 1991.

———. "The New Historicism and the Privileging of Literature." *Annals of Scholarship* 4 (1987): 23–48.

Thomas, Keith. "Women in the Civil War Sects." *Past and Present* 13 (1958): 42–62.

Thomas, Vivian. *The Moral Universe of Shakespeare's Problem Plays.* London: Croom Helm, 1987.

Tillyard, E. M. W. *Elizabethan World Picture.* New York: Vintage, 1946.

———. *Shakespeare's History Plays.* 1944. New York: Collier, 1962.

———. *Shakespeare's Problem Plays.* 1950. Toronto: U of Toronto P, 1971.

Trewin, J. C. *The Edwardian Theatre.* Oxford: Blackwell, 1976.

Tricomi, Albert. *Anticourt Drama in England, 1603–1642.* Charlottesville: U of Virginia P, 1989.

———. "The Dates of the Plays of George Chapman." *English Literary Renaissance* 12 (1982): 242–66.

———. "Philip Earl of Pembroke and the Analogical Way of Reading Political Tragedy." *Journal of English and Germanic Philology* 85 (1986): 332–45.

————. "The Social Disorder of Chapman's *The Widow's Tears.*" *Journal of English and Germanic Philology* 72 (1973): 350–59.

Tudor Royal Proclamations. 3 vols. Ed. Paul L. Hughes and James F. Larkin. New Haven: Yale UP, 1964–69.

Turner, James G. "The Sexual Politics of Landscape: Images of Venus in Eighteenth-Century English Poetry and Landscape Gardening." *Studies in Eighteenth-Century Culture* 11 (1982): 343–66.

Turner, Victor. *The Ritual Process: Structure and Anti-Structure.* Ithaca: Cornell UP, 1969.

Underdown, David. *Revel, Riot, and Rebellion: Popular Politics and Culture in England, 1603–1660.* 1985. Oxford: Oxford UP, 1987.

Ure, Peter. *William Shakespeare: The Problem Plays.* 3rd ed. London: Longman, 1970.

Veeser, H. Aram. Introduction. *The New Historicism.* Ed. H. Aram Veeser. New York: Routledge, 1989. ix–xvi.

Vesalius, Andreas. *De humani corporis fabrica.* [The construction of the human body.] 1543.

Vico, Giambattista. *The New Science of Giambattista Vico.* 1744. Trans. Thomas Goddard Bergin and Max Harold Fisch. Ithaca: Cornell UP, 1968.

Waddington, Raymond B. "Prometheus and Hercules: The Dialectic of *Bussy D'Ambois.*" *English Literary History* 34 (1967): 21–48.

Waith, Eugene. *The Herculean Hero in Marlowe, Chapman, Shakespeare and Dryden.* New York: Columbia UP, 1962.

Walkowitz, Judith, Myra Jehlen, and Bell Chevigny. "Patrolling the Borders: Feminist Historiography and the New Historicism." *Radical History Review* 43 (1989): 23–43.

Wallerstein, Immanuel. *The Modern World-System.* New York: Academic P, 1970.

Ward, Adolphus. *A History of English Dramatic Literature to the Death of Queen Anne.* 3 vols. London, 1895.

The Wasp or Subject's Precedent. [Anon]. Ed. J. W. Lever. Oxford: Malone Society Reprints, 1976.

Weales, Gerald. *Edwardian Plays.* New York: Hill and Wang, 1962.

Webster, John. *The Duchess of Malfi.* Ed. Elizabeth M. Brennan. London: Ernest Benn and Norton, 1964.

Weedon, Chris. *Feminist Practice and Poststructuralist Theory.* Oxford: Blackwell, 1987.

Weidner, Henry M. "Homer and the Fallen World: Focus of Satire in George Chapman's *The Widow's Tears.*" *Journal of English and Germanic Philology* 62 (1963): 518–32.

Wells, Susan. *The Dialectics of Representation.* Baltimore: Johns Hopkins UP, 1981.

Wheeler, Richard P. *Shakespeare's Development and the Problem Comedies.* Berkeley: U of California P, 1981.

Whigham, Frank. "Sexual and Social Mobility in *The Duchess of Malfi.*" *Papers of the Modern Language Association* 100 (1985): 167–86.

White, Hayden. "New Historicism: A Comment." *The New Historicism.* Ed. H. Aram Veeser. New York: Routledge, 1989. 293–302.

——. *Tropics of Discourse: Essays in Cultural Criticism.* Baltimore: Johns Hopkins UP, 1978.

White, Stephen D. *Sir Edward Coke and "The Grievances of the Commonwealth," 1621–1628.* Chapel Hill: U of North Carolina P, 1979.

Whitney, Geoffrey. *A Choice of Emblemes.* [1586]. Ed. Henry Green, 1866. New York: B. Blom, 1967.

Williams, Penry, and G. L. Harriss. "A Revolution in Tudor History?" *Past and Present* 25 (1963): 3–58.

Williams, Raymond. *Marxism and Literature.* Oxford: Oxford UP, 1977.

Willson, David Harris. *King James VI and I.* 1956. London: Jonathan Cape, 1963.

Wilshire, Bruce. *Role Playing and Identity: The Limits of Theatre as Metaphor.* Bloomington: Indiana UP, 1982.

Wilson, F. P. *Elizabethan and Jacobean.* Oxford: Clarendon P, 1945.

Wrightson, Keith. *English Society, 1580–1640.* 1982. New Brunswick, N.J.: Rutgers UP, 1984.

Index